The Catholicity of
the Church

AVERY DULLES, SJ

D0218435

CLARENDON PRESS · OXFORD

Oxford University Press, Walton Street, Oxford OX2 6DP

Oxford New York Toronto
Delhi Bombay Calcutta Madras Karachi
Petaling Jaya Singapore Hong Kong Tokyo
Nairobi Dar es Salaam Cape Town
Melbourne Auckland
and associated companies in
Berlin Ibadan

Oxford is a trade mark of Oxford University Press

Published in the United States
by Oxford University Press, New York

© Avery Dulles, SJ 1985
First issued in paperback 1987
Reprinted 1989

All rights reserved. No part of this publication may be reproduced,
stored in a retrieval system, or transmitted, in any form or by any means,
electronic, mechanical, photocopying, recording, or otherwise, without
the prior permission of Oxford University Press.

This book is sold subject to the condition that it shall not, by way
of trade or otherwise, be lent, re-sold, hired out or otherwise circulated
without the publisher's prior consent in any form of binding or cover
other than that in which it is published and without a similar condition
including this condition being imposed on the subsequent purchaser

British Library Cataloguing in Publication Data
Dulles, Avery
The catholicity of the church
1. Catholicity
I. Title
262'.72   BX8.2
ISBN 0–19–826695–2 (pbk)

Library of Congress Cataloging in Publication Data
Dulles, Avery Robert, 1918–
The Catholicity of the church
Includes index.
1. Church—Catholicity—Addresses, essays, lectures.
I. Title.
BV601.3.D85   1985   262'.72   85–7258
ISBN 0–19–826695–2 (pbk)

Printed in Great Britain by
Courier International Ltd.,
Tiptree, Essex

Preface

THE present book reproduces, in slightly revised form, the Martin C. D'Arcy Lectures which the author was privileged to deliver at Campion Hall, Oxford University, in the Michaelmas Term, 1983.

Catholicity, the focus of this study, has long been recognized as an essential attribute of the Church of Christ and has been of particular concern to those churches which designate themselves as 'Catholic'. It is not possible to analyse catholicity without speaking of other traditional attributes of the Church: unity, holiness, and apostolicity. In the context of planetization, in which the cultures of diverse peoples are interacting and interpenetrating, catholicity takes on new and challenging aspects, decisive for the future of Christianity. Catholicity has ramifications in many different areas of ecclesiology. The present work, although brief, necessarily touches on many problems of historical and contemporary theology. But it does not pretend to be, even in outline, a complete ecclesiology. Retaining the basic structures of the original lecture series, this work is limited in scope.

As the reader will perceive, I personally am committed both to catholicity, in the sense of universalism, and to Catholicism, in the sense of adherence to a specific tradition and affiliation. I do not foresee that this dual commitment on my part will be offensive to persons who do not consider themselves Catholics. In the present climate of candour and pluralism, authors are generally encouraged to declare their point of view, rather than pretend to an unreal impartiality. I hope that readers of other persuasions may be able to recognize the validity of my descriptions of Catholic positions, so that they can say: 'This is what I would have to accept if I were a Catholic.' Few Christians, in fact, repudiate catholicity as a whole. Nearly all acknowledge the universal and permanent value of the gifts of God in Jesus Christ, and wish to live by these. To that extent they are implicitly committed to what I call the Catholic principle. 'Catholic' structures such as Scripture, ordained ministry, preaching, and sacramental worship function in one way or another in all churches. Hence the theology of catholic Christianity has a rather wide ecumenical interest.

I hope that my readers will bear with me in my rather fluid use of the term 'Catholic', which has various levels of meaning, distinguished in the course of this book. In some cases I use it practically as a synonym for 'Roman Catholic' (a term I use sparingly, for reasons explained later), and in other cases with a broader meaning, which I hope will be clear from the context. I have generally spelt 'Catholic' with a capital 'C' when it refers to Catholicism, as a particular structured form of Christianity. When it is simply an adjective referring to catholicity, I have used a small 'c', but in some cases, where the two meanings are both connoted, I have found it hard to make a choice. Also, in some cases my punctuation has been influenced, legitimately I believe, by the authors I am paraphrasing. I do not insist on any particular orthography, and in fact I envy authors writing in languages in which the question of capitalization is less vexing.

This study would never have been undertaken except for the kind invitation extended to me some years ago by Father Benjamin Winterborn, SJ, then Master of Campion Hall, to deliver the D'Arcy Lectures. I wish to acknowledge my indebtedness to him and to express my sincere regrets at his premature death on 7 December 1980, shortly after the end of his term of office. Father Paul Edwards, SJ, who succeeded him as Master, and all the tutors and residents of Campion Hall, made my stay at Oxford a pleasant and profitable one.

In my revisions of the original lectures I have been assisted by the advice of several gracious readers. Professor Reginald H. Fuller of Virginia Theological Seminary, Alexandria, Virginia, was able to bring to my attention some important literature and ideas coming from an Anglican perspective. I have also received helpful suggestions from two Catholic theologians: the Reverend Patrick Granfield of The Catholic University of America and the Reverend Robert P. Imbelli of the Maryknoll School of Theology, Maryknoll, New York. Susan E. Nowak,

SSJ, has generously and ably assisted me in compiling the Indexes.

Finally, I am indebted to the kind patience of my various editors at the Oxford University Press, and especially to Miss Audrey Bayley, who first encouraged me to proceed with publication.

Washington, D.C.   AVERY DULLES, SJ
15 January 1985

Contents

Abbreviations

Documents of Vatican II are abbreviated according to the two first words of the Latin text; thus:

AG   *Ad gentes*: Decree on the Church's Missionary Activity

CD   *Christus Dominus*: Decree on the Bishops' Pastoral Office in the Church

DH   *Dignitatis humanae*: Declaration on Religious Freedom

DV   *Dei Verbum*: Dogmatic Constitution on Divine Revelation

GS   *Gaudium et spes*: Pastoral Constitution on the Church in the Modern World

LG   *Lumen gentium*: Dogmatic Constitution on the Church

NA   *Nostra aetate*: Declaration on the Relationship of the Church to Non-Christian Religions

SC   *Sacrosanctum Concilium*: Constitution on the Sacred Liturgy

UR   *Unitatis redintegratio*: Decree on Ecumenism

Other abbreviations include:

AAS   *Acta Apostolicae Sedis* (Rome, 1909 ff.).

CSEL   *Corpus Scriptorum Ecclesiasticorum Latinorum* (Vienna, 1866 ff.).

DS   *Enchiridion symbolorum*, edited by H. Denzinger and A. Schönmetzer, 32nd edn. (Freiburg: Herder, 1963).

Mansi   *Sacrorum Conciliorum nova et amplissima collectio*, edited by J. D. Mansi, continued by L. Petit and J. Martin (Florence, 1759 ff.; Paris and Leipzig, 1901–27).

PG   *Patrologiae cursus completus, series graeca*, edited by J.-P. Migne (Paris, 1857 ff.).

PL   *Patrologiae cursus completus, seris latina*, edited by J.-P. Migne (Paris, 1844 ff.).

INTRODUCTION

The Catholic Principle

As stated in the Preface, this work grows out of a series of
lectures given at Campion Hall, Oxford University, in the
autumn of 1983. A variety of convergent reasons seemed to
favour the selection of catholicity as the theme.

(1)

First, the theme seemed appropriate for a lectureship dedicated
to the memory of Martin D'Arcy, SJ. Not only had he written a
splendid little book entitled *Catholicism*;[1] he was in his own
person an embodiment of catholicity. His tastes and interests
extended to religion, philosophy, literature, and the arts. Many
of the books and works of art that he collected are still to be seen
in Campion Hall, where my lectures were held.

A further consideration was the place and the time. Oxford
University has over the centuries done much to infuse a
Catholic outlook into the Church of England and the world-
wide Anglican communion. The year 1983, moreover, marked
the 150th anniversary of the Oxford Movement, which is
commonly reckoned to have taken its rise from John Keble's
famous sermon on National Apostasy preached in 1833 at the
University Church of St. Mary the Virgin. The anniversary
was marked by several important conferences and
publications.

An additional reason for my theme was the relative scarcity
of recent Roman Catholic literature on catholicity. The most
recent monograph known to me was that of Wolfgang Beinert,
published in 1964, too early to take into account the changes
introduced by Vatican Council II (1962–5).[2] A new study of

---

[1] Martin C. D'Arcy, *Catholicism* (Dublin: Clonmore & Reynolds, 1927; reprinted
1954).
[2] Wolfgang Beinert, *Um das dritte Kirchenattribut* (Essen: Ludgerus-Verlag, 2 vols.,
1964).

the subject seemed to be demanded both by the results of that council and by other forward-looking documents such as the report on 'The Holy Spirit and the Catholicity of the Church' adopted by the World Council of Churches at its Uppsala Assembly in 1968.[3]

Yet another consideration was the broad ecumenical interest in the topic. In the past few decades prominent theologians of practically all the major Christian traditions have been speaking of catholicity as an essential characteristic of the Church. Hardly any seem to reject the aphorism of Karl Barth: 'A Church is catholic or else it is not the Church.'[4] The Orthodox theologian, John Meyendorff, states his conviction that the notion of the Church's catholicity 'is a central one for the understanding both of what authentic ecumenism should be and of the mission of the Orthodox Church in the world today'.[5] Lutherans, who at one time hesitated to use the word 'catholic' in the creed (Luther himself substituted 'Christian'), increasingly identify themselves as 'a theological movement in the church catholic'.[6] Freechurchmen write books with titles such as *The Catholicity of Protestantism*.[7] Presbyterians frequently designate their own churches as both catholic and reformed.[8] Even conservative evangelicalism, historically suspicious of things catholic, is experiencing a strong trend towards 'evangelical catholicity'.[9]

The theme of catholicity is a very old one, treated in hundreds of volumes gathering dust on the shelves of theological libraries. Today, however, the topic is taking on new

[3] Report of Section I, 'The Holy Spirit and the Catholicity of the Church', in Norman Goodall (ed.), *The Uppsala Report 1968* (Geneva: World Council of Churches, 1968), pp. 11–19.

[4] Karl Barth, *Church Dogmatics*, vol. iv/1 (Edinburgh: T. & T. Clark, 1956), p. 702.

[5] John Meyendorff, *Orthodoxy and Catholicity* (New York: Sheed & Ward, 1966), p. vi. See also his *Catholicity and the Church* (Crestwood, NY: St. Vladimir's, 1983).

[6] Eric W. Gritsch and Robert W. Jenson, *Lutheranism* (Philadelphia: Fortress, 1976), pp. vii and 207.

[7] R. Newton Flew and Rupert E. Davies, *The Catholicity of Protestantism* (London: Lutterworth (1951), and Philadelphia: Muhlenberg (1954)).

[8] E.g. Robert McAfee Brown, *The Spirit of Protestantism* (New York: Oxford University Press, 1961), chap. 2, 'The Catholicity of Protestantism', pp. 13–23, and in chap. 4, 'The Spirit of Protestantism', pp. 44–8.

[9] Donald G. Bloesch, *The Future of Evangelical Christianity* (Garden City: Doubleday, 1983), pp. viii–ix, 48–52. Cf. Robert Webber and Donald G. Bloesch, *The Orthodox Evangelicals* (Nashville: Nelson, 1978).

vitality, not only within communions traditionally called 'Catholic' but in the wide spectrum of Christianity. Nearly all Christian churches are for the first time in history engaged in a common reflection on the meaning and importance of the Church's catholicity in a world where many cultures, economies, political blocs, and religions are coming together into new relationships, whether friendly or hostile, on a planetary scale. These pages are written with the confidence that a Roman Catholic voice, speaking in the perspectives opened up by Vatican Council II, may be able to make a contribution to this ecumenical reflection.

A final factor influencing my decision was the renewed interest, especially within the Roman Catholic communion, in the nature of Catholicism. After the unsettling changes of the past twenty years many are searching out their roots and seeking a clearer sense of their own identity. Numerous books and articles have appeared attempting to specify the essentials of Catholic Christianity. Few of these works, however, have taken advantage of the abundant literature on the idea of Catholicism produced by idealists, liberal Protestants, Anglo-Catholics, Modernists, and others in the nineteenth century.

(2)

A number of approaches to the meaning of Catholicism will be mentioned in the course of this work. To introduce this topic, however, it may be useful to mention two recent efforts to summarize, in compact form, the essentials of Catholicism.

The final chapter of Richard P. McBrien's massive work, *Catholicism*, is entitled 'Catholicism: A Synthesis'. Catholicism, he states, 'is characterized by a *radical openness to all truth and to every value*. It is *comprehensive* and *all-embracing* toward the totality of Christian experience and tradition, in all the theological, doctrinal, spiritual, liturgical, canonical, institutional, and social richness and diversity of that experience and tradition'.[10] Theologically speaking, Catholicism is characterized, he maintains, by a *both/and* rather than an *either/or* approach.

It is not nature *or* grace, but graced nature; not reason *or* faith, but reason illumined by faith; not law *or* Gospel, but law inspired by the

---

[10] Richard P. McBrien, *Catholicism* (Minneapolis: Winston, 1980), p. 1173.

Gospel; not Scripture *or* tradition, but normative tradition within Scripture; not faith *or* works, but faith issuing in works and works as expressions of faith; not authority *or* freedom, but authority in the service of freedom; not the past *versus* the present, but the present in continuity with the past; not stability *or* change, but change in fidelity to stable principle, and principle fashioned or refined in response to change; not unity *or* diversity, but unity in diversity, and diversity which prevents uniformity, the antithesis of unity.[11]

A few pages later, McBrien inquires into the theological foci of Catholicism, and finds that they are three: sacramentality, mediation, and communion. By the principle of sacramentality he means the acceptance of tangible and finite realities as actual or potential carriers of the divine presence. The principle of mediation is a corollary of that of sacramentality. The universe of grace, for the Catholic, is mediated by Christ, the Church, and other signs and instruments. Communion is a further corollary. The mediation of the divine occurs in and through a community, which is in turn strengthened by the encounter; 'there is no relationship with God, however intense, profound, and unique, that dispenses entirely with the communal context of *every* human relationship with God'.[12]

The three theological foci, for McBrien, emerge most clearly in the Catholic understanding of the Church both as the sacrament of Christ, mediating salvation through institutional means of grace, and as the Communion of Saints. In the latter aspect the Church is a foretaste of the eternal communion which we hope to enjoy in the final Kingdom of God.

Robert Imbelli, writing in the autumn of 1982, presents a similar characterization of Catholicism.[13] Beneath the successive empirical forms of Catholicism he finds a consistent 'depth structure' that may be described as 'sacramental consciousness'. This consciousness, he says, may be expressed in a variety of cultural forms, but all such expressions must be governed by certain foundational sensitivities. These he groups under five headings:

1. The corporeal, inasmuch as body sacramentalizes spirit.

[11] Ibid., p. 1174.
[12] Ibid., p. 1181.
[13] Robert P. Imbelli, 'Vatican II: Twenty Years Later', *Commonweal*, vol. cix, no. 17 (8 Oct. 1982), pp. 522–6.

2. The communal, for the community is the matrix of sacramental consciousness.

3. The universal, inasmuch as the Catholic sacramental consciousness addresses the private and the public, the natural and the cultural, the personal and the institutional.

4. The cosmic, since the whole of creation is involved in God's redemptive work in Christ.

5. The transformational, because of the Catholic conviction that the human is capable of being graced and glorified in Christ.

Imbelli then goes on to speak of the comprehensiveness of Catholic thought and language, which seek, in his opinion, 'to promote and sustain the creative tension of "both/and" rather than succumb to the easier, but often reductionist, language of "either/or" '.[14]

Certain authors, attempting to express the ideas of mediation and comprehensiveness, speak of the Catholic *via media* or of the Catholic centre.[15] These terms, while expressing a valid insight, can easily lead to the impression that Catholicism refuses to make a clear decision in the face of contradictories or that it contents itself with weak compromises. Walter Kasper here provides a much needed corrective:

The center is not a harmless geometrical point but a field of tension that endures in spite of all that is extreme and in fact can be described only in relation to the extreme. For this reason it is easier to maintain extreme positions, whereas mediation demands spiritual strength. We need an increase of the strength to fight 'between the front lines'.[16]

This increase of strength, I would suggest, can come only from the Catholic consciousness as a comprehensive theological vision. The Catholic insistence on mediation as against false mysticism, on communion as against individualism, and on plenitude as against sectarianism or reductionism, must be a matter of principle. But what principle is at stake?

(3)

In recent years it has become commonplace to contrast the Catholic substance of Christianity with the Protestant

---

[14] Ibid., p. 525.

[15] See, for example, Edward I. Watkin, *The Catholic Centre* (New York: Sheed & Ward, 1939), esp. chap. 1.

[16] Walter Kasper, *An Introduction to Christian Faith* (New York: Paulist, 1980), p. viii.

principle. Paul Tillich especially popularized this polarity.[17] By the Catholic substance he meant the embodiment of the Spiritual Presence in holy persons and institutions, in word and sacrament. By the Protestant principle he meant the critical or prophetic mandate to protest against any claims to divine dignity made on behalf of these embodiments. Tillich's point of view, as we shall see, had its basis in a whole line of Protestant thinkers beginning with Hegel and Schelling. Lutherans of our day, such as Jaroslav Pelikan and George Lindbeck, continue to warn that the Protestant principle is needed to prevent Catholicism from becoming ossified, magical, demonic, and idolatrous.

At an informal dialogue with Professor Lindbeck at Gettysburg Lutheran Seminary in 1980, Professor Carl Peter asserted the necessity of admitting not only a Catholic substance but a Catholic principle. His point, as I understand it, was that unless the substance is protected by a principle it will gradually be eroded by a criticism that does not know where to stop. As one formulation of the Catholic principle he proposed: 'Be not so prone to expect abuse that you fail to recognize God's grace as working, as having worked, and as hopefully going to work again' through the means that have been given.[18] The Catholic principle, he went on to say, prevents one from calling sin what God has made clean (cf. Acts 10: 14). It enables one to hear the command, 'Put off your shoes from your feet, for the place upon which you are standing is holy ground' (Exod. 3: 5). The Catholic principle thus keeps Christianity, whether Protestant or Catholic, from falling into sins of irreverence, scepticism, and sacrilege, which are no less deleterious than magic, superstition, and idolatry.

Reflecting on this recent development in ecumenical discussion, I would be inclined to speak of a Christian substance and of two principles. The Protestant principle, as a critical norm, prevents one from blurring the distinction between God and creature and from attributing divine status to that which is finite and defectible. The Catholic principle, conversely, criti-

---

[17] This theme is pervasive in the writings of Paul Tillich. See, e.g., his *Systematic Theology*, vol. iii (Chicago: Univ. of Chicago Press, 1963), pp. 6 and 245.

[18] Carl J. Peter, 'Justification and the Catholic Principle', *Lutheran Theological Seminary Bulletin*, vol. lxi, no. 1 (Feb. 1981), pp. 16–32, quotation from p. 22.

cizes the critics. It warns them not to banish God from his creation and not to minimize the gifts of God in Christ and in the Holy Spirit.

The Catholic principle is an acceptance of mediation, and indeed of visible mediation. It asserts that God ordinarily comes to us through the structures that are given, especially those to which his gracious promises are attached, such as Incarnation, Scripture, sacrament, and apostolic ministry. The first attitude of the believer toward Christ, the Bible, the Church, and tradition ought not to be one of suspicion but, on principle, one of trusting receptivity. If it later appears that there are reasons for suspecting that the mediation has been faulty, the time will come for criticism and even protest. But if criticism comes too early it can be corrosive of faith.

The concept of a Catholic principle is not a new invention. When Johann Adam Möhler in 1825 wrote his masterful work, *Unity in the Church*, he gave it the sub-title, 'The Principle of Catholicism'.[19] For the young Möhler the Catholic principle signified the quasi-organic unity brought about by the abiding presence of the Holy Spirit in the Church as a whole and in all its parts. Möhler stressed that the Holy Spirit, as divine reconciling principle, blends the differences among the members into a rich, diversified harmony. In his later work Möhler gave greater attention to the incarnational and institutional aspects of Catholicism. His focus became Christological rather than primarily Pneumatological, but he retained the theme of a synthesis of contrasting elements.

It is significant that Tillich, who particularly insisted on the 'Protestant principle', had difficulty in accepting the doctrine of the Incarnation. Although he was quite prepared to acknowledge the symbolic value of the biblical picture of Jesus as the Christ, he seemed unable, consistently with his own principles, to admit a real union of the divine with the human in Jesus Christ. George Tavard rightly observes of Tillich: 'When he himself tried "to find new forms in which the Christological substance of the past can be expressed," the Christological substance vanished'.[20]

[19] Johann Adam Möhler, *Die Einheit in der Kirche oder Das Prinzip des Katholizismus*, ed. J. R. Geiselmann (Cologne: J. Hegner, 1956).

[20] George H. Tavard, *Paul Tillich and the Christian Message* (New York: Scribner's, 1962), p. 132. He here quotes from Tillich's *Systematic Theology*, vol. ii, p. 145.

Something resembling Tillich's dialectic of Catholic substance and Protestant principle was proposed from the
Catholic side by the French lay theologian, Jean Guitton. The
essence of Protestantism, he suggested, lies in its quest for
purity. As the religion of separation and transcendence, it is on
guard against alloys and compromises. Catholicism, while
striving for purity, accepts the provisional combination of the
pure and the impure. 'It is afraid of disturbing the indwelling
presence of the good by detaching it too soon from the less good
and even the evil, which are bound up with it.'[21] Catholicism,
according to Guitton, insists more than does Protestantism on
composition, on the immanence of eternity in time, and on the
impregnation of nature by grace.

Guitton would seem to be here putting in different words the
same basic idea that we have found in McBrien and Imbelli:
that of sacramental consciousness or sacramental mediation.
All three of these authors help to spell out in greater detail what
Professor Peter apparently means by the Catholic principle.

(4)

The relationship between catholicity and Catholicism cannot
be settled at the beginning of our investigation, since the terms
are used with different nuances in different theological systems.
However the two terms may be distinguished, they cannot be
entirely separated, for both are derived from the same Greek
root (*kath'holou*) which, as we shall see, implies not only
extensive universality but also qualitative wholeness. Catholicity, like Catholicism, stands in opposition to incompleteness,
partiality, diminishment, factionalism, sectarianism, and
heretical selectivity. In general usage, however, the two terms
have different connotations. Catholicity suggests universality
in a rather abstract sense, whereas Catholicism is more closely
connected with the structures that make for the transmission
and retention of that particular fullness which was given in
Christ to the apostles and the apostolic community. In this
sense Catholicism may be said to include not only universality
but also unity, holiness, and apostolicity, or, more generally, all
that is required for the essential fullness of the Church.

[21] Jean Guitton, *The Church and the Gospel* (Chicago: Regnery, 1961), p. 225.

In intellectual circles today catholicity is commonly praised, whereas Catholicism is an object of suspicion. Whoever is catholic, in the sense of having *catholicity*, is esteemed as open-minded, tolerant, and undogmatic. But to be Catholic in the sense of professing *Catholicism* is regarded as signifying a closed, intolerant, and dogmatic spirit. According to the view I shall propose, catholicity and Catholicism are closely correlated. Catholicity always implies, in principle, adherence to the fullness of God's gift in Christ. Christianity is inclusive not by reason of latitudinarian permissiveness or syncretistic promiscuity, but because it has received from God a message and a gift for people of every time and place, so that all can find in it the fulfilment of their highest selves.

Catholicity, no less than Catholicism, depends upon the free disposition of God whereby his transcendence makes itself present in our world, thanks to the missions of the Son and the Holy Spirit. Catholicity demands that we accept Jesus as Lord, not because God demonstrably had to come to us in this way, but because he has in fact willed to make himself present in this wandering rabbi of first-century Palestine. Jesus Christ is, so to speak, the concrete universal, for in the particularity and contingency of his human existence the plenitude of divine life is made available to all who will receive it. Without Christ and the Holy Spirit the Church would not have the fullness of power and holiness that founds its claim to be Catholic. The 'Catholic principle' enables the Christian to adhere to the fullness that has been given.

(5)

The positions briefly indicated in this introduction will be set forth in greater detail in the chapters that follow. In Chapter 1 we shall briefly consider the history of the concept of catholicity and pose the problem of catholicity in the context of the contemporary world. In the next four chapters we shall consider four facets of catholicity, which may be designated as its height, depth, breadth, and length. Chapter 2 will take up the divine source of catholicity, particularly in Christ as Incarnate Word. In Chapter 3 we shall reflect on the way in which Catholic Christianity accepts, completes, corrects, and elevates

what is given in nature, and in this connection we shall have
occasion to touch on the relationship between Christianity and
the other religions. In Chapter 4 we shall turn our attention to
the universal expansive dynamism of Catholic Christianity and
to the type of unity to be sought in the universal Church.
Chapter 5 will be concerned with catholicity in time; it will deal
with the idea of development and with the preservation of
continuity through change.

The remaining chapters will deal more particularly with
Catholicism as a specific ecclesial type. Chapter 6 will be
devoted to the sacramental principle and the visible structures
of authority. Chapter 7, continuing the same theme, will
discuss the unifying role of the 'Petrine' see and the bishop of
Rome. In Chapter 8 we shall return to a question already
broached in the Introduction regarding the relationships
between Protestant and Catholic Christianity. In a final con-
cluding reflection we shall touch on the prospects of Catholicism as it struggles to become a world Church in what some
have called a 'diaspora situation'.

Each of these chapters may be seen as developing a particular aspect of the Catholic principle, which underlies and
sustains all the features I shall present as distinctively Catholic:
the Incarnation, the essential goodness of nature, the universal
expansiveness of the Church, its inner unity, its continuous life,
the reliability of sacramental mediation, the authority of the
hierarchical ministry, and the truth of dogmatic teaching.

Appendix I, which I regard as an integral part of the book,
may best be studied in connection with Chapter 1. The six
testimonies reveal, in my estimation, the richness of the traditional concept of catholicity, its relative stability through time,
and the gradual shifts made to accommodate new situations.

Cyril of Jerusalem, our first witness, representing the Greek-
speaking communities of the fourth century, brings out what
modern theologians call the qualitative aspects of catholicity,
especially its fullness of truth and healing power. The next
representative, Thomas Aquinas, is heir to the Augustinian
tradition. Like Augustine, he emphasizes the Church's universality in space and time, its origins with Abel, and its survival
into eternity. Philipp Melanchthon, a sixteenth-century
Lutheran, exemplifies the acceptance of the classic concept of

catholicity in early Protestantism with a slighly stronger accent on the Bible ('the prophets and apostles') as the norm of sound doctrine.

The fourth testimony, drawn from a committee report commissioned by the Archbishop of Canterbury in 1947, represents a modern Anglo-Catholic point of view. Notable is the emphasis on adherence to, and recovery of, the objectively given structures, ecclesial, creedal, and sacramental.

For a contemporary Roman Catholic position I have selected a passage from Vatican Council II's Constitution on the Church. It brings out the Christological and Pneumatological dimensions of catholicity, as well as the inner diversity implied by the term. I hope I have succeeded better than other translators in conveying the exact force of the Latin text. In many translations much is lost: for example, one misses the term 'recapitulate', which the council took over from the New Testament (Eph. 1: 10) and from the Greek Fathers.

Finally, I have reproduced a passage from the Uppsala Report of 1968 to illustrate how the traditional concept of catholicity is reaffirmed by the World Council of Churches in a more secular framework. The passage is also striking for its eschatological emphasis.

The Concept of Catholicity:
Yesterday and Today

THE catholicity of the Church, which will be the primary theme of the next five chapters and a central concern of this whole book, is today under severe challenge, while at the same time it challenges every Christian and every human being. In order to perceive these reciprocal challenges one must have some clarity about what catholicity means. The present chapter is intended to convey a preliminary working notion. The concept of Catholicism will be left for analysis in later chapters.

(1)

In the Apostles' Creed Christians profess their belief in 'the holy catholic Church'. In the Nicene–Constantinopolitan Creed this article is amplified to say, 'We believe in one holy catholic and apostolic Church'. The four adjectives in this sentence are often understood as identification marks, all of which must be present for the Church to be what it must be.

Even if this be granted, some problems remain. It is not clear on the surface whether the creed is asserting a fact about the Church as it actually exists, an ideal of what it ought to be, or a promise about what it eventually will be. If a present fact, is catholicity verifiably present in the visible, institutional Church or perceptible only by faith in an invisible Church? If visible, is the catholic Church some one particular body (e.g. Roman Catholic or Orthodox), or several bodies of a certain type ('catholic churches'), or the entire collectivity of baptized believers, regardless of their ecclesiastical affiliation? As for catholicity, does it mean universal extension, fullness of grace, purity of doctrine, apostolic ministry, or what? On all these points controversies have raged.

The meaning of catholicity cannot be settled from the Bible, for the Bible never uses the term in a theological sense. Except in the canonical titles to certain epistles, the only occurrence in the New Testament is the adverb *katholou* which, in combination with the negative particle *me*, translated as 'not at all' (Acts 4: 18).

Greek profane usage gives little help, for the term *katholikos* (derived from *kath'holou*) has a wide range of meanings such as general, total, complete, and perfect.

Theologians have often tried to base their concept of catholicity on the earliest Christian usage in Ignatius of Antioch and the *Martyrdom of Polycarp*, but unfortunately the fleeting appearances of the adjective *katholikos* in these authors lend themselves to various interpretations. Some patristic scholars favour the sense of 'pure' or 'authentic'; others, 'universal' or 'total'.[1] By the middle of the fourth centry the term begins to take on a more precise meaning. It generally refers to the great Church in opposition to dissident Christian groups. Cyril of Jerusalem in his *Catechetical Lectures* gives the fullest discussion of the term in Christian antiquity. He assigns five reasons why the Church is called catholic: it extends to the ends of the earth; it teaches all the doctrine needed for salvation; it brings every sort of human being under obedience; it cures every kind of sin; and it possesses every form of virtue.[2]

The next major step in the history of the term occurred in Northern Africa in the fourth and fifth centuries. Against the Donatists, who identified catholicity with the strict observance of the commandments, orthodox controversialists such as Optatus and Augustine held that catholicity meant communion with the Church spread over the whole world.

In Augustine this contention was linked to a high spirituality of Christian love as emanating from God and sealed by the Eucharist, the sacrament of universal communion. The communion of grace for Augustine extended to all times and places. In its full extension the Body of Christ, he believed, includes

---

[1] Discussion may be found in J. N. D. Kelly, ' "Catholic" and "Apostolic" in the Early Centuries', *One in Christ*, vi (1970), 274–87, esp. pp. 275–8. Further literature is indicated in Yves Congar, *L'Église: une, sainte, catholique et apostolique. Mysterium Salutis* 15 (Paris: Cerf, 1970), pp. 150–1. See also Wolfgang Beinert, *Um das dritte Kirchenattribut* (Essen: Ludgerus-Verlag, 1964), pp. 36–45.

[2] Cyril of Jerusalem, *Catecheses*, 18: 23; *PG* 33: 1047. See Appendix I.

members from Abel, the righteous one, to the final consummation of the heavenly Kingdom.[3]

In the Middle Ages there was no major shift. Bonaventure,
Albertus Magnus, and Thomas Aquinas follow the patristic
authors, especially Augustine. St. Thomas, with his metaphysical perspective, sees catholicity as freedom from all the
limitations of particularity. Because it possesses this property
the Church, he says, is able to transcend the frontiers of place
and time and to include people of every kind and condition.[4]

(2)

The fifteenth and sixteenth centuries witnessed what one may
call the first great crisis of catholicity. After the Council of
Florence the separation between the Eastern and Western
churches, which had previously appeared to be a temporary
rupture of communion, became definitive. In the sixteenth
century the Western church itself broke up into a multiplicity of
contending factions, Lutheran, Reformed, Anglican, and
Roman—bodies which in the ensuing centuries continued to
subdivide. As a result of these multiple fractures certain shifts
occurred in the very meaning of catholicity, which was differently understood by different groups. I can here speak only
of the most important trends.

The Orthodox churches have continued to claim catholicity,
which for them means, above all else, adherence to the fullness of
the faith as handed down from the Fathers. Orthodox writers, as
we shall see, insist that each local church is catholic if it embodies
this qualitative plenitude and celebrates it in the liturgy.[5]

Roman Catholics, faced by the dissolution of Western
Christendom, went back to Augustine's arguments against the
Donatists to prove that their own communion, by reason of its

[3] On Augustine see Beinert, *Kirchenattribut*, pp. 55–63, which provides references to
important literature. Beinert does not overlook passages in which Augustine teaches
that the Church is called 'catholic' also because it retains the totality: e.g. Ep. ad
Vincentium 93, 23 (*CSEL* 34: 468).

[4] On Aquinas see Beinert, *Kirchenattribut*, pp. 83–5. Of special interest is Aquinas's
commentary *In Symbolum Apostolorum, Opusculum VII* (Parma edn., vol. xxi, pp. 135–51,
esp. art. IX, p. 148). See Appendix I.

[5] e.g., Vladimir Lossky, 'Concerning the Third Mark of the Church: Catholicity',
chap. 4 of his *In the Image and Likeness of God* (New York: St Vladimir's Seminary Press,
1974), pp. 169–81.

wider geographical extension, was the true Church of Christ. Gustave Thils, in his important study of Counter–Reformation apologetics,[6] adverts to this focus on universality in the spatial sense. In the nineteenth century this emphasis on extension was coupled with a special concern for visible unity, understood as an adherence to the same set of doctrines, rites, and hierarchical leaders. In this school all four attributes or marks of the Church tended to be reduced to apostolicity, in the sense of obedience to the bishops who were in union with the pope, and thus ultimately obedience to the pope himself as supreme vicar of Christ. Some nineteenth-century Catholics in effect treated *romanitas* as a fifth mark of the Church.[7]

Setting the trend for some Protestants, Luther was unhappy with the term 'catholic' in the Creed. Perhaps because the word was imported from Greek, he translated it by the German word *christlich* (Christian). Many of the early Lutheran theologians, however, including Philipp Melanchthon and John Gerhard, contended that their own church was catholic because it adhered to the doctrine of Scripture and to the common teaching of the Fathers of the ancient, undivided Church. They accused Rome of having introduced doctrinal innovations and of having thereby departed from catholicity.[8]

In the period of the Enlightenment many theologians saw pure reason as the principle of universality and lost interest in the Church and its catholicity. But in the early nineteenth century, under the stimulus of Romanticism, a new enthusiasm for the catholic tradition arose both in Germany and in England. In Germany the chief bearers of this revival were the leaders of the Catholic Tübingen school, Johann Sebastian Drey and Johann Adam Möhler. In England this new impetus was promoted by the Oxford movement under the leadership of John Keble, Edward Pusey, and John Henry Newman. In both these movements scholars went back to the Greek Fathers and found in them a richer, more imaginative, and more appealing

---

[6] Gustave Thils, *Les Notes de l'Église dans l'Apologétique catholique depuis la Réforme* (Gembloux: Duculot, 1937).

[7] Congar, *Église une*, pp. 259–61. See below, Chapter 7.

[8] On Luther, Melanchthon, and J. Gerhard, see Beinert, *Kirchenattribut*, pp. 93–109; also, from a Lutheran perspective, Peter Steinacker, *Die Kennzeichen der Kirche* (Berlin: Walter de Gruyter, 1982), chap. 4, pp. 102–41. Steinacker includes a section on Calvin, pp. 126–40.

presentation of the faith than had been seen at any later time. Catholicity for these nineteenth-century theologians meant primarily the religion of incarnation and divine indwelling. Looking upon the life of grace as necessarily mediated by the Church and the sacraments, these authors professed a highly ecclesial and liturgical piety.[9]

The liberal Protestantism of the late nineteenth and early twentieth centuries offered still another, rather unfavourable, vision of catholicity. For Adolf von Harnack and Rudolph Sohm, primitive Christianity had not been Catholic, but the Church became Catholic in the third century or thereabouts as it struggled against heresies such as Gnosticism. The marks of catholicity for Harnack were traditionalism, orthodoxy, ritualism, and monasticism, but in the West, under the influence of Rome, it took on an additional mark, namely, legalism. The Church with its rules of thought and behaviour, according to these liberals, set itself in place of the gospel. Human authority took the place of the divine Spirit, which was no longer immediately experienced. Catholicity was therefore a kind of original fall from grace which overtook the Church in the course of its history. The Reformation was seen as a protest against this defection and as a call to evangelical renewal.[10]

Between the Reformation and the Second World War, therefore, the concept of catholicity was presented under four principal aspects, partly overlapping but partly antithetical.

1. Especially among Greek Orthodox theologians, catholicity was understood to mean adherence to the full apostolic heritage as expressed in the great councils and patristic theologians of the fourth and fifth centuries.

2. In the Roman Catholicism of the Counter-Reformation and neo-Scholasticism, catholicity meant wide geographical extension combined with manifest unity under a single governing authority.

3. For the Catholics of the Tübingen school and for the

---

[9] See Geoffrey Rowell, *The Vision Glorious: Themes and Personalities of the Catholic Revival in Anglicanism* (Oxford: Oxford Univ. Press, 1983), pp. 1–97; James E. Griffiss, *Church, Ministry and Unity* (Oxford: Blackwell, 1983), pp. 1–40.

[10] For Harnack's basic position see his *What Is Christianity?* (New York: Harper Torchbooks, 1957), pp. 207–68. In his *The Constitution and Law of the Church in the First Two Centuries* (New York: Putnam's, 1910), Harnack compares his views with those of Sohm.

Anglicans of the Oxford movement, with the disciples of both groups down to our own day, catholicity meant incarnational and sacramental religion, in which divine life was mediated by the living Church.

4. For the liberal Protestants, Catholic Christianity meant legalistic religion in which divine authority was falsely claimed for human ecclesiastical regulations. This suspicion of things Catholic has been shared by many evangelical Protestants professing to follow biblical religion.

When the World Council of Churches held its First Assembly at Amsterdam in 1948, the question of catholicity inevitably came to the fore. The Assembly reported that the deepest difference among the member churches was between those of the Catholic and those of the Protestant type. The former put primary emphasis on 'the visible continuity of the Church in the apostolic succession of the episcopate', whereas the latter emphasized 'the initiative of the Word of God and the response of faith, focused on the doctrine of justification *sola fide*'.[11]

(3)

Prior to the middle of the present century the principal challenge to catholicity seemed to come from liberal or evangelical Christianity. But in the last few decades other challenges have been more strongly felt. Civilization has become increasingly pluralistic and intercultural. European dominance in culture and religion as well as in politics and economics has been on the decline. All traditions, moreover, are threatened by the acceleration of social change. Attention is focused more on the future than on the past. Threatened by the products of human technology, people are more alarmed by the destructive capacities of earthly weapons than by divine retribution. Religion is asked to address the human predicament rather than to pursue its traditional otherworldly goals. This volatile situation poses a new crisis for Christian catholicity, possibly more serious than the crisis that had arisen from the break-up of the 'undivided Church' at the end of the Middle Ages. Each of the conceptions of catholicity that has been prevalent

---

[11] Willem A. Visser 't Hooft (ed.), *The First Assembly of the World Council of Churches* (London: SCM, 1949), p. 52.

in the past few centuries finds itself called into question.

1. In many parts of the world, the Orthodox view of catholicity as adherence to patristic tradition seems anachronistic. However much one may admire the Greek Fathers of the fifth century, the contemporary secular mind is unable to accept their views and practices as definitive. The Fathers, it is said, were men of their times whose limitations must be frankly acknowledged. A church that failed to admit change and development beyond the patristic age would commonly be regarded as no more than an interesting relic of the past.

2. The apologetics of the Counter-Reformation and of neo-Scholasticism is no more acceptable than patristic restorationism. In the expanded horizons of the mid-twentieth century the alleged universality of the Roman Catholic Church no longer makes any great impression. Like other branches of Christianity, it appears embarrassingly Western and particularist. Roman Catholicism makes up scarcely half of Christianity, and all Christians taken together are only about one-third of the human race. Because of the population growth in Asia and Africa, the percentage of Christians and Catholics in the world is continually decreasing. In view of the ecumenical movement, moreover, non-Roman Christianity can no longer be dismissed as a Babel of confusion. There is a new emphasis on World Confessional Families, Lutheran, Reformed, and Anglican. Regional and denominational bodies have begun to enter into co-operative relationships and in some cases to unite. The World Council of Churches, for all its internal dissension, offers an impressive spectacle of multiform unity.

Meanwhile other universalisms have begun to appear. The international expansion of Islam and Buddhism enables them to claim a catholicity comparable to that of the Christian churches. Various non-religious ideologies such as Marxist socialism can boast of large international membership and of disciplined internal unity. Organizations such as the United Nations, for all their failings, surpass any given church in their inclusiveness. Although the United Nations has not succeeded in preventing hostility and armed conflict among its members, it is believed by some to hold greater promise as an instrument of reconciliation than dogmatic religions, such as Christianity and Islam, with their long record of polemics, persecutions, and holy wars.

In their search for a truly international civilization many turn to the arts and sciences rather than to religion. In our own day peoples of many nations and cultures can experience community in their appreciation for music and the visual arts and in their acceptance of the findings of modern science. United in their taste for beauty and their respect for reason, they feel divided from one another by their religious faith. The inner unity within any given religious group serves only to sharpen its antagonism to other groups.

3. The Catholic revivals of the Tübingen school and of high church movements, such as that of Oxford in the nineteenth century, can still be appreciated, but the ecclesiocentrism of these revivals is often criticized. More specifically, their liturgical piety incurs the suspicion of being a flight from the harsh realities of a world in which so many people lack the most elemental human necessities. In desperate circumstances it can seem almost obscene for Christians to seek communion with God in ornate, incense-filled sanctuaries. It is widely felt that catholicity cannot be viable in our time unless it includes the entire redemptive plan of God, extending to the whole of humanity and even to the inanimate material world.

4. The authoritarianism and legalism attacked by liberal Protestantism have become even less popular than a century ago. In the mass culture of our technological age, any vision of catholicity that ascribes divine authority to a hierarchical caste tends to be met with scorn and resentment. Catholicity cannot be credible unless it respects the freedom and dignity of every human being and gives scope for initiatives from below.

(4)

In the remainder of this chapter I should like to examine three corporate efforts to reinterpret catholicity in the light of this changed situation. The first of these in time is the teaching of Vatican Council II (1962–5). I cannot here go into the council's teaching on subjects such as collegiality, the ministry, the laity, religious freedom, the liturgy, development of doctrine, and the Church in the modern world, all of which would be pertinent to our topic, but it will be possible to indicate what the council had to say on the specific point of catholicity.

Since the Reformation it had become common in Roman Catholic apologetics to assert that the Church of Christ, with its four marks of unity, holiness, catholicity, and apostolicity, was simply identical with the Roman Catholic communion, and that catholicity, consequently, belonged to it alone. In opposition to the Anglo-Catholics, the Holy Office declared in 1864: 'No other church is catholic except that which is built on the one individual Peter, and which grows up into one body closely joined and knit together [see Eph. 4: 16] in the unity of faith and love.'[12]

Vatican Council II, without directly contradicting this doctrine, nuanced it in a remarkable way. In its Constitution on the Church it predicated catholicity not directly of the Roman Catholic Church but rather of the Church of Christ, which the council depicted as 'subsisting' in the Catholic Church (*LG* 8), so that the fullness of catholicity was not obtainable except in communion with Rome (*UR* 4). But the Church of Christ was held to be present in some measure in other Christian communities, which could participate in catholicity to the extent that they continued to accept and live by the authentic Christian heritage. The Decree on Ecumenism could therefore teach that the 'entire heritage of spirituality and liturgy, of discipline and theology' in the various traditions of the Orthodox churches 'belongs to the full catholic and apostolic character of the Church' (*UR* 17), and that 'some Catholic traditions and institutions continue to exist in certain Western communities, such as the Anglican Communion' (*UR* 13). Vatican II's concept of catholicity may therefore be called cautiously ecumenical rather than narrowly confessional.

The council's vision of the Church, moreover, was not limited to the Christian arena. While acknowledging that the Church may at times appear as a 'little flock', the council asserted that Christ, the universal Saviour, continues to use it as an instrument for the redemption of all (*LG* 9). 'All are called to be part of this catholic unity of the People of God' (*LG* 13). The Constitution on the Church goes on to assert that all human beings, even those to whom the gospel has not as yet

[12] Letter of the Holy Office to the Bishops of England, 16 Sept. 1864 (DS 2888).

been preached, are related to the Church of Christ (*LG* 16). This general statement is then specified with respect to four groups: Jews, Muslims, adherents of other religions, and atheists. None of these groups is excluded from the redemptive influence of Christ, which impels its recipients toward the catholic unity of the Church. The grace of Christ thus operates in a secret way in all persons of good will, ordering them toward salvation and disposing them to accept the gospel if and when they hear it credibly proclaimed (*LG* 16–17).

The Church, according to Vatican II, achieves its catholicity in a historically palpable way by evangelizing all peoples. Missionary activity is therefore seen both as an expression and as an intensification of the Church's catholicity. By evangelizing the world the Church can become in manifest actuality what in principle it has been from its origins—the universal communion of all men and women with God in Christ. 'It is plain, then', we read in the Decree on Missionary Activity, 'that missionary activity wells up from the Church's innermost nature and spreads abroad her saving faith. It perfects her Catholic unity by expanding it' (*AG* 6). The New Covenant, according to the same Decree, calls for a Church that speaks all tongues and 'thus overcomes the divisiveness of Babel' (*AG* 4). Inspired by this vision, the Church 'prays and labors in order that the entire world may become the People of God, the Body of the Lord, and the Temple of the Holy Spirit' (*LG* 17).

At various points in its documents, Vatican II acknowledged that the catholicity of the Church is in fact limited. One reason has already been indicated: the failure of Christian missionary activity to have effectively reached all peoples and all individuals with the good news of Jesus Christ. A second reason, chiefly treated in the Decree on Ecumenism, is the inner dividedness of Christianity itself. To overcome this, the Church is under grave obligation to pursue the apostolate of Christian unity. 'The divisions among Christians', says the Decree, 'prevent the Church from effecting the fullness of catholicity proper to her in those of her children who, though joined to her by baptism, are yet separated from full communion with her' (*UR* 4). This renders it 'difficult for the Church to express in actual life her full catholicity in all its aspects' (ibid.). In other words, the Catholic Church itself is a less splendid expression than it ought to be of Christ's universal redemptive power.

A third obstacle to catholicity is the failure of Catholics themselves to realize in their own household the kind of unity God wills for the Church. In this connection the Decree on Ecumenism insists on the importance of preserving a healthy freedom and diversity in styles of spirituality, discipline, and liturgy, and in the formulation of revealed truth (*UR* 16–17). The council at this point echoes the axiom popularized by Pope John XXIII: unity in necessary matters, freedom in others, and charity in all. As we shall see more in detail in the coming chapters, this principle has important applications to the local church. 'The variety of local churches with one common aspiration', says the Constitution on the Church, 'is particularly splendid evidence of the catholicity of the undivided Church' (*LG* 23). Elsewhere the Constitution asserts that legitimate differences, far from impeding catholic unity, can actually enrich and strengthen it (*LG* 13).

Aloys Grillmeier, in his reflections on catholicity in chapter II of the Constitution on the Church, rightly highlights the idea of *communio*—a fellowship achieved through the mutual sharing of spiritual gifts.

Thus catholicity is understood as a union of opposites. The people of God represents one pole, in its unity and unicity, but also in being graced by the Spirit. The other pole is formed by the multiplicity of the peoples of the earth, with their various customs, talents, and energies, which are to be preserved for them insofar as they are genuine values and used to bring into the family of Christ all those who are called to the one people of God. . . . One of the achievements of the Council was the rediscovery of the universal Church as the sum and communion of the local Churches, understood as fully themselves, and the rediscovery of the universal Church in the local Church (see Article 28).[13]

A new development in Vatican II, in comparison with previous official Catholic teaching, is the doctrine that the whole Catholic Church is present and operative in the local church. This dynamic presence is variously attributed to the

---

[13] Aloys Grillmeier, Commentary on *Lumen gentium*, chap. 2, in Herbert Vorgrimler (ed.), *Commentary on the Documents of Vatican II* (New York: Herder and Herder, 1967), vol. 1, p. 167.

bishop, the gospel, and especially to the Eucharist, as the sacrament of unity in which Christ himself is truly present with his grace (*LG* 26, *CD* 11).

In summary, Vatican II presents catholicity not as a monotonous repetition of identical elements but rather as reconciled diversity. It is a unity among individuals and groups who retain their distinctive characteristics, who enjoy different spiritual gifts, and are by that very diversity better equipped to serve one another and thus advance the common good. Individual Christians and local churches are bound to one another in mutual service and mutual receptivity. This relationship is founded not upon domination but on a free exchange of trust and respect. Thanks to Christ's faithfulness to his promise to be with his people, catholicity is never lacking to the Church. But it is dynamic and expansive; it continually presses forward to a fullness and inclusiveness not yet attained. It is a ferment at work in the Catholic Church and in every authentic Christian community. Even beyond the borders of explicit Christianity, the grace of Christ, working in the hearts of all who are open to it, brings individuals and groups into a saving relationship with the Church catholic, the God-given sign and sacrament of the ultimate unity to which the entire human race is called. Thus the Catholic Church is, according to the teaching of Vatican II, 'a lasting and sure seed of unity, hope, and salvation for the whole human race' (*LG* 9).

Vatican II's doctrine of catholicity is not, to be sure, a totally new invention. It is for the most part a selection and recombination of elements taken from the tradition. It draws heavily on the New Testament and on ancient theologians such as Irenaeus and Eusebius, Augustine and Aquinas. Here and there one can perhaps detect the influence of a Johann Adam Möhler, a John Henry Newman, an Henri de Lubac, and especially an Yves Congar. Although securely rooted in the tradition, the council's teaching on catholicity is attuned to the new situation that became evident after World War II. It takes cognizance of the plurality of cultures, the other Christian churches, the non-Christian religions, and atheism. Optimistic without being overweening, modest without being abject, this treatment of catholicity is serene and attractive. In comparison with papal teaching of the nineteenth centry, Vatican II shows a remarkable respect for freedom and diversity, both within the Church and in the larger sphere of human relations.

(5)

Let me now turn, more briefly, to a second collective statement on catholicity. In 1968 a Joint Theological Commission of eighteen members, half from the World Council of Churches and half from the Roman Catholic Church, drew up an important study document on 'Catholicity and Apostolicity'.[14] The treatment of catholicity in this document is remarkable for its focus on Christ and the Holy Spirit. The Church, according to this statement, possesses catholicity as a gift it can never lose because, thanks to the messianic outpouring of Pentecost, it inalienably bears the mystery of Christ, in whom all things have been summed up. The Church, however, lives and effectively achieves its catholicity inasmuch as it expresses in its actual conduct the integral truth and unbounded charity of Christ and his divine Spirit. The full consummation of this universal communion in the truth will never occur on earth, but is an eschatological gift reserved for the day of Christ's return in glory. Through missionary endeavour the Church continually strives for a fuller realization of its catholicity.

The concept of catholicity, finally, is clarified by contrast with the ways in which catholicity is betrayed. The Joint Theological Commission signals four aberrations: the restriction of Christian communion to certain races, nations, or classes; the formation of sects or parties within the Church; pride in one's own confession to the detriment of others; and finally, misuse of the term 'catholic' to support ideas or practices destructive of Christian identity.

Having left certain difficulties unresolved, the study document relegated to appendices disputed questions concerning matters such as conciliarity and primacy, unity and plurality, the local church and the universal Church.

Although it has no authority comparable to the teachings of an ecumenical council, this study document is important for registering the broad consensus that can be attained between

[14] Text in *One in Christ*, vi (1970), pp. 452–83.

Roman Catholics, Orthodox, Anglicans, Lutherans, and Reformed. The text is valuable also for the attention it gives to the Christological and pneumatological foundations of the Church's catholicity. This special emphasis may well be due to the strong participation of Orthodox theologians.

(6)

The most significant ecumenical statement on catholicity in recent decades, and the last I shall here consider, came from the Fourth Assembly of the World Council of Churches, which met at Uppsala in 1968. Its first section report was on the subject, 'The Holy Spirit and the Catholicity of the Church'.[15] This report represents a notable advance from 1948 when, as we have seen, the World Council was content to use the term 'catholic' as a label for churches of a certain orientation. The Uppsala Report, by contrast, affirms that the Church is and should be catholic in all her elements and in all aspects of her life (no. 7). It self-consciously strives to make the idea of catholicity palatable and credible to the secular mind, which in 1968 was at the height of its assertiveness. Adverting to the 'secular catholicities' now challenging the Church, Uppsala points out both the distinctiveness of the Church's catholicity and the value of that catholicity for answering the aspirations of the human spirit for wholeness and unity.

The concept of catholicity in this document may be described as qualitative rather than quantitative. Gone is the traditional stress on geographical extension, presumably because the modern mind, accustomed to global perspectives, finds the Church all too Western. No effort, moreover, is made to exploit catholicity as a visible mark of the true Church. Aware of the attraction of worldly solidarities, the Assembly cautions against confusing them with the catholicity of the Church which issues from the unifying grace of the Holy Spirit, uniting men and women in faith, love, and service for the sake of the world. In a key sentence catholicity is described as 'the quality by which the Church expresses the fullness, the integrity, and the totality of life in Christ' (no. 7).

[15] Text in Norman Goodall (ed.), *The Uppsala Report* (Geneva: World Council of Churches, 1968), pp. 11–18.

Since the grace of Christ requires a human response, catholicity is both a divine gift and a human task. While both these aspects are affirmed, the Uppsala Report puts greater emphasis on the task. To this extent it reflects the social awareness and activism of the 1960s.

Like Vatican II, the World Council gives considerable scope for inner diversity within the Church. Catholic unity is held to be compatible with manifold ways of presenting doctrinal truth, with diverse styles of worship, and with different patterns of church organization.

Although not reduced to any secular reality, catholicity is described as being intimately connected with human aspirations for peace, justice and community. The Church is designated as a sign of the coming unity of mankind (no. 20). Committed to this vision, Christians are obliged to work against all forces of division and alienation such as prejudice, discrimination, oppression, and excessive loyalty to one's own party or nation (nos. 10, 22). The evils of racism are particularly stressed.

In a full account many other points in this eight-page document would deserve discussion; for example, its contention that catholicity is inseparable from unity, holiness, and apostolicity; its treatment of the criteria for distinguishing between healthy and unhealthy diversity; its search for balance between continuity and renewal; its discussion of the ecumenical movement as a means of achieving a broader catholicity; and finally its attention to eschatology. 'Catholicity reaches its completion when what God has already begun in history is finally disclosed and fulfilled' (no. 6).

Chief credit goes to the Lutherans, it would seem, for having cautioned against the demonic aspects of secular catholicities and against over-estimating the value of human effort for achieving the fullness of catholicity. They apparently stressed the need for patience and prayer for the coming of the Lord in glory. In the final version of the report eschatology serves as a check on excessive activism.

Bishop Karekin Sarkissian of the Armenian Orthodox Church criticized the draft at one stage for promoting a 'futuristic and utopian attitude', as though the Church could become catholic only at the end of history.[16] It was the

---

[16] Ibid., p. 8.

Orthodox, apparently, who particularly insisted on catholicity as a permanent endowment of the Church, and who introduced some mention of the liturgy and the Eucharist as means of preserving and actualizing the Church's catholicity.

Thanks to interventions such as these the final document achieves a fair measure of balance. It does not contradict the teaching of Vatican II or any firm Catholic positions. Among its merits are the attention it gives to the challenges of contemporary secularity, its sensitivity to the social implications of catholicity, and its qualitative description of catholicity as the fullness of life in Christ.

Notwithstanding these merits, the Uppsala document in some respects suffers by comparison with Vatican II's statements on catholicity.[17] Composed by representatives of mutually divided churches, the report could not point to any given church as the place where catholicity subsists. Its concept of catholicity consequently remains rather abstract, floating like a soul in search of its body.

In an important sentence the Church is said to be a sign of the coming unity of mankind. This assertion reminds one of Vatican II's description of the Church as a kind of sacrament of the unity of the human family in Christ (*LG* 1). But unlike Vatican II, Uppsala says 'sign' rather than efficacious sign or sacrament, and thus leaves unexplained the connection between the sign and the reality to which it points. In general the report may be said to neglect the human and visible mediations of grace.

Uppsala's treatment of diversity within the Church leaves something to be desired. The criteria for identifying legitimate diversity are left vague. Missing is Vatican II's idea of the universal Church as a communion of local churches having different gifts for the benefit of all.

The three documents analysed in the second half of this chapter, despite their distinctive emphases, exhibit a significant convergence regarding the nature and importance of catholicity. None of them views catholicity simply, or even

---

[17] For Roman Catholic reactions see Jérôme Hamer, 'Le Saint-Esprit et la catholicité de l'Église', *Angelicum* xli (1969), pp. 387–410; Patrick W. Fuerth, *The Concept of Catholicity in the Documents of the World Council of Churches (1948–1968)* (Rome: Anselmiana, 1973), pp. 184–252.

primarily, as a matter of sheer numbers or geographical extension. None of them writes as though the evident catholicity of a
single communion could be used as proof that it alone is the
Church of Christ. Nor is it claimed that catholicity has been
achieved in perfect or unsurpassable form at any point in time.
All these documents see catholicity as involving an imperative.
They view it as linked not to uniformity but to reconciled
diversity. They present it as demanding different forms in
different times and different cultural settings. Catholicity, as
presented in these documents, is distinctive to the Church but
positively related to the total human community and the
aspirations of that community for peace and harmony. Above
all, these documents insist that catholicity, having its source in
Christ and in the Holy Spirit, is a gift from above, continually
renewed in the celebration of word and sacrament. This gift,
they assert, is destined to reach its completion when Christ
returns in glory.

The various positions set forth in this chapter may serve to
illustrate what catholicity has meant in the Christian tradition.
In subsequent chapters we shall consider the theological
foundations for the kinds of generalizations that make up the
current ecumenical consensus. We shall also seek to cast some
light upon the questions that are still disputed or unresolved.

2

Catholicity from Above: The Fullness of God in Christ

As we read in the Letter to the Ephesians, Paul prays that his readers may be enabled to comprehend 'the breadth and length and height and depth' of the love of Christ, even though this 'surpasses knowledge' (Eph. 3: 18–19). Like the love of Christ, the Church may be viewed as a mystery with four dimensions: height, depth, breadth, and length. In this and the three following chapters we shall consider this fourfold catholicity. In the present chapter we shall reflect on the divine component of catholicity, as the gift of the Father who communicates himself through his incarnate Word and the Holy Spirit. In Chapter 3 I shall turn to the depth dimension of catholicity, its rootedness in the natural and the human. In the following two succeeding chapters I shall discuss the spatial universality of the Church, which may be called catholicity in breadth, and its temporal extension, or its catholicity in length.

Although these aspects will be separately considered, they are interconnected. The geographical extension of the Church and its durability in time come about because it is deeply rooted both in God and in cosmic and human nature. To the extent that the Church is a created participation in the fullness of divine life, it is capable of realizing itself in variety without detriment to its unity. Precisely because of its ontological richness, the Church demands a plurality of forms in which to actualize and express its essence.

(1)

As a general principle we may assert that the higher any entity is on the scale of being, the greater is its inner diversity. Living beings are organic: they contain a multiplicity of powers and organs. The parts and faculties of such beings are mutually ordered to one another and are bound together by dynamic internal relations. The most perfect kind of unity is not static and homogeneous but dynamic and heterogeneous.

This principle, if it is valid, must apply to God as the absolute plenitude of being. His ontological richness may be inferred from the world he has created. The Scriptures assert as much. According to the Wisdom of Solomon (13: 1–9), God possesses in a pre-eminent way all the goodness and beauty found in his creatures; and Paul points out that God's eternal power and deity can be perceived from the things that have been made (Rom. 1: 20). Thus there is good biblical foundation for the doctrine of the analogous knowledge of God, developed with great precision in high Scholasticism. We can attain a real, though obscure, knowledge of God by attributing to him the perfections we find in the universe, and by denying the imperfections, keeping in mind that every perfection in God immeasurably surpasses all its created likenesses. In the famous phrase of Anselm, God is the one than whom no greater can be conceived. He has, or rather is, the unsurpassable fullness of being.

The term *plērōma* (fullness) is perhaps the nearest biblical equivalent for what we call catholicity. Col. 2: 9 speaks of 'the fullness of divinity'. The idea of God's fullness occurs already in the Old Testament, but chiefly in texts about how he fills other things with his presence. Jeremiah, for instance, asks in the name of God, 'Do I not fill heaven and earth?' (23: 24). Isaiah affirms: 'The whole earth is filled with his [God's] glory' (6: 3). And according to Ben Sira, God 'has filled the earth with his good things' (Sir. 16: 29).

Besides implying plenitude, catholicity connotes differentiated unity. This, too, is verified in God, who is, in the phrase of Nicholas of Cusa, *coincidentia oppositorum*. In him knowledge and love, justice and mercy, coincide. The doctrine of the Trinity makes it evident that God's unity is not static and monotonous but consists in a dynamic interaction. The Father and the Son are constituted by the mutually opposed relations of paternity and filiation; the Holy Spirit originates through the mutually opposed relations of active and passive spiration. These inner differentiations, far from impairing the divine unity, bring the divine persons into the closest possible union. The Father communicates the fullness of his own being to the Son, and the

Father and Son, as a single co-principle, communicate that same being to the Holy Spirit, so that each of the divine persons has one and the same nature, not partially but totally. The Father is God, the Son is God, and the Holy Spirit is God, not three Gods but one. God, then, is both one and many; he is the supreme instance of both unicity and communication.

The divine catholicity, as I like to call it, does not remain sealed up in the godhead. Out of the fullness of his love, God wills to communicate his goodness and share it with others. Created beings are likenesses and participations of God's absolute perfection. In him, as we read in the Acts, 'we live and move and have our being' (17: 28), so that the one God, as the Letter to the Ephesians puts it, 'is above all and through all and in all' (4: 6). God is universal, not in the sense of being a metaphysical abstraction, but as a concrete reality. He is, as some theologians say, the supreme concrete universal.

(2)

With this introduction I should like to turn to the main theme of the present chapter: the catholicity of Christ. The phrase may sound somewhat odd, but it is not my own invention. Professor Jan Witte of the Gregorian University says of Jesus Christ: 'He bears catholicity within himself'.[1] And a contemporary high-church Lutheran, Ernst Fincke, describes the event of the Incarnation as the *urkatholische Ereignis*, the foundational catholic event.[2] Theologies that go by the name of catholic are quite properly described as incarnational. They take the words *et incarnatus est* in the creed with utmost realism, and, reading the Gospels in the light of this doctrine, they look upon the sayings and deeds of Jesus as outward manifestations of the inner mystery of his being.

While deliberately reading the Scriptures in the light of the Church's historic faith, Catholic theology does not yield to the subjectivist view of faith as a freely adopted but arbitrary perspective. Contemporary religious relativism all too casually

[1] Johannes L. Witte, 'Die Katholizität der Kirche: eine neue Interpretation nach alter Tradition', *Gregorianum* xlii (1961), pp. 193–241.

[2] Ernst Fincke, 'Ein neuer Blick für die Katholizität der Kirche', *Una Sancta* x (1955), pp. 14–23, quotation from p. 18.

dissolves the Christ of dogma into a mere cult-object of the Church, so that he is viewed as the product of Christian piety rather than as the source and norm of Christian existence. Catholic realism, on the contrary, concerns itself with Christ because it is convinced that by the very nature of things he demands our attention and reverence. Faith for the Catholic is not a projection of religious needs and desires but a submission to the real.

The catholicity of Christ, understood in this realist tradition, may conveniently be considered under three aspects. In one sense catholicity belongs to Christ by his very constitution as Incarnate Word. In a further sense he is catholic by reason of his primacy over all other creatures, and in a third sense, in so far as he is head of the Church. The catholicity of the Church cannot be adequately understood except in the light of Christ's threefold catholicity. In making this application to the Church we should keep in mind that Christ's own catholicity ought not to be understood in a merely static sense, as though it were complete from the beginning. Rather, it dynamically works itself out in the ministry of Jesus, and achieves its fullest manifestation and actualization in his death and resurrection, so that, by becoming the 'first-born from the dead', he reconciles all things to himself, 'whether on earth or in heaven, making peace by the blood of his cross' (Col. 1: 18–20).

Considered in itself, the Incarnation is a mystery of divine plenitude. In the Johannine and Pauline writings the term *plērōma* (fullness) is repeatedly predicated not only of God, as we have seen, but also of Christ. According to the Fourth Gospel, Christ is full (*plērēs*) of grace and truth, and of his fullness (*plērōmatos*) we have all received (1: 14, 16). Col. 1: 19 tells us that all fullness (*plērōma*) has been pleased to dwell in Christ, and Col. 2: 9 adds that the fullness of divinity dwells in him corporeally (*sōmatikōs*). This last text, by pointing up the visible and palpable aspects of Christ's humanity, converges closely with John's assertion, 'The Word was made flesh' (1: 14).

The Incarnation deserves to be called Catholic because, besides being a mystery of plenitude, it is a mystery of reconciled opposites. This latter aspect is celebrated in the chorus of Richard Crashaw's Christmas ode:

> Wellcome, all Wonders in one sight!
>   Aeternity shutt in a span.
> Sommer in Winter. Day in Night.
>   Heaven in earth, and God in Man.[3]

What could be more opposed than God and creature, Word
and flesh? Yet here they are drawn into the unity of a single
person. The human nature, taken on by the Word of God, is
itself a complex unity, in which rationality coexists with physical, chemical, vegetative, and sentient levels of being, so that
man, containing all the basic elements of the universe, has been
called a microcosm. The Word of God, in assuming a full
human existence, entered into a kind of union with the cosmos.

(3)

We are thus brought to our second aspect of Christology, Christ
as head of creation. This theme, central to the New Testament
and dear to the Greek Fathers, became obscured in the West,
where an unfortunate cleavage was made between body and
spirit, nature and person. In modern Western theology Christ
is often seen as having entered the sphere of the human but not
of the cosmic. His career is treated as a phenomenon in the
history of the spirit, but not of the physical. Nineteenth-century
philosophers, especially in the Kantian school, introduced
dichotomies not only between faith and reason but also
between the natural sciences and the humanities. Nature was
seen as an endless process of self-repetition, whereas history
was viewed as consisting of unique, unrepeatable events.

   In recent years, however, there has been a reintegration.
Nature is no longer considered, as it was by earlier ages, to be a
mere backdrop for history, but is understood as being impli-
cated in an evolving history and as capable of engendering
successively higher forms of life. In the eyes of contemporary
science the human phenomenon is an inner moment of the
history of the cosmos, a history that extends far beyond the
earth to the remotest galaxies. To merit the significance that
Christian faith attributes to it, the Incarnation of the Word

---

[3] From 'A Hymn of the Nativity, sung by the shepheards' in George Walton
Williams (ed.), *The Complete Poetry of Richard Crashaw* (Garden City, NY: Doubleday
Anchor, 1970), p. 83.

must have a bearing not only on human destiny but on that of the larger universe of nature.

Joseph Sittler, in a celebrated address at the New Delhi Assembly of the World Council of Churches (1961), pleaded in the name of catholicity for a Christology of nature and a cosmic soteriology. Commenting on the first chapter of Colossians, he remarked: 'It is here declared that God's restorative action in Christ is no smaller than the six-times repeated *ta panta*. . . . All things are permeable to his cosmic redemption because all things subsist in him.'[4] The Greek Fathers, Sittler noted, avoided any dualism between nature and history. They developed a daring, penetrating, life-affirming Christology of nature. We therefore face the question, he declared: 'Is it again possible to fashion a theology catholic enough to affirm redemption's force enfolding nature, as we have affirmed redemption's force enfolding history?'[5]

Sittler was of course aware that some twentieth-century theologians had already embarked upon this quest, but he was probably not acquainted with the work of a whole school of French Catholic theologians since the turn of the century. As early as 1919 the French philosopher, Maurice Blondel, wrote to his friend Auguste Valensin:

Our world has expanded through the social and natural sciences. One cannot remain true to Catholicism and be content with a mediocre explanation, a limited outlook which represents Christ as an accident of history, isolating Him in the Cosmos as if He were an episode without proper time and place. One cannot represent Him as an intruder, an alien in the crushing and hostile immensity of the universe.[6]

Blondel in this passage went on to observe that Christianity was here confronted by two options: either to fall back into a doctrine of subjective symbolism, as Loisy had done, or to move forward toward a thoroughgoing realism, a 'metaphysics of Christianity' that harmonized with the mystical theology lived by the saints.

---

[4] Joseph A. Sittler, 'Called to Unity', *Ecumenical Review*, xiv (1961–2), pp. 177–87, quotation from p. 177.

[5] Ibid., p. 182.

[6] 'Maurice Blondel's First Paper to Auguste Valensin', in *Pierre Teilhard de Chardin—Maurice Blondel Correspondence* (New York: Herder and Herder, 1967), p. 23. Cf. A. Feuillet, *Le Christ Sagesse du Dieu* (Paris: Gabalda, 1966), pp. 10 and 276.

Inspired in part by Blondel, speculative theologians such as Pierre Rousselot and Pierre Teilhard de Chardin, with the support of exegetes such as Ferdinand Prat and Jules Lebreton, rediscovered the ancient Catholic heritage regarding the universal headship of Christ. They relied principally on biblical texts from the Fourth Gospel, Hebrews, the Apocalypse, Romans, First Corinthians, and especially the Pauline Captivity Epistles. I shall here touch on only a few of these texts.

According to Col. 1: 15–17 all things were created in Christ, through him, and for him; he is before all things, and in him all things hold together (*synestēken*, which some translate as 'continue in being'). Col. 2: 10 goes on to say that Christ is the head of all rule and authority. In Eph. 1: 23 we have an obscure text in which Christ is said either to fill, or, according to other interpreters, to be filled by, all in all. Reinforcing this association between Christ and fullness, Eph. 4: 10 describes Christ as having descended and ascended in order to fill all things. Gathering up the sense of these and similar passages, one may conclude that the coming of Christ, according to these canonical authors, has an importance far beyond the community of the disciples and even beyond the whole of humanity. His existence and career have constitutive and transformative importance for the entire universe, including both the material and the spiritual realms.

In Eph. 1: 10 we find a statement that it has pleased the Father to bring all things to a head—to recapitulate them—in Christ. Scholars tend to interpret the term *anakephalaiōsis*, here used, as meaning that Christ is the summit or compendium in which everything is both preserved and brought to its proper perfection.[7]

Certain eschatological assertions in the New Testament enhance the power of the statements we have just examined. According to 1 Cor. 15: 28, Christ at the end will hand over the completed creation to the Father so that God may be all in all. Only then, it would seem, will the universe as a whole be fully penetrated by what I have been calling the catholicity of God. Again, in the final chapter of the Apocalypse, the risen Jesus says: 'I am the Alpha and the Omega, the First and the Last, the beginning and the end' (Apoc. 22: 13). Because the whole

---

[7] See Yves Congar, *Jesus Christ* (New York: Herder and Herder, 1966), pp. 136–7.

creation takes its origin in the divine Logos (cf. John 1: 3), it fittingly reaches its consummation in him.

Teilhard de Chardin, as is well known, engaged in a lifelong meditation on Christ's relationship to the cosmos.[8] He developed a highly personal theory to the effect that God could not have created the world except through the Incarnate Word as its bond of inner unity or, to use his own Leibnizian term, as *vinculum substantiale*. Teilhard, moreover, posited in Christ not only a divine and a human nature but a third nature, which he called cosmic, and regarded as coextensive with the entire material universe. Thus he could hold that Christ, the physical centre, literally fills all things and is filled by them. Teilhard coined the term 'pleromatization' to signify the completion received by the expanding universe as all things are brought into convergence by the Christic energies of love.

Without necessarily accepting these intriguing but idiosyncratic theories, many representative contemporary theologians agree that Christ is the focus of all creation. To cite only one, Karl Rahner describes the Incarnate Word as 'the unambiguous goal of the movement of creation as a whole'. He adds: 'If Col. 1: 15 is true, and is not attenuated in a moralistic sense; if then in Christ the world as a whole, even in its "physical" reality, has really reached historically through Christ that point in which God becomes all in all', it cannot be false in principle to conceive of the evolution of the world as a gradual ascent that comes to its peak in Christ.[9]

This consideration of Christ's role in creation brings us to the further question, broached by Sittler, of Christ's role in redemption. From the creeds we are familiar with the idea that he became incarnate for us human beings and for our salvation. But if Christ is the creative centre of the entire universe, one must ask whether his redemptive role does not extend beyond the human sphere. Here again it is Teilhard de Chardin who proposed the boldest theories. For him creation itself is a process of introducing unity into multiplicity without sacrificing the distinct identity of each individual. Christ's reconciling

---

[8] Among other books see George A. Maloney, *The Cosmic Christ from Paul to Teilhard* (New York: Sheed & Ward, 1968) and especially James A. Lyons, *The Cosmic Christ in Origen and Teilhard de Chardin* (Oxford: Oxford Univ. Press, 1982).

[9] Karl Rahner, 'Current Problems in Christology', *Theological Investigations*, vol. i (Baltimore: Helicon, 1961), p. 165.

activity therefore pertains to creation in its full range. As he
continually creates the universe, God must overcome fragmentation, deviation, and evil of every kind. Creation therefore is
inseparable from redemption.[10]

Without clearly identifying creation with redemption, the
New Testament gives some support to the idea of cosmic
redemption. Rom. 8: 19–23 speaks of the entire creation as
being subject to futility and groaning in travail as it awaits
redemption. The biblical doctrine of the 'new heavens and the
new earth' likewise suggests that the material world will be
renewed and transformed (see Isa. 65: 17; 66: 22; 2 Pet. 3: 13;
Apoc. 21: 1–8). In Christ's risen body the glorification of the
material universe has already begun.

Pondering issues such as these, Yves Congar saw their
pertinence to the theme of catholicity. 'Our theology of catholicity (mine in any case)', he wrote, 'is certainly too timid,
insufficiently cosmic. The Pauline theology of Christ in his
cosmic role and that of the *plērōma* permit and require one to
go further.'[11] If Christ is the universal principle of creation
and redemption, he has, so to speak, a cosmic catholicity. In
his incarnate existence he is, under God, the concrete universal.

The 'pan-Christic' universalism of Blondel and Teilhard de
Chardin has, in some respects, become official Catholic teaching in Vatican II's Pastoral Constitution on the Church in the
Modern World. It states that God's Word, in whom all things
were made, became flesh so that as perfect man he might save
all humanity and sum up all things in himself (*GS* 45). It speaks
of how, when Christ hands over his kingdom to the Father, the
whole of creation, made on man's account, will be unchained
from the bondage of vanity (*GS* 39). And, in a most interesting
sentence, the Pastoral Constitution declares that 'by His
incarnation the Son of God has united Himself in some fashion
with every human being' (*GS* 22). This sentence, on which
Pope John Paul II commented at length in his first encyclical,[12]
seems to endorse the opinion of many Greek Fathers to the
effect that human nature is intrinsically modified by the

---

[10] Lyons, *Cosmic Christ*, p. 156.
[11] Yves Congar, Preface to Feuillet, *Le Christ*, pp. 14–15.
[12] John Paul II, Encyclical *Redemptor hominis* (1979), esp. no. 13.

Incarnation, inasmuch as all men and women are newly related to God in Christ their brother.

(4)

The third aspect of Christ's catholicity, his relationship to the Church, is a further specification of his universal relationship to creation. Christ's relatedness to the Church is described in the New Testament through a variety of images, such as shepherd and flock, vine and branches, bridegroom and bride. The most pervasive of these images is that of the head and the body. Already in Romans and First Corinthians Paul uses this metaphor, but it is further elaborated in the Captivity Epistles, especially in the Letter to the Ephesians which, according to Friedrich Heiler, 'is in Catholic eyes the Magna Carta of the idea of the Universal Church'.[13] In Romans and First Corinthians the body of Christ corresponds to the local church, and there is as yet no reference to Christ as head. In Colossians and Ephesians, by contrast, the body of Christ stands for the universal Church, and Christ is designated as its head.

How does Christ's headship over the Church differ from his headship (*anakephalaiōsis*) over all creation? When Paul speaks of the latter he apparently means only that Christ is the highpoint, or that he exercises universal dominion. There is no statement in Paul that the cosmic and angelic powers, though they be subject to Christ, belong to his body. Unlike *plērōma* (fullness), which can embrace the whole universe in its relation to Christ, *sōma* (body) includes only the Church. Pauline usage is in this respect narrower than that of Teilhard de Chardin, who spoke of the entire cosmos as the body of Christ.

Some Greek and Roman rhetoricians had used the metaphor of the body politic, in which different classes of citizens corresponded to different organs in the body.[14] Unlike these authors, Paul is not thinking of a merely moral or juridical union. He has in mind a real physical incorporation effected

---

[13] Friedrich Heiler, 'Catholicism', in Jaroslav Pelikan (ed.), *Twentieth Century Theology in the Making*, vol. iii (New York: Harper & Row, 1971), pp. 109–37, quotation from p. 111.

[14] Frequently compared with St. Paul's treatment of the body of Christ is the fable Titus Livy attributes to Menenius Agrippa in his *Annals of the Roman People*, Bk. II, chap. 32. The fable recurs in Shakespeare's *Coriolanus*, Act II, scene i.

through the sacraments and especially the Eucharist. Paul builds on the tradition that Jesus at the Last Supper uttered the words, 'This is my body' (1 Cor. 11: 24). By receiving holy Communion, Paul infers, we are ingested into that body. 'Because there is one bread', writes Paul, 'we who are many are one body, for we partake of the one bread' (1 Cor. 10: 17). Hence it is sacrilegious for a communicating Christian to join himself with a prostitute, becoming one body with her (1 Cor. 6: 16).

Although J. A. T. Robinson and others are correct in stressing physical aspects of the Church as body of Christ, it would be an exaggeration to say that Paul uses the term in a perfectly literal sense.[15] He is quite conscious of speaking figuratively when he speaks of some Christians as eyes and others as ears, or when he speaks of Christ and his members becoming, like bride and groom, one flesh. The body of Christ, like any analogy, is in some respects inadequate. The analogy breaks down at a certain point because in the Church the head and members do not make up a single organism. The members are complete and distinct persons, having their own freedom and responsibility. The union between head and body is therefore a unique, supernatural one, which many theologians call 'mystical'.

A further weakness is that the image of the head and body, if taken literally, would not do justice to the very intimate union between Christ and the Church. In an organic body the head is not in the arms and legs, but is above and external to them. Christ, although he transcends the Church, is interior to it. According to Augustine, Aquinas, and the great Catholic tradition, the head and members together make up the total Christ, one mystical person. Christ is in all the members, and they in him.

The image of the body of Christ, since it implies both plenitude and inner diversity, is very helpful for illuminating the catholicity of the Church. Christ, who is the very fullness of God, communicates himself to the Church, which can therefore be described in Eph. 1: 23 as 'the fullness of him who fills the universe in all its parts'. Even if one prefers to translate the last

[15] John A. T. Robinson holds that Paul did not understand the body of Christ as a metaphor but as a literal fact (*The Body: A Study in Pauline Theology* (Naperville: Allenson, 1957), p. 51.).

clause, 'who is filled by the universe in all its parts',[16] the previous words still affirm that the Church is the fullness or completion of Christ. Because the head and body make up one mystical person, they prolong Christ's very self in space and time. By a kind of exchange of properties, similar to that between the human and divine natures in Christ, what belongs to the head can be predicated of the body, and vice versa. So closely does Christ identify himself with his disciples that the New Testament can speak of them as though they were Christ himself. In showing kindness to them one does a favour to Christ (Matt. 10: 42; 25: 40), and in persecuting them one persecutes him (Acts 9: 5).

Because Christ is personally present in his body, the catholicity of the Church, as a participation of Christ's own fullness, is more than an idea or a hope; it is a present reality. According to the fifth chapter of Ephesians, Christ has suffered and sacrificed himself in order to gain his bride, sanctify her, and present her to himself 'holy and without blemish' and 'without spot or wrinkle or any such thing' (Eph. 5: 27). Like the marriage bond, the union between Christ and the Church is indissoluble. Thanks to his sanctifying action, the Church has a definitive share in his fullness of life.

Notwithstanding this intimate association, the body of Christ suffers from a certain incompletion. As we read in Ephesians, the Church grows gradually toward the perfect stature of the fullness of Christ (Eph. 4: 13). The whole body of the Church receives from Christ its head the impulses it needs to build itself up in love (4: 16). We seem to have here an echo of the Greek medical tradition, for Hippocrates and Galen, according to the scholars, regarded the head of any organism as the source of life, energy, movement, and growth in the body.[17] The risen Christ distributes a variety of ministries and callings for the building up of his body (4: 11–12). In this way all the members of the body can be strengthened; they can grow in knowledge of the love of Christ, which surpasses knowledge, and thus 'be filled with all the fullness of God' (3: 19).

[16] This translation is favoured by Pierre Benoit, 'Body, Head, and Plērōma in the Epistles of the Captivity', in his *Jesus and the Gospel*, vol. ii (New York: Seabury, 1974), pp. 89–91. See also Feuillet, *Le Christ*, pp. 276–87.

[17] Benoit, *Jesus and the Gospel*, vol. ii, p. 74.

Can Christ the head be said to lack completion? In some
ways, no. The fullness of divinity is present inalienably in him
as Incarnate Word, and since the Ascension his sacred humanity is definitively established in glory. But in his members he
still suffers and progresses toward full union with God. In Col.
1: 24 Paul says: 'I rejoice in my sufferings for your sake, and in
my flesh I complete what is lacking in Christ's sufferings for the
sake of his body, that is, the Church'. Commentators generally
explain this as a statement that although Christ is perfect the
Church has an insufficiency that needs to be filled.[18] But if it is
true, as suggested above, that Christ is filled or completed by
the cosmos, it seems permissible to say also that the Church is
his completion. Even though his sufferings lack nothing inten-
sively, they must be complemented by those of his disciples. In
a world alienated from God, redemptive suffering is the road to
perfection not only for Christ as an individual but for the whole
Christ, head and members, as one mystical person. The
Church therefore supplies a certain extensive catholicity to the
sufferings of Christ.

Catholicity implies not only fullness of being but also, as we
have said, diversified unity. In speaking of the Trinity and the
Incarnation we have seen that the highest unity is compatible
with, and even demands, multiplicity. The same principle
holds for living organisms, in which the form of the whole gives
both unity and distinction to the parts, so that all together
collaborate for the benefit of the whole. In the Church, which is
comparable to a living organism, Christ as the living centre
draws the members together and at the same time impels them
to actualize their individuality to the utmost. Teilhard de
Chardin, who coined the formula 'union differentiates', applied
this principle to the cells of a living organism, to the members of
a civil society, and to the elements of the body of Christ. Christ,
he believed, as the bond of union, exerted an influence that
intensified the differences between the assimilated elements
and at the same time drew them together in love. Thanks to this
principle Teilhard could affirm the closest possible unity in the
Church without falling into pantheistic monism.[19]

[18] For a helpful discussion of this problem see Louis Bouyer, *The Church of God*
(Cincinnati: Franciscan Herald Press, 1983), pp. 255–6.
[19] See Lyons, *Cosmic Christ*, pp. 164–70.

The Teilhardian formula, 'union differentiates', casts additional light on the concept of catholicity. According to Möhler the Greek Fathers understood catholicity as a union of diverse parts in a community of mutual support. Applied to the Church, this meant reciprocal communion between all the elements in the great, diversified body of the faithful. The distinctive trait of heresy, in Möhler's estimation, was separation from the multitude for the sake of some particular insight. Such withdrawals could produce only fragmentary communities, each of which fell into distortions because deprived of the full context of Catholic truth and life.[20]

In this analysis of the ancient heresies, Möhler undoubtedly had his eye on the Protestantism of his day. For contemporary Protestantism, with its more ecumenical spirit, Möhler's analogy may be less appropriate. But his basic point still holds. To separate oneself from the great Church for the sake of cultivating some particular insight is to guarantee deformation and impoverishment. If ecumenism is to become a search for plenitude through mutual enrichment, the churches that engage in it will find themselves embarked on a recovery of catholicity.

The catholicity of the Church is admittedly less comprehensive than that of Christ, which extends to the whole universe. The Church may be called in the terminology of Teilhard de Chardin, the 'consciously Christified portion of the world'.[21] Towards it all the energies of the universe must converge as they come to a focus in Christ. The catholicity of the Church must finally be understood as a participation in Christ's dynamic power to recapitulate both humanity and the cosmos under his universal headship.[22] Since it is not a self-contained society, the Church does not have its catholicity in itself. Hans Urs von Balthasar puts the matter well. 'The Church', he writes, 'has the norm of her catholicity—the norm that intrinsically shapes that catholicity—not from or in herself but over her: in the mystery of Christ. But this mystery is itself

---

[20] Johann Adam Möhler, *Die Einheit in der Kirche* (Cologne: J. Hegner, 1957), chap. 3, pp. 57–113 and Appendix 5, pp. 253–8.
[21] Émile Rideau, *The Thought of Teilhard de Chardin* (New York: Harper & Row, 1967), p. 597.
[22] Witte, 'Katholizität', p. 223; cf. p. 238.

inseparable from the witness of the *catholica*.'[23] In other words, the Church's catholicity is continually borrowed from her Lord; it may be called a *catholicitas aliena*, and yet it does belong to the Church, for Christ lives in her and identifies himself with her. She, in turn, bears witness to him, and in so doing realizes in herself the mystery of Christ.

(5)

I have mentioned above that the catholicity of Christ is to be understood not statically but dynamically. It is a self-communicating energy of love, and for this reason it may properly be attributed to the Holy Spirit as the principle of shared divine life.

In the history of theology authors have hesitated whether to trace the Church and its catholicity primarily to Christ or to the Holy Spirit. Möhler, in his youthful work, *Unity in the Church*, began with the assertion that the communication of the Holy Spirit is the condition of our acceptance of Christianity. The Spirit unites all the faithful into a mystical communion and enables them to receive Christ as Lord. 'Where the Spirit of Christ is', he quotes from Irenaeus, 'there is the Spirit of God, and where the Spirit of God is, there is the Church and the fullness of grace.'[24] In his later work, *Symbolism*, Möhler focused on Christ as the ground of the Church. He called the Church 'the permanent incarnation of the Son of God everlastingly manifesting himself, perpetually renewed and eternally young'.[25] Like Christ, he added, the Church is a union between the human and the divine.

The similarity between the Church and the Incarnation is real, but the differences must not be overlooked. In the Incarnation the human element is not a pre-existing person, but the assumed nature, and the personality is that of the divine Word. In Christ, therefore, there is no multiplicity of persons. In the Church, however, pre-existent persons are drawn into a community of faith and love that leaves intact their distinctness as individual subjects.

[23] Hans Urs von Balthasar, *Katholisch: Aspekte des Mysteriums* (Einsiedeln: Johannes Verlag, 1975), p. 9.

[24] Irenaeus of Lyons, *Adversus haereses*, III. xxiv. 1 (*PG* 7: 966), quoted by Möhler, *Einheit*, chap. 1, sec. 2, p. 9.

[25] Johann Adam Möhler, *Symbolism* (New York: E. Dunigan, 1844), p. 333.

Vatican Council II both used Möhler's comparison and indicated its limitations. The Church, it declared, comprises a divine and a human element, and for this reason, by an excellent analogy, may be compared to the mystery of the Incarnation (*LG* 8). But the council went on to say that in Christ, the assumed nature is united to the divine Word, whereas in the Church the visible society is vivified by the Holy Spirit. Thus we have a proportionality consisting of four terms: the human nature of Christ is to the divine Word analogously what the Church as a human society is to the Holy Spirit.

Specialists on the theology of the Holy Spirit point out that while the divine Word is capable of becoming incarnate, the Holy Spirit is not. It is the very nature of the Holy Spirit to be one person in many persons.[26] Within the Trinity the Spirit is the subsistent love breathed forth by the Father and the Son. He is the personal bond of union expressing and sealing their mutual love, and proceeding from them. The role of the Spirit in the Church is similar. Once again, he is one person in many persons—in this case, Christ and us. He who sanctified Jesus in his humanity inhabits and sanctifies the members of Christ, drawing them into union with one another. The Spirit does not become incarnate in the Church or its members, so that they can claim to be the Holy Spirit, but he dwells in subjects who already have their own personal existence.

The immediate relationship of the Church to the Holy Spirit as its animating principle does not prevent the Church from being the body of Christ, but on the contrary causes it to be his body. The whole function of the Spirit, as sent forth from the risen Christ, is to mediate Christ's presence. The Holy Spirit is self-effacing. He does not speak on his own authority, but as sent by Jesus (John 16: 13). 'He will glorify me', says Jesus, 'for he will take what is mine and declare it to you' (John 16: 14). He testifies in our hearts that we are children of God, incorporated into the only-begotten Son (Rom. 8: 16; cf. Gal. 4: 6).

In communicating his own Spirit to us as the gift of Pentecost, the risen Christ completes his own work. Without the

---

[26] See Heribert Mühlen, *Una Persona Mystica* (3rd edn.; Paderborn: Schöningh, 1968), especially pp. 65–71.

interior fructifying influence of the Spirit, catholicity would remain an empty shell. By operating within each believer the Holy Spirit enables the gifts of Christ to be received according to each one's capacities and needs, and thus to be interiorized. It is the Spirit who gives warmth and relish to the Christian life and who causes the dry bones of doctrine, ritual, and discipline to come alive.

Within the Holy Trinity, the Spirit is the principle of unity in diversity. He spans the mutual opposition of Father and Son: he is the bond of union and the seal of peace. Similarly, in the Church the Spirit fosters communion without effacing differences. Paul in First Corinthians attributes the variety of gifts or charisms to 'one and the same Spirit, who apportions to each one individually as he wills' (1 Cor. 12: 11). Far from tearing the Church apart, the diversity of gifts serves to build up the whole in unity. The Holy Spirit can accomplish this because he instils God's love in human hearts. Authentic love does not dominate and suppress, but rather preserves and develops the gifts of the beloved. To love is to appreciate and cherish the other precisely as other. To the extent that they love, the members of the Church are able to place their gifts at one another's disposal and thus to build up the community. As the gift of love, the Holy Spirit places the seal of perfection on the catholicity that the Church receives from Christ.[27]

Bestowed on Pentecost, the gift of the Spirit is the sign of the fullness of time, the messianic age of completion and perfection. According to Peter's sermon on the first Pentecost, it is only in the last days that the Lord pours forth his Spirit upon all flesh, thus fulfilling the prophecy of Joel (Acts 2: 17–21; cf. Joel 2: 28–9). Through this event the saying of Wisdom becomes true: 'The Spirit of the Lord has filled the world' (Wisd. 1; 7). Thanks to the gift of Pentecost, the early Christian community burst out of its Jewish shell and became, as we shall see in a later chapter, catholic in scope. Whereas the gift of Christ, taken in itself, is a past event that has occurred once and for all, the gift of the Holy Spirit renders the fruits of Christ's redemptive action continually present in new and unexpected ways.

---

[27] The functions of the Holy Spirit in the Trinity and in the Church are compared by Emile Mersch, *Theology of the Mystical Body* (St. Louis: B. Herder, 1951), chap. 14, pp. 415–52.

The theology of catholicity, therefore, must avoid both a Christological and a Pneumatological constriction. It must be comprehensively Trinitarian. The triune God, who communicates himself in the incarnate Word and in the Holy Spirit, is the source and ground of catholicity.

3

Catholicity from Below: The Aspirations of Nature

In Chapter 2 we considered what may be called the 'height' of catholicity. We saw that it has its source in Christ, who ascended 'above all the heavens so that he might fill all things' (Eph. 4: 10), and that the risen Christ perpetuates his presence through the Holy Spirit. Now, turning to the second aspect of catholicity, we must ask whether there is anything in it corresponding to depth. If so, how deep are its roots in the world? Presenting a basic Catholic answer to this question, Yves Congar writes: 'The fullness that is in Christ does not communicate itself to an empty and inert humanity. It has a source of richness likewise in human beings or in human nature.'[1] According to the Catholic understanding, the Spirit of God does not merely hover above the world, nor does it simply touch the world as a tangent touches a circle, but it reaches into the depths. Divine life, when it enters the human realm, penetrates not only the spiritual faculties of intellect and will, but the person's whole being, including the sensory and bodily aspects.

Just as in Chapter 2 we considered chiefly the triune God and only in that connection the Church, so in this chapter I shall be speaking principally about the Christian understanding of nature, especially human nature, and only from that point of view about the Church. Working at the lower limits of ecclesiology, we shall be exploring, so to speak, the human material that goes into the Church. Since the Church is made up of human beings, differences in anthropology have an inevitable impact on ecclesiology. This will become apparent in later chapters, especially when we turn to sacramentality.

---

[1] Yves Congar, *L'Église: une, sainte, catholique, et apostolique.* Mysterium Salutis 15, p. 165.

(1)

The relationship of nature to the Christian life is treated by theologians most directly under the heading of justification. On this subject there are three main tendencies. The first is the naturalist tendency, represented in antiquity by Pelagianism, which puts the accent on continuity. The Pelagian, denying that original sin makes us inwardly corrupt, regards human nature in its present condition as sound and healthy. Hence it follows that if we are sinful, this is the result of our own free activity, and that the same freedom makes us capable of rising again. Grace is understood as a set of favourable conditions, such as the good example and admonition that come from other human beings. Conversely, original sin, if the term is used at all, means the bad example and moral influence of Adam or our predecessors. According to the Pelagian, the justified person is inherently righteous and does not need to rely on the merits of Christ as imputed. Finally, the virtuous person can perform good and meritorious works by the powers of unaided nature. Positions approaching the Pelagian occasionally reappeared in late medieval Nominalism, in Renaissance humanism, and in liberal Protestantism.

The second major tendency is the Manichaean, which has its analogues in certain strands of Lutheranism (especially the extreme positions of Matthias Flacius Illyricus), as well as in the rigid Augustinianism of Baius (Michel de Bay) and Jansenius (Cornelius Jansen). In reaction against Pelagianizing movements, this tendency stresses the discontinuities. In the old Manichaeanism nature itself was regarded as evil and as produced by an evil demiurge rather than by the God of Jesus Christ. In its Protestant and Jansenist forms, this tendency is expressed in the view that human nature, since the Fall, is irreparably corrupt and incapable of doing anything but sin.[2] The Christian life therefore consists in allowing the sufferings of Jesus Christ to serve as a substitute for the meritorious works

---

[2] The Lutheran Formula of Concord (1577) goes very far in stressing the 'abominable corruption' and incapacity of fallen nature. See Solid Declaration, art. 1, Original Sin, sec. 10 and 25. Text in Theodore G. Tappert (ed.), *The Book of Concord* (Philadelphia: Fortress, 1959), pp. 510, 512.

that we ourselves are incapable of performing.[3] In the transition from sin to grace, according to some Lutheran formularies, the human subject is totally passive, so that the change is attributable to God alone. By faith, God imputes to us the merits of Christ as if they were our own.[4]

The third tendency, proposed most officially by the Council of Trent in its Decree on Justification (1547), may be called the Catholic position. Striking a middle path between the other two, this position emphasizes, as catholicity always does, continuity within discontinuity. Nature is fundamentally good, and remains so, even though it is wounded by the effects of original sin. The human person is and remains an image of God. Retaining the essential powers of intelligence and free will, the sinner is able to act responsibly, and does not necessarily sin (as some Protestants held) in every act.

Justification, according to the Catholic view, is freely accepted. With the help of grace we freely consent and dispose ourselves for the further gift of new life in Christ. Thus faith and conversion are not simply God's acts in us but human acts elicited under the influence of grace.

After justification, according to this view, we truly participate in the righteousness of Christ, who with the Holy Spirit dwells in us. Notwithstanding this transformation, sinful tendencies remain. We are in constant danger of falling into sin; we cannot promise ourselves that we shall persevere in grace, nor at any moment can we be empirically certain of our own state of righteousness. Our hope of salvation, therefore, must be placed in God, not in ourselves.

Although God is not under any obligation to his creatures, his own fidelity (or, if one prefers, his self-consistency) requires him to acknowledge the good works of the justified, which he rewards. These works are 'theandric' in the broad sense that they follow not simply from human effort but from the working of divine grace in us. 'In rewarding our good works,' says St. Augustine, 'God does nothing else than crown his own gifts.'[5]

In general we may say that the Catholic position—con-

---

[3] Our natural free will is said to be capable of activity only in ways that are displeasing to God, ibid., art. 2, Free Will, sec. 7 (Tappert, p. 521).

[4] Ibid., art. 3, Righteousness, sec. 4 (Tappert, p. 540).

[5] Augustine, Epistle 194: 5, 19 (*CSEL* 57: 190).

cerned, as is the Lutheran, to glorify God—differs from the latter by insisting that we do not glorify God by denigrating his gifts. What is given to the human is not taken away from God. On the contrary, we must, without vainglory, humbly acknowledge and celebrate all God's gifts, for in so doing we best magnify the goodness and mercy of the Giver.

(2)

From a Catholic point of view, the redemptive action of God ought to be studied not simply in the quasi-juridical categories of justification and imputation, but also in the ontological categories of creation and re-creation. The Anglican Report on *Catholicity*, commissioned by the Archbishop of Canterbury and submitted in 1947, makes this point. In Holy Scripture, it declares, justification stands in a cosmic setting. It is a renewal of creation, a second creative act.

Hence Luther, in neglecting the doctrine of man as made in God's Image, and in affirming the 'total depravity' of man as the ground of the 'bondage of the will', was isolating Redemption from its proper setting; and this failure to provide a theology of the created order has remained as a permanent characteristic of orthodox Protestantism.[6]

This Catholic criticism of Luther and Lutheranism is paralleled, in similar terms, by some ecumenically-minded Lutherans. Dietrich Bonhoeffer wrote:

The concept of the natural has fallen into discredit in Protestant ethics. . . . [T]his was a disastrous mistake, for its consequence was that the concept of the natural no longer had a place in Protestant thought. . . . Before the light of grace everything human and natural sank into the night of sin, and now no one dared to consider the relative differences within the human and the natural, for fear that by their so doing grace as grace might be diminished.[7]

Bonhoeffer then goes on to explain that in Lutheran theology the natural was treated as antithetical to the Word of God, so that consequently there was no room for an antithesis between the natural and the unnatural. He pleads for a recovery of the concept of the natural on the basis of the gospel. The natural, he

---

[6] E. S. Abbott and others, *Catholicity* (Westminster: Dacre Press, 1947), p. 24.
[7] Dietrich Bonhoeffer, *Ethics* (London: Collins, 1964), pp. 143–4.

holds, 'is that which, after the Fall, is directed towards the coming of Christ. The unnatural is that which, after the Fall, closes its doors against the coming of Christ.'[8] Thus the natural is 'the form of life presented by God for the fallen world, and directed towards justification, redemption, and renewal through Christ'.[9] This positive evaluation of the natural, though expressed by a Lutheran, stands in sharp contrast to the anti-naturalism of the Formula of Concord.

In the early modern period Roman Catholics, reacting against certain Protestant exaggerations, stressed the element of continuity. Their main intent was to prove that reason and free will survived in fallen nature and took part in the process of justification. Influenced by the reigning neo-classicism, Catholic theology became a defender of the order of nature and was inclined to confuse continuity with the absence of change.

In a more integrally Catholic view, nature is seen as being preserved intact and yet as undergoing a certain impairment as a result of sin, and as being rehabilitated by the working of grace.[10] This continuity within change could be verified in detail for each of the powers that make up the human composite. The faculty of reason merits special attention, for it has long been considered the distinctive feature of the human species.

Vatican Council I, in its Constitution on the Catholic Faith (1870), taught that human reason, in the present state of fallen nature, retains its ability to establish the existence of God (DS 3004–5, 3026). This statement was, however, carefully worded to avoid exaggerations. The council did not say that anyone had constructed a satisfactory natural theology without the assistance of divine revelation, which the council regarded as necessary in practice. Against certain fideistic tendencies, Vatican I taught that the act of faith was in full accord with the demands of reason (DS 3009). It asserted further that reason, enlightened by faith, is able to probe more deeply into the mysteries of revelation (DS 3016). By its recognition that God,

---

[8] Ibid., p. 144.

[9] Ibid., p. 145.

[10] 'Grace does not destroy nature but perfects it', Thomas Aquinas, *Summa theol.* I.i. 8 ad 2. In Roman Catholic theology the present order is commonly described as that of fallen and redeemed nature. See John Paul II, quoted in *L'Osservatore Romano*, Eng. edn. (18 Feb. 1980), p. 1.

even after revelation, remains essentially mysterious, Vatican I
avoided the pitfalls of rationalism. It recognized the role of
grace in making faith possible (DS 3010), and distinguished the
different capacities of reason when influenced respectively by
sin and grace.

Vatican Council II at several points reaffirmed the key
positions of Vatican I on the capacities of reason (*DV* 6, *GS* 59).
In its Pastoral Constitution on the Church in the Modern
World it particularly emphasized the necessity of faith in order
to illuminate the riddles of suffering and death and the mystery
of human destiny (*GS* 22). The same emphasis is present in the
closing message of the council Fathers to intellectuals and
scientists, which contains the typically Catholic appeal: 'Have
confidence in faith, this great friend of intelligence. Enlighten
yourselves with its light in order to take hold of truth, the whole
truth.'[11]

A sympathetic Protestant critic of Catholicism, Langdon
Gilkey, holds that the drive toward rationality has been one of
the distinctive strengths of Catholic Christianity. While making certain reservations, he praises Roman Catholicism for its
insistence that the revealed mysteries must be as far as possible
'penetrated, defended, and explicated by the most acute
rational reflection'.[12] This commitment to rationality has
prevented Catholicism, generally speaking, from falling into
'revelational positivism' (the fault of which Dietrich Bonhoeffer
accused Karl Barth) and the kind of anti-intellectual
fundamentalism so prevalent in some sectors of the United
States today. Catholic Christianity, valuing both faith and
reason, accepts the necessary tensions involved in working out
a synthesis that does justice to both.

The Catholic reverence for human nature involves respect
not only for reason but also, secondly, for human freedom. The
thesis of Luther most quickly and emphatically condemned
was his apparent rejection of the freedom of the will, at least in
the all-important sphere of the spiritual life. Some of Luther's
Catholic critics, such as the humanist Erasmus, may have
veered too far in the direction of Pelagianism, but the Council of

[11] Text in Walter M. Abbott (ed.), *The Documents of Vatican II* (New York: America
Press, 1966), p. 731.

[12] Langdon Gilkey, *Catholicism Confronts Modernity* (New York: Seabury, 1975), p. 22.

Trent successfully maintained the tension between grace and freedom. Against the determinism of Baius and Jansenius, church authorities in the ensuing centuries repeatedly insisted on the freedom of fallen human nature, and thus on human responsibility in the matter of sin and salvation. Thus it was no break with the Catholic tradition when Vatican II issued its Declaration on Religious Freedom. 'It is one of the major tenets of Catholic doctrine', said this Declaration, 'that man's response to God must be free. . . . The act of faith is of its very nature a free act' (*DH* 10). Vatican II, like previous councils, recognized that human freedom has a history as it is successively affected by sin and redemption. It accordingly speaks of this freedom as having been 'damaged by sin' (*GS* 17) and as being brought 'by the grace of Christ and the power of the Holy Spirit to the sublime and unending "freedom of the glory of the sons of God" (Rom. 8: 21)' (*DH* 15).

Catholic respect for human nature is not confined to the higher faculties of intelligence and will. It extends also to the senses and the body itself. Although the councils have little to say on this point, Catholic authors make much of it. 'By the fact of the Incarnation,' wrote Cardinal Newman, 'we are taught that matter is an essential part of us, and, as well as mind, is capable of sanctification.'[13] In an essay on 'The Essentials of Catholicism', Friedrich von Hügel contended that Catholicism, by its incarnational character, recognizes grace in nature and spirit in body.[14] The spiritual, he says, cannot be separated from the material, but grows by insertion in it.[15] About the same time, George Tyrrell spoke in similar terms: 'It seems to us that Catholicism is, more than other systems, a religion of the whole man, body, soul, and spirit.'[16] In his masterful work, *The Spirit of Catholicism* (1924), Karl Adam identified as one of the elements of the Church's catholicity 'that she loves and understands man's nature, his bodily and sensitive structure,

[13] John Henry Newman, *Essay on the Development of Christian Doctrine* (London: Longmans, Green, 1909), chap. 7, sec. I, no. 4, p. 326. Passages such as this should be taken into account by those tempted to describe the sacramentalism of the Tractarian movement as Platonic or dualistic.

[14] Friedrich von Hügel, *Essays and Addresses on the Philosophy of Religion* (1st series; London: J. M. Dent, 1921), p. 238.

[15] Ibid., p. 230.

[16] George Tyrrell, *Through Scylla and Charybdis* (London: Longmans, Green, 1907), p. 28.

as well as his mental powers'.[17] He goes on to say: 'Art is native to Catholicism, since reverence for the body and for nature is native to it.'[18]

This reverence for the body and for beauty is reflected in the liturgy of Catholicism, which appeals not simply to the ear but to all the senses. Already at the dawn of the nineteenth century, Drey sought to show how Catholicism affects human hearts by means of its cult, reaching the spirit through the beauty of sight and sound.[19] Newman, opposing the iconoclastic spirit, builds on the work of St. John Damascene in defence of images.[20] Tyrrell, in like manner, criticizes what he calls 'the pedantry of a purely reasonable religion that would abolish the luxuriant— doubtless at times too luxuriant—wealth of symbolism in favour of a "ministry of the word" alone, taking "word" in its baldest literal sense'. According to Tyrrell, God speaks to us through all the senses and bids us answer him again in his own tongue.[21] A similar thought appears in the apologetic work of Isaac Hecker, significantly entitled *Aspirations of Nature*: 'Catholicity seizes hold of our whole nature, puts all our faculties in action, and directs all our energies to the attainment of our divinely-appointed end.'[22]

(3)

According to the perspective set forth in Chapter 2, catholicity is a reconciliation of opposites in terms of a transcendent fullness that unifies. Having glanced at some of the elements to be preserved and unified, we must now turn to the transcendent principle. For a Catholic theology of grace it is crucially important that the new creation is far more than a cancelling out of human guilt. The gift of God in Christ, as the new Adam, infinitely excels the offence of the old Adam (cf. Rom. 5: 15). Christ does not simply repair the damage to nature inflicted by

[17] Karl Adam, *The Spirit of Catholicism* (Garden City, NY: Doubleday Image, 1954), p. 162.

[18] Ibid.

[19] Johann Sebastian Drey, 'Beziehung des Katholizismus auf christliche Religiosität und christliche Gottesverehrung', part III of his *Vom Geist und Wesen des Katholizismus*, first printed in *Tübinger theologische Quartalschrift* 1 (1819), pp. 369–92.

[20] Newman, *Development of Doctrine*, chap. 8, sec. I, no. 2, pp. 376–7.

[21] Tyrrell, *Through Scylla*, pp. 32–3.

[22] Isaac T. Hecker, *Aspirations of Nature* (New York: Kirker, 1857), p. 261.

sin; he raises nature to an intimate union with God. The New
Testament speaks in this connection of participation in the
divine nature (2 Pet. 1: 4), the inhabitation of the divine
persons (John 14: 22; 17: 21, 26), and of the outpouring of the
Holy Spirit in our hearts (Rom. 5: 5).

The Catholic theology of grace never ceases to celebrate
what Scheeben in the title of one of his most popular books
called 'The Marvels of Divine Grace'.[23] Not satisfied to con-
centrate on justification considered as a mere non-imputation
of sin, Catholicism emphasizes the realities of adoptive filiation, sanctification, reconciliation, and intimate sharing in the
life of the triune God. Many Catholic theologians in the West
have appealed to the concept of divinization (*theōsis*), so prominent in the Greek Fathers and in modern Orthodox theology.[24]
While some other Christian traditions put primary emphasis
on human sinfulness and need for mercy, Catholic theology is
especially concerned to acknowledge the full range of God's
gifts and the dignity that God has conferred on those whom he
has redeemed.[25] The Roman Breviary for Christmas Day
reproduces a sermon of Leo I in which he states:

Learn, O Christian, how great is your dignity! You have been made a
partaker of the divine nature. . . . Remember of whose body you are a
member, and who is its head. Remember that you have been snatched
from the power of darkness, and transported into the light and
Kingdom of God.[26]

If Christians are called to this exalted destiny, further
questions arise with regard to the theology of human nature.
How is the old creation related to the new? How is human
nature disposed toward participation in the divine nature?
Does it have an intrinsic orientation toward the divine gift
whereby it is perfected and marvellously transformed?

In much of the Catholic theology from the sixteenth century
until the 1940s, this last question was answered in the negative.

---

[23] Matthias-Josef Scheeben, *Die Herrlichkeiten der göttlichen Gnade* (Freiburg: Herder,
1863).

[24] See Charles Moeller and Gérard Philips, *The Theology of Grace and the Ecumenical
Movement* (Paterson, NJ: St Anthony Guild, 1961, 1969), pp. 13–17, 30–1.

[25] Cf. USA Lutheran–Roman Catholic Dialogue, 'Justification by Faith', *Origins*,
vol. 13, no. 17 (6 Oct. 1983), par. 112, p. 292.

[26] Pope Leo I, First Sermon on the Nativity (*PL* 54: 192–3).

Theologians divided the world all too neatly into two realms, the natural and the supernatural, recognizing no clear and positive relation of the first to the second. Nature, it was admitted, is capable of being supernaturally elevated, but it was thought to have no native tendency or inclination in that direction. Thus it could achieve its own proper and proportionate end—a kind of natural beatitude—without any assistance from God.

This theological schematization is widely rejected in the twentieth century. Catholic theologians such as Blondel, von Hügel, de Lubac, and Rahner have gone back to the Fathers and the medieval theologians, who were able to do without the hypothesis of pure nature having a purely natural finality. In place of this modern dualism, current theology prefers the earlier idea that human nature is intrinsically ordered toward the goal of eternal blessedness in God through Christ. It seeks to unfold the implications of St. Augustine's cry of wonder: 'You have made us for yourself, O Lord, and our hearts cannot find rest until they rest in you!'[27] Maurice Blondel held that human nature, as it concretely exists, is in a 'transnatural' state, having a certain restlessness to be raised to supernatural communion with God.[28] According to von Hügel, following Blondel, 'this development fully reveals the profoundly Catholic, alone Catholic, doctrine that "the state of 'pure nature' might, without doubt, have existed, but that, in fact, it does not exist, and that, in fact, it never has existed" '.[29]

The theology of nature at this point dovetails with the Christology proposed in Chapter 2 on the basis, primarily, of the Pauline Captivity Epistles. If everything was created in Christ, and has in him its centre of coherence and meaning, it stands to reason that nature cannot be adequately understood except in reference to him, who came to fill all creation with the fullness of God. Human nature, having been constituted from the beginning in Christ, must be interpreted as having an inherent tendency to be perfected and brought into union with God through him.

[27] Augustine, *Confessions*, Book I, chap. 1.
[28] Testis [pseudonym for Maurice Blondel], 'La "Semaine Sociale" de Bordeaux', *Annales de philosophie chrétienne* ix (1909–10), p. 268.
[29] Von Hügel, *Essays and Addresses*, p. 235.

This view does not, as might be feared, do away with the concept of the supernatural. Nature is the prior subject that receives the self-communication of God in grace. It cannot achieve this goal by its own powers, or even merit that the gift be given. No creature can put God under obligation to do anything, least of all to give himself. Thus his self-gift is pre-eminently supernatural.

It might seem that God is unjust in calling all men and women to a goal that they lack the power to achieve. Can people fairly be required to do anything that lies beyond their capacities? For Catholic theology the answer has always been that what they cannot do by their unaided powers they can do with the divine assistance. Do they, then, have a right to demand God's grace? What, then, becomes of its gratuity? Here we meet one of the most persistent and vexing problems in the theology of grace, but not, I think, an unanswerable one. As Henri de Lubac explains, the problem has been badly stated. We ought not to think of God first issuing a call and then at some later time providing the means whereby such a call can be answered. From God's point of view man's supernatural voca-tion and the offer of the means of grace are simultaneous; they represent two aspects of the same disposition of God's loving mercy. What the offer of grace expresses in the moral sphere, the call to the supernatural expresses in the ontological sphere.[30]

Because all human beings are called to the same supernatural end, and because the offer of grace is inseparably bound up with that call, it follows, in Catholic theology, that the offer of grace must be universal. We can speak in this sense of the 'catholicity' of grace. Against heresies such as Jansenism, Catholic Christianity has always insisted on the extension of God's real salvific will to every individual who comes into the world. Vatican II, in a number of important texts, asserted this doctrine. It taught that no one who is inculpably ignorant of God, Christ, the gospel, or the Church was on that account excluded from eternal life (*LG* 16; *AG* 7). These texts make it clear that such 'unbelievers' do not save themselves; that they are not saved by their good will or sincerity (as a Pelagian might hold) but by the grace of Christ, which works in an

---

[30] Henri de Lubac, *Mystery of the Supernatural* (London: Chapman, 1967), p. 239.

unseen way in the hearts of all persons of good will (*GS* 22). 'The Holy Spirit in a manner known only to God offers to every man the possibility of being associated' with the Paschal mystery of Christ's death and resurrection (ibid.).

In some contemporary Catholic theologians, such as Karl Rahner, there is a marked tendency to look on actual grace less as an occasional occurrence than as a constant atmosphere in which we live and move. However that may be, it would appear that the offer of grace is never totally absent. From this it follows that, as Rahner puts it, 'Every morally good act of man is, in the actual order of salvation, also a supernaturally salutary act.'[31]

Does this imply that persons born into a situation where Jewish or Christian revelation is not available must be saved by means of a purely individual, invisible, spiritual relationship to God? Such a suggestion would be directly in conflict with what I have been calling catholicity in depth. In terms of the anthropology proposed in this chapter, it would be erroneous to imagine that God's grace and truth could come to individuals without any historical and institutional mediation. Relying on the views of Juan de Lugo, Friedrich von Hügel rejected any such 'verticalism' as uncatholic. Whoever is saved, he wrote:

is saved, here also, by God's working with and in and through the senses of this soul's body, the powers of this soul's mind and will, and the varingly rich or poor history, society, institutions which (during centuries or millenniums before this soul's existence and throughout our most various humankind now around it) have experienced, articulated, and transmitted, and are at this moment more or less mediating, the touch, the light, the food of God. Thus only do we get a fully Catholic, because an organic, an incarnational conception, not only of the Catholic Church or even of Christianity, but, in their various seekings and stages, of every sort of religion, indeed of all spiritual life at all.[32]

(4)

These words of von Hügel may serve to introduce the next

[31] Karl Rahner, 'Nature and Grace', *Theological Investigations*, vol. vi (Baltimore: Helicon, 1966), p. 195.

[32] Von Hügel, *Essays and Addresses*, p. 236.

question to be considered in this chapter: is there a distinctively Catholic attitude towards the world's religions?

In the course of the centuries, Christian theologians have taken many different positions regarding the non-Christian religions. The most negative view, still found in some types of sectarian Protestantism, regards these religions as false, diabolical, and idolatrous. A more moderate but still negative position, characteristic of much contemporary Protestantism, holds that in these religions there are some elements of natural revelation, but that these sound elements are so distorted by human sinfulness that the religions are evil. A central position, favoured by many contemporary Catholics, is that these religions are human creations, admirable in their own way, but reaching out in vain towards a transcendence they cannot achieve. A more optimistic position, held by many progressive theologians, is that these religions come from authentic supernatural experience and that they are ordinary means of salvation for those who do not know Christ. Finally, there is the liberal position, favoured by some humanistically oriented Protestants, that all the religions are essentially good and inspired, and that in this respect Christianity must be put in a class with the others.

On the basis of the conception of catholicity we have thus far developed, the first two positions and the fifth would seem to be deficient. The first two positions correspond to the kind of anthropology which, in the early pages of this chapter, has been described as Lutheran or Jansenistic. The fifth position, on the other hand, is difficult to reconcile with the high Christology presented in Chapter 2. If Christ is the incarnate Word of God, it would seem to follow that the religion that recognizes the Incarnation is in a class by itself. Every faith that fails to confess Jesus as divine Saviour is still ignorant of 'the way, the truth, and the life' (John 14: 15).

Setting the framework for the current discussion within Roman Catholicism, Vatican Council II laid down two general principles that stand in tension with each other. First, on the ground that non-Christian faiths 'often reflect a ray of that Truth which enlightens all men', the council stated that 'the Catholic Church rejects nothing which is true and holy in these religions' (*NA* 2). But secondly, it stated that the Church must always proclaim Christ as the one in whom the fullness of religious life is to be found, and in whom God has reconciled all things (ibid.). The council left open the question whether the non-Christian religions contain revelation and are, in themselves, salvific.

Our aim in these pages cannot be to settle these disputed questions, but only to identify a characteristically Catholic approach to the religions. Among the prominent theologians who have made this attempt, Newman, Tyrrell, Karrer, and von Balthasar would seem to deserve special mention.

In a review article on Henry Milman's *History of Christianity*,[33] John Henry Newman wrote that the Church gathers up the 'seeds of truth' scattered far and wide by the Moral Governor of the universe. Like a pilgrim, she wanders through the cultures of the nations 'claiming to herself what they said rightly, correcting their errors, supplying their defects, completing their beginnings, expanding their surmises, and thus gradually by means of them enlarging and refining the sense of her own teaching'. Milman had objected: 'These things are in heathenism, therefore they are not Christian.' Newman replied: 'These things are in Christianity, therefore they are not heathen.' Rejecting Milman's quest for 'some fabulous primitive simplicity', Newman preferred, as he put it, to 'repose in Catholic fullness'.

George Tyrrell wrote enthusiastically of the inclusiveness of Catholic Christianity, as the closest approximation to 'a microcosm of the world's religions'.[34] In contrast to the severe rationality of Puritanism, he contended, Catholicism paganizes Christianity in order to Christianize paganism.[35] 'Catholicism is but the most fully developed branch of a tree that springs from the very roots of humanity, and bears traces and proofs of its kinship with every other branch of the religious process.'[36] To be Catholic, Tyrrell affirmed, is 'to possess this sense of solidarity with all the religions of the world; to acknowledge

[33] John Henry Newman, *Essays Critical and Historical*, vol. ii (London: Longmans, Green, 1919), pp. 186–248, esp. pp. 230–4; partly quoted in his *Development of Doctrine*, chap. 8, sec. I, no. 2, pp. 380–2.

[34] George Tyrrell, *Christianity at the Cross-Roads* (London: Longmans, Green, 1909), pp. 254–5.

[35] Tyrrell, *Through Scylla*, p. 46.

[36] Ibid., p. 47.

that they are all lit, however dimly, by the same Logos-light which struggles, unconquered, with even their thickest darkness'. Catholicity thus requires one to rise above exclusiveness and sectarianism without in any way falling into indifferentism.[37]

Tyrrell did not advocate a syncretistic fusing of different religions. On the contrary, he regarded the law of development as tending towards greater distinctiveness. If a truly Catholic religion is ever realized, he wrote, 'it will not be by a sinking of differences . . . nor by an impossible unification of essentially incompatible systems', but rather by the survival of one religion that surpasses all the others and contains all the principal advantages of each.[38] Catholic Christianity was for him this pre-eminent, unifying faith.

In a pioneering study of the religions, published in 1934, Otto Karrer expressed a remarkably positive outlook. By virtue of its catholicity, he said, Christianity is the fulfilment of every religion; it comprehends to the utmost values that are elsewhere scattered and fragmentary.[39] 'Because the Church rejects as sectarian every deliberate "selection" from the whole, she preserves the scattered "seeds of the Logos" from degenerating into fragmentary religions and proves herself their comprehensive fulfilment, the *Catholic* Church.'[40]

In practice, Karrer recognizes, some Catholics seem to regard their Church as a self-contained body restricted to its own visible members, but this attitude, he holds, is 'Catholicist' rather than authentically Catholic.[41] To be truly Catholic, in his view, is to be open to all truth, goodness, and holiness. At bottom, Karrer concludes, there is only one religion, namely the Catholic religion 'which lives in all men and saves all men insofar as they share the treasures of truth bestowed upon that religion in their fulness'.[42]

A balanced Catholic theology of the religions must acknowledge the continuities, as does Karrer, but also the discontinuities. Hans Urs von Balthasar, one of the greatest living

---

[37] Ibid., p. 23.
[38] Tyrrell, *Christianity at the Cross-Roads*, p. 156.
[39] Otto Karrer, *Religions of Mankind* (London: Sheed & Ward, 1936), p. 210.
[40] Ibid., p. 215.
[41] Ibid., p. 265.
[42] Ibid., p. 276.

exponents of catholicity, is reserved towards the Eastern religions, which he regards, in general, as human efforts to attain the divine through an ecstatic leap that never, in fact, achieves its objective.[43] Revealed religion, by contrast, attains the divine in so far as it freely bestows itself in an incarnational way in the crucified Christ and the Eucharist.[44] Von Balthasar does not deny that there are seeds of truth in other religions, but these, he says, are always distorted until integrated into the fullness of Christ. A pagan custom such as ancestor worship, for example, demands deep transformation before it can be integrated into the Catholic communion of the saints.[45]

As is evident from the disagreements among the authors, there is no one Catholic approach to the non-Christian religions. Catholicism, as I have indicated, is irrevocably bound to affirm that the fullness of grace and truth came into the world in Jesus Christ, and is disposed to find elements of truth and goodness in religions that have developed without benefit of exposure to Judaism or Christianity. Contemporary Roman Catholicism, as represented by Vatican Council II, holds that God's saving grace is operative among all peoples, even the unevangelized. Catholic theology favours the idea of a social mediation of grace. One channel for the mediation of divine grace could presumably be the religions in which people attempt to articulate their relationship to the divine. If the religions are shaped by authentic spiritual experience, it would seem that they must contain supernatural elements worthy of being respected and preserved.

It may be admitted, however, that any religion not firmly based on God's self-revelation in Christ will suffer from human distortion, for sin is at work among all peoples. Hence it is to be expected that many elements in the non-Christian religions are in need of being corrected, and not simply supplemented. The precise ratio between grace-filled elements and sinful structures in particular religions cannot be determined in advance by deduction from Christian theological principles. The appli-

---

[43] Hans Urs von Balthasar, *Pneuma und Institution* (Einsiedeln: Johannes Verlag, 1974), pp. 83–7.

[44] Ibid., pp. 101–8.

[45] Hans Urs von Balthasar, 'Die Absolutheit des Christentums und die Katholizität der Kirche', in W. Kasper (ed.), *Absolutheit des Christentums*, Quaestiones Disputatae 79 (Freiburg: Herder, 1977), pp. 131–56, esp. pp. 152–3.

cation has to be made in each case on the basis of a detailed study of the religion in question. It may be that some are in part demonic, that others are pitiful attempts to rise above the human condition, while still others are predominantly fruits of the Holy Spirit. The Christian theologian cannot set a priori limits to the heights to which grace can raise persons and social groups that are inculpably ignorant of the gospel.

(5)

A final question that requires treatment in connection with the problem of nature and grace is that of the Church's relationship to culture and politics. Under this rubric special consideration may be given to the ancient question of Church–State relations. The State has been recognized in Catholic thought as a natural society, whereas the Church is evidently supernatural. Thus the relationship between nature and the supernatural has a bearing on the questions to which we now turn.

In the light of what has already been said about catholicity, Christianity and secular culture may be seen as interconnected and yet diverse. Perceiving the whole of creation as an object of Christ's redemptive concern, and as destined to be transformed in the final Kingdom, the Church cannot simply abandon the world to its own devices or accept an unresolved dualism between the sacred and the secular. Neither sectarian withdrawal from the world nor secularist absolutization of the world is compatible with the Catholic mentality. Catholicism is characteristically the religion of those who, while committed to Christianity, operate within the social structures of their secular environment. In Ernst Troeltsch's categories, Catholicism belongs not to the sect-type but to the church-type of Christianity.[46] The Catholic Church has in fact had a long history of involvement with the arts and sciences, education and science, law and social policy.

On the other hand, authentic Catholicism does not totally equate Church and society. It recognizes a distinction between the Church, as the body of Christ and the world, as the larger sphere of his redemptive action. Even though sometimes tend-

[46] Ernst Troeltsch, *The Social Teaching of the Christian Churches* (Chicago: Univ. of Chicago, 1981), *passim*.

ing towards an excessive union between Church and State, Catholicism has traditionally recognized, in principle, that each is a distinct society having autonomy in its own sphere of competence.

The ways in which Catholic Christianity has influenced the social order have varied from one age to another. Under Constantine and his successors, Catholicism was imposed as the law of the Empire, and the emperors assumed quasi-episcopal authority. In the medieval West the papacy, representing the 'spiritual' power, claimed supremacy over the temporal rulers who, however, became increasingly restive and rebellious. In modern times, when Christianity has been generally disestablished, medieval sacralism is little more than a fading memory. Instead of dictating to the secular authorities, the Church now seeks to promote Christian values by shaping the ideas and attitudes of citizens and rulers, especially those who are also members of the Church.

Maurice Blondel, as a layman deeply concerned by the rift between the Church and the secular society of France in his day, approached the problem in terms of his own philosophy of action.[47] He argued that, while the respective rights of Church and State could be endlessly debated in the abstract, the only real answer could come through the lived experience of persons engaged in collaborative action on behalf of peace and justice. Social Catholicism, by seeking to achieve concrete solutions of a practicable kind, could come to appreciate the secret workings of grace in the hearts of men and women who, without formal adherence to Christianity, sought to promote truth and community. Such persons, he believed, were secret allies of the Church, which knew that peace, prosperity, and justice could not be maintained in the long run without the support and guidance of the gospel. Blondel disagreed with Catholics who wanted the hierarchical Church to formulate Catholic social teaching on the basis of abstract doctrine. He preferred to look upon the gospel as a leaven within the secular.

In the increasingly secularized situation of the modern West,

---

[47] See the entire series of articles by Maurice Blondel (under the pseudonym, Testis), 'La "Semaine Sociale" de Bordeaux', *Annales de philosophie chrétienne*, ix (1909–10), pp. 5–21, 162–84, 245–78, 272–92, 449–71, 561–92; x (1910), pp. 127–62; reprinted under the title *La Semaine Sociale de Bordeaux et le Monophorisme* (Paris: Bloud, 1910).

when Christianity is no longer backed up by social sanctions and popular culture, the preservation of a Catholic point of view offers special difficulties. The Church may find it necessary to give a more rigorous formation to its own members so that their attitudes will not simply mirror the ideas and values of the dominant culture. In some respects, therefore, the Church may be expected to assume a 'sectarian' stance precisely in order to make a distinctively Catholic contribution.

Michael Novak warns against excesses in this regard. The sectarian mentality, which is 'absolutist, pure, certain, and righteous', must in his opinion be resisted. 'The Catholic spirit', he writes, 'does not believe that the church is a church of the saved, the saints, the true believers. It is, rather, a gathering of the struggling, the voyaging, the weak, those in whom there remains much unbelief, and sinners.'[48] All of this may be conceded, provided that efforts are continually made to combat the weakness and to attain true holiness.

In recent years there have been some disagreements among Catholic Christians regarding the ways in which it is best for the Church to address contingent matters of social policy. Should such questions be left to the informed judgement of individual lay persons? Should the hierarchy take official positions? If so, can these positions be binding on the consciences of the faithful? This is not the place to settle debates of this kind. It may suffice to observe that, in spite of such disputed points, Catholic Christians can agree that grace and sin are at work in the socio-political order and that this order falls within the Church's sphere of concern. Catholicism does not settle for a purely privatized religion or for a rigid division between the 'two kingdoms' of Christ and the world.

The Catholic view of the Church–world relationship is therefore another instance of unity in difference. The Church must walk a fine line between sectarian withdrawal from the world and secularist absorption into it. Depending on which is the greater temptation at a particular time, Catholic practice,

---

[48] Michael Novak, *Confession of a Catholic* (San Francisco: Harper & Row, 1983), p. 103. In several of his later works, Cardinal Jean Daniélou warned against the danger that Christianity might become a small sect of the elect and cease to be the religion of the great multitude. See his *Prayer as a Political Problem* (New York: Sheed & Ward, 1967), esp. chap. 1. On the values and pathologies of popular Catholicism see Leonardo Boff, *Church; Charism and Power* (New York: Crossroad, 1985), pp. 86–8.

as a corrective, may have to lean more in one direction or the other.

(6)

Throughout this chapter the fundamental Catholic principles of plenitude and mediation have been kept in view. The fullness of the divinity, as we previously saw, is present and active in Christ and in the Holy Spirit. But Christ is to be found as represented and reflected in created realities, which have their final meaning only in relation to him. The Holy Spirit makes himself present by the secret action of grace, which inheres in nature, heals, and transforms it. Nature is oriented towards grace as its transcendent fulfilment. Grace, when it comes, corrects what is faulty, supplies what is lacking, ratifies and elevates what is sound. These principles, as we have seen, are applicable to culture, economics, politics, and religion. In each of these areas the Catholic tendency is to accept provisionally the composition of the pure and the impure, the saintly and the sinful, not in order to rest in what is deficient but in order to pass by means of it into deeper communion with God.

4

Catholicity in Breadth: Mission and Communion

In the last two chapters we have seen that catholicity derives from the confluence of two streams. The divine plenitude of catholicity comes from above, as God freely communicates his own life in Christ and the Holy Spirit. This gift, however, could not be received and appropriated unless nature were oriented towards it. Human nature, according to the Catholic understanding, has an enduring capacity to receive and be inwardly transformed. Theologians often speak of 'qualitative' or 'vertical' catholicity, meaning the participation of individuals and groups in the divine fullness of truth and life. Even if there were only one true Christian in the world, that individual would be Catholic in the qualitative sense. Using the term 'catholic' in this sense, Henri de Lubac points out that the Church was as Catholic on the day of Pentecost as it was ever to become in the course of its history.[1] Even a 'small flock' can be Catholic.

Yet there is another aspect of the Church's catholicity, sometimes called quantitative or horizontal. These terms designate the union of Christians with one another in a community that is expansive and inclusive. Catholicity in this sense is opposed to schism, sectarianism, and whatever would tend to confine or isolate Christians in a closed, particularist group. Quantitative catholicity, as we shall see, is connected with qualitative. It is the self-diffusiveness of the fullness of God's gift in and through the Church—the capacity of that gift to communicate itself without limit to persons of every kind and condition.

(1)

The universalism of the Church is anticipated—but only

[1] Henri de Lubac, *Catholicism: A Study of Dogma in Relation to the Corporate Destiny of Mankind* (London: Burns, Oates, and Washbourne, 1950), p. 17. The same point is made by Yves Congar in *Divided Christendom* (London: G. Bles, 1939), p. 253.

anticipated—in the public ministry of Jesus. When he sent his disciples to proclaim God's Kingdom, Jesus enjoined them to go only to the lost sheep of Israel (Matt. 10: 6). Matthew, who supplies this information, quotes Jesus as saying, 'I was sent only to the lost sheep of the house of Israel' (Matt. 15: 24), thus indicating the divine will as the reason for his self-limitation. Yet the faith and obedience of the Syro-Phoenician woman, to whom Jesus spoke these words, moved him to make an exception. In the future Church, faith and obedience were to prevail over descent from Abraham as criteria for admission.

In his preaching, Jesus repeatedly inveighed against restrictive interpretations of God's law that would give a privileged status to observant Jews. In one of his best-known parables he extolled the merciful Samaritan in contrast to the Levite and the priest (Luke 10: 29–37). On another occasion he congratulated a Roman centurion for showing greater faith than had been found in Israel. He then predicted that many would come from the East and the West and would sit down with Abraham, while the natural heirs of the Kingdom would be cast out (Matt. 8: 10–12). He depicts all nations as being called to judgement before the throne of the Son of Man (Matt. 25: 31–46). According to a recent study there can be little doubt that Jesus' prophetic challenge to defined boundaries of membership in God's people 'was a prime cause of the hostility directed against him' and a major factor leading to his execution.[2]

According to the Gospels Jesus looked forward to a future proclamation of the gospel to the Gentiles. His reference to the sign of Jonah, as reported by Luke points to the future conversion of the Gentiles as a sign of judgement upon unbelieving Jews (Luke 11: 29–32). When anointed by the sinful woman at Bethany, Jesus alluded to a time when the gospel would be preached throughout the world (Mark 14: 9; Matt. 26: 13). On another occasion he said that he had sheep who did not belong to the fold of Israel (John 10: 23). While the historicity of individual sayings is difficult to verify, the convergent testimony of the Evangelists would seem to be trustworthy.

A certain universalism in the thinking of Jesus would not be surprising, since the conversion of all nations to the God of

---

[2] Donald Senior and Carroll Stuhlmueller, *The Biblical Foundations of Mission* (London: SCM, 1983), p. 155.

Israel had been predicted by the prophets. The Judaism of Jesus' day was already breaking out of its natural confines. Aware of this, Jesus spoke of those who travelled over land and sea to make converts (Matt. 23: 15). He did not disapprove of this missionary zeal, though he did rebuke the scribes and Pharisees for turning their converts into children of hell like themselves.

The universalism of the Gospel accounts of Jesus' ministry is no doubt heightened in the light of Easter and Pentecost. The glorification of Jesus and the sending of the Spirit were seen by the early community as a fulfilment of the eschatological promise of the prophets. At the moment of final revelation, writes the exegete Joachim Jeremias, God 'summons the nations of Zion, and by constituting the universal people of God from Jews and Gentiles abolishes all earthly distinctions'.[3] Luke, when he described Peter's Pentecost sermon as being heard in their own languages by 'devout men from every nation under heaven' (Acts 2: 5), unquestionably has in mind the eschatological significance of the descent of the Holy Spirit. The New Testament authors were convinced that Jesus had laid down his life not for one nation alone, but 'to gather into one the children of God who are scattered abroad' (John 11: 52).

A serious problem was posed for the early Church by the conversion to Christianity of many pagans from the Hellenistic world. The Jerusalem leadership had assumed that to become a Christian one would first have to become a Jew, submitting to circumcision and the precepts of the Mosaic law. The Acts and Pauline letters reflect the intensity of the struggle between those who wanted to insist on the Mosaic law and those who did not. The so-called council of Jerusalem, as portrayed in the fifteenth chapter of Acts, reached a compromise settlement which, if implemented at all, could only have been transitory. The end-result was the dissolution of the barriers between Jews and Gentiles and the formation of a truly international Church.

Some of the most eloquent passages in the New Testament celebrate this universalism. The First Letter of Peter, for instance, portrays the Church as a holy nation, God's own

---

[3] Joachim Jeremias, *Jesus' Promise to the Nations* (Naperville, Ill.: Allenson, 1958), pp. 70–1.

people (1 Pet. 2: 9–10), born anew through the living and abiding word of God (1: 23). Paul is especially impressed by the ability of this new people to overcome all discrimination and hostility due to social differences. 'As many of you as were baptized into Christ,' he writes to the Galatians, 'have put on Christ. There is neither Jew nor Greek, there is neither slave nor free, there is neither male nor female; for you are all one in Christ Jesus' (Gal. 3: 27–8). This teaching is repeated almost verbatim in Col. 3: 10–11), where the writer ascribes the vanquishing of natural social barriers to the fact that all Christians have put on a new nature, so that for them 'Christ is all and in all.' Rebirth in Christ does not, of course, eliminate human differences but it makes them non-divisive.

The Letter to the Ephesians focuses on the new-found communion between Jews and Gentiles who had until that time been enemies. Only in Christ could this deep antagonism be overcome. 'He is our peace,' writes the author, 'who had made us both one and has broken down the dividing wall of hostility' (Eph. 2: 14). Christ has reconciled both groups by the Cross, and has created in himself one man in place of the two.

From these New Testament texts it was only a short step to the boast of the early apologists that Christians were neither Jews nor Greeks, but belonged to a new people, a 'third race' (*triton genos*) created in Jesus Christ, the new Adam.[4]

(2)

The catholicity of the early Church was not only inclusive but also expansive. We have already seen how the preaching of Jesus, though restricted for the most part to Jews, fore-shadowed the universal mission of the Church. From Pentecost onwards the Church felt itself driven by an inner compulsion to disseminate its faith. The whole Church could collectively say what Paul said of himself, 'Woe to me if I do not preach the gospel' (1 Cor. 9: 16). The Apocalypse accordingly depicts an angel flying across the sky 'with an eternal gospel to proclaim to those who dwell on earth, to every nation and tribe and tongue and people' (Rev. 14: 6). The main theme of Acts is the outward

---

[4] This theme is richly illustrated in Adolf Harnack, *The Mission and Expansion of Christianity in the First Three Centuries* (New York: Putnam, 1908), chap. 7, pp. 240–78.

thrust of the Church's mission, especially through Paul as the Apostle of the Gentiles.

The New Testament traces the Church's universal mission-ary mandate to the risen Christ. According to Mark, Jesus before his Ascension instructed the Eleven to go into the whole world and preach the gospel to every creature (Mark 16: 15). In Luke and Acts the apostles are directed by the risen Lord to preach and bear witness to the ends of the earth (Luke 24: 27; Acts 1: 8). The most explicit text is the great commission at the end of Matthew: 'All authority in heaven and on earth has been given to me. Go therefore and make disciples of all nations . . .' (Matt. 28: 18–19). In this passage the word 'all' occurs four times in three verses: Jesus has received all authority, all nations are to be evangelized, they are to be taught all that Jesus has commanded, and Jesus himself will be with his commissioned witnesses all days. If catholicity signifies totality, this fourfold 'all' abundantly certifies the Catholic character of Christian mission.

Throughout the ages Catholic Christianity has accepted this global missionary obligation. According to Henri de Lubac, the medieval writers, though ignorant of other continents, were willing to exclude from their missionary concern

neither the 'Pygmies', the fabulous long-eared Scythians, nor the grotesque 'dog-headed ones'. From the very first she [the Church] had always kept her objective before her. A Christian age which deliberately turned away from it would be worse than an age of heresy. . . . It would amount to a denial of her very being, what Newman would have called her 'Idea'. Her Catholicity is both her strength and at the same time a continual demand upon her. . . . So long as the Church does not extend and penetrate to the whole of humanity, so as to give it the form of Christ, she cannot rest.[5]

In the Middle Ages the impression was widespread that the gospel had been disseminated almost everywhere, and that little evangelization remained to be done. Under these circum-stances it did not seem unduly harsh to maintain that, with certain rare exceptions, the salvation of individuals depended on their actual incorporation in the Church. After the great voyages of discovery in early modern times this illusion was

---

[5] Henri de Lubac, *Catholicism*, pp. 114–15.

shattered. It gradually became apparent that the majority of the human race were not Catholic Christians and that vast multitudes had never even heard the name of Christ.

The first reaction to this situation, at least in Roman Catholicism, was an admirable intensification of missionary effort. The solid achievements of this effort should never be forgotten, even though certain shortcomings must be deplored. The missionaries were too much under the spell of the medieval view of the Church as the sole ark of salvation; they were consequently too pessimistic about the possibilities of salvation for non-Christians. They were also in many cases insufficiently respectful of the cultures and religions of the peoples to whom they came. In some cases the missionaries, either willingly or reluctantly, were too closely linked to the colonial powers. Each of these faults involved a certain lack of catholicity.

Between the sixteenth century and the twentieth, Catholic theology has become aware of these shortcomings. In particular, it has come to a deeper realization that the sphere of Christ's redemptive work is much wider than the Church as a visible society. Vatican Council II, as we have seen, teaches that those who, without personal fault, are ignorant of God, Christ, the gospel, or the Church are not thereby excluded from eternal life (*LG* 16; *AG* 7). The council affirms that such persons may, by God's grace, be associated in a mysterious way 'with the Paschal mystery of Christ's death and resurrection' (*GS* 22).[6]

While the mercy of God towards those inculpably ignorant of Christ must not be minimized, this point should not be allowed to cloud the universal significance of the Christian message. The catholicity of the Church became manifest when the Gentiles turned to the gospel as giving the answers to their own questions about the meaning of life and death.[7] Subsequent history has confirmed the capacity of men and women of every kind and condition to find faith and hope in the Christian proclamation that God loves them, that they have been redeemed, and that they are called to eternal life in the redeeming Christ. The invitation to share this faith and

---

[6] See above, chap. 1, sec. 4; chap. 3, sec. 3.

[7] On this subject see Wolfhart Pannenberg, *Revelation as History* (New York: Macmillan, 1968), pp. 131–5.

hope brings with it a call to join the believing community.

As the Church spreads her faith, she shows forth the transcendence of the gospel and the universal working of the grace of the Holy Spirit. At the same time, the Church actualizes her own catholicity. Constituted in the world as a sacrament, or efficacious sign, of God's universal redemptive will in Christ, the Church is driven by an inner dynamism to represent the whole of humanity as the recipient of redemption. If the Church were content to exist only in a single portion of humanity, she would lack what I have in one place called 'semeiological catholicity', i.e., universality in her capacity as sign.[8]

The missionary obligation does not cease where the message encounters resistance. Like her founder, the Church is required to proclaim to the hard of hearing and even to the deaf. Time and again the temptation has arisen to limit the scope of evangelization, either on the ground that some do not need the gospel, or that they are beyond hope of being reached by it. Hans Urs von Balthasar points out that any such contraction introduces a fateful distortion into the Church's inner life. 'When Catholicism renounces pressing into these realms,' he writes, 'it begins to recede in its own realm.'[9] His analysis is, I think, correct. Once we begin to conceive of Christianity as the religion of a certain segment of humanity—the religiously disposed, the Semitic, the Western, or whatever—the very basis of the Church is falsified. One begins to wonder whether Christ is just the saviour of the few who believe in him, whether rival faiths are equally true, and at length whether the whole class of saviour figures, including Krishna, Buddha, and Jesus Christ, are just arbitrary symbols manufactured by the religious consciousness. Thus horizontal and vertical catholicity stand or fall together.

(3)

The extensive catholicity of the Church manifests itself only gradually, and in continually varying ways. Originally centred

---

[8] Avery Dulles, *The Dimensions of the Church* (Westminster, Md.: Newman, 1967), p. 51.

[9] Hans Urs von Balthasar, *Katholisch: Aspekte des Mysteriums* (Einsiedeln: Johannes Verlag, 1975), p. 86.

in the Mediterranean countries, Catholic Christianity later found its primary home in Europe. Writing early in the present century, Hilaire Belloc propounded the thesis, 'The Faith is Europe. And Europe is the Faith.'[10] As a plea to Europeans to recover the religious roots of their former unity, this slogan could be defended. Christianity was in possession as the religion of Europeans, and the Christianity that had united Europe was Catholic. But what about people of different stock? Did Belloc mean to imply that to become Christian they would first have to be Europeanized? If so, his thinking was too particularist.

Vatican Council I (1869–70) was the first council in history to include members from outside Europe and the Mediterranean world. Some of the council Fathers were North and South Americans, but all of them, it would seem, were either born in Europe or descended from Europeans. At Vatican II, less than a century later, the picture was vastly different. Present were indigenous bishops from many continents. Organizing themselves into national and regional conferences, many of the non-Europeans saw to it that their collective insights were reflected in the council documents. For Roman Catholicism Vatican II marks the emergence of what Karl Rahner aptly called the 'world Church'.[11] Unlike Vatican I, this council exhibited a consciousness of cultural pluralism.

It is not surprising, therefore, that Vatican II in its documents gave greater acknowledgement to legitimate differences within the universal Church than had ever been given before. According to the Constitution on the Church, Catholic Christianity fosters and takes to itself, in so far as they are sound, the abilities, resources, and customs of each people (*LG* 13). The Decree on Missionary Activity adds that, while syncretism and false particularism are to be avoided, the Christian life should be accommodated to the genius and dispositions of each culture so that, by a wonderful exchange, all the riches of the nations may be given to Christ as an inheritance, as suggested by the Christological interpretation of Psalm 2: 8 (*AG* 22). The Pastoral Constitution on the Church

[10] Hilaire Belloc, *Europe and the Faith* (London: Constable & Co., 1920), p. 331.
[11] Karl Rahner, 'Basic Theological Interpretation of the Second Vatican Council', in his *Theological Investigations*, vol. xx (New York: Crossroad, 1981), pp. 77–89.

in the Modern World declares that the accommodated preaching of the gospel ought to remain the law of all evangelization, so that each nation may develop the ability to express Christ's message in its own way (*GS* 44). And finally, the Decree of Ecumenism, in its chapter on Eastern Christianity, asserts that the legitimate variety of customs and observances, modes of worship and styles of doctrinal expression, should present no obstacle to the restoration of communion (*UR* 14–18). Several other texts of similar tenor have already been cited from Vatican II in Chapter 1, above.

In this context the complicated question of the relationship between Christianity and culture takes on new actuality. The distinction between the faith and its cultural embodiments was already made in principle when Christianity detached itself from its Jewish matrix and became inculturated in the Hellenistic world. But that inculturation, by reason of its very success, presents new problems for the 'world Church'. Can the faith with equal right be inculturated into the civilizations of other races and continents? Vatican II indicated a basically positive answer to this question:

. . . the Church, sent to all peoples of every time and place, is not bound exclusively and indissolubly to any race or nation, nor to any particular way of life or any customary pattern of living, ancient or recent. Faithful to her own tradition and at the same time conscious of her universal mission, she can enter into communion with various cultural modes, to her own enrichment and theirs too. (*GS* 58)

Since the council this process of multiple inculturation has been promoted, and in some ways restrained, by the worldwide voyages of Popes Paul VI and John Paul II, as well as by many official documents. Paul VI linked this development to the Church's catholicity:

In fact the Church, by virtue of her essential catholicity, cannot be alien to any country or people; she is bound to make herself native to every clime, culture, and race. Wherever she is, she must strike her roots deep into the spiritual and cultural ground of the place and assimilate all that is of genuine value.[12]

With this kind of encouragement the inner diversification of

---

[12] Paul VI, Radio Message to Asia from Manila, 26 Nov. 1970, in *AAS* lxiii (1971), pp. 35–40; quotation from p. 39.

the Catholic Church has notably increased. The Latin American bishops, in general conferences such as those of Medellín (1968) and Puebla (1979), have taken the lead. Other regional and national bishops' conferences, such as that of the United States, have likewise assumed a distinctive identity. The differing concerns and orientations of different portions of the world Church have been aired at the biennial and triennial meetings of the international Synod of Bishops since 1967. The tensions between different constituencies in the Catholic Church since Vatican II are inevitable accompaniments of the movement from monolithic to pluriform unity. It seems safe to predict that the Catholic Church from now onwards will be less Eurocentric, in the sense of being dominated by European culture, though it will doubtless continue to use European languages in its official documents and universal assemblies. Without loss of its unity in the essentials of faith, worship, and morality, the Church will exhibit greater internal diversity than ever before.

A similar analysis would hold for many other branches of Christianity. The great denominations, such as Lutheranism, Presbyterianism, and Anglicanism, are increasingly seen as World Confessional Families. Some nineteenth-century American sects, such as the Seventh-day Adventists, are shedding their original fundamentalism as they take on international membership. In the World Council of Churches, since its origins in 1948, leadership has in great part shifted from mainline European churches to the budding churches of the Third World.

(4)

In this discussion of pluralism we have begun to raise the very delicate question of distinguishing between acceptable and unacceptable diversity. This, of course, is the heart of the ecumenical problem. When Christian bodies disagree about whether one another's doctrines and practices are authentically Christian, they fall into a state of schism. There is a sense in which all churches today are in this state, inasmuch as they are cut off from communion with others which possess elements of authentic Christianity. In Roman Catholic circles, however, schism will be more narrowly conceived as meaning lack of communion with the body in which the Church of Christ 'subsists' intact—that is to say the Roman Catholic communion.

In an effort to clarify the difference between acceptable and unacceptable diversity, Johann Adam Möhler made an important distinction between a contrast (*Gegensatz*) and a contradiction (*Widerspruch*). He illustrated this distinction by means of an analogy:

A choir is constituted when the voices of different persons, men and women, boys and girls, each singing in its own way, are blended into a harmony. Without the multitude and variety of the voices we would have only a tiresome and crippling monotony, and without their blending, only a painful dissonance. The art of the choir master, who must have a keen sense of harmony in order to be able to train others, enables him to recognize the discordant voice, but his wisdom prompts him to correct that voice, so as to be able to keep it as a constituent part of the choir.

When encouraged by the choir master, he who sings the bass must not be led to imagine that because his specialty is the strong, deep note, the lower he sings the better, but he must strive to put the depth and power of his voice in harmony with the sweetness and gentleness of the others. If, unable to notice by himself the dissonance of his voice, he were to take no account of the conductor who is in charge of the performance as a whole, or still worse, if he imagined that he alone could produce the entire melody, he would have to be excluded as incapable of being trained and as hindering the common achievement. He would represent no longer a contrast (*Gegensatz*), since true contrasts are compatible with unity, but would rather constitute a contradiction (*Widerspruch*).[13]

Catholic ecumenism has, on the whole, followed along the lines here indicated by Möhler. Catholicism, as Newman frequently observed, has the power of holding together in unity elements that in all other schools are incompatible. But, as Newman himself observed, there is a point at which certain opinions must be rejected as repugnant to the Christian idea.[14] Following up this line of thought, George Tyrrell, in his posthumously published *Christianity at the Cross-Roads*, warned

[13] Johann Adam Möhler, *Die Einheit in der Kirche* (Cologne: J. Hegner, 1957), sec. 46, pp. 152–3.
[14] John Henry Newman, *Essay on the Development of Christian Doctrine*, chap. VI, sec. 2, nos. 15–17 (Garden City, NJ: Doubleday Image, 1960), pp. 261–5.

against a 'syncretic catholicism' that would attempt to embrace all religions in one overarching synthesis.[15] Such an amorphous unity would be condemned to sterility. Much of the theology of reunion in his own day, Tyrrell contended, was born of weariness and scepticism rather than of visionary faith.[16] In our own day it remains important to distinguish between a reductionist ecumenism that would achieve unity by discarding what is distinctive to each tradition, and an authentically Catholic ecumenism that would enrich the total Church by a critical appropriation of what is valid in the separate traditions.

Building upon the approval given to legitimate pluralism by Vatican II, Catholic ecumenists have often reflected about the extent to which the existing differences between communions such as the Anglican, the Orthodox, the Roman Catholic, and the Lutheran might be retained in a reunited Church. In a sermon delivered in Cambridge, England, on 18 January 1970, Cardinal Jan Willebrands, President of the Secretariat for Promoting the Unity of Christians, spoke of the ecumenical importance of the principle that the Church Catholic must embody diversity as well as unity, and can therefore comprise distinct ecclesial types, which he called by the Greek term, *typoi*. 'Where there is a long coherent tradition, commanding men's love and loyalty, creating and sustaining a harmonious and organic whole of complementary elements, each of which supports and strengthens the other, you have the reality of a *typos*.'[17] A *typos*, he went on to say, is ordinarily specified by the presence of four elements: a characteristic theological approach, a characteristic liturgical expression, a characteristic spiritual and devotional tradition, and a characteristic canonical discipline.

Cardinal Willebrands evidently intended to suggest that Anglicanism contains many of the elements of a legitimate *typos*, and that in the event of reunion with Rome it might be able to preserve the essentials of its own heritage. Pope Paul VI gave additional backing to this suggestion when, on the occa-

---

[15] George Tyrrell, *Christianity at the Cross-Roads* (London: Longmans, Green, 1909), p. 232.

[16] Ibid., pp. 229, 233.

[17] 'Cardinal Willebrands' Address in Cambridge, Eng.', in *Documents on Anglican/ Roman Catholic Relations* (Washington, DC: US Catholic Conference, 1972), pp. 32–41; quotation from p. 39.

sion of the canonization of the forty English martyrs (25 Oct. 1970), he declared:

... on the day when—God willing—the unity of faith and of Christian life is restored, no offense will be inflicted on the honor and sovereignty of a great country such as England. There will be no seeking to lessen the legitimate prestige and the worthy patrimony of the piety and usage proper to the Anglican Church when the Roman Catholic Church—this humble 'Servant of the servants of God'—is able to embrace her ever-beloved sister in the one authentic Communion of the family of Christ. . . .[18]

The question of ecclesial 'types' is closely connected with that of inculturation, mentioned above. In principle it is not only possible but desirable for Christianity to assume different forms suited to different socio-cultural situations. Some cultures are more individualistic, others more collectivist; some more mystical, others more rational; some more traditional, others more innovative; some more sacral, others more secular. These and other factors make for different spiritualities, different ways of thinking about the faith, different styles of worship, different administrative structures and practices. In a multicultural church a variety of such expressions is to be encouraged, for, as the common expression has it, unity is not the same as uniformity.

These cultural factors have not always been recognized in the past. This oversight has itself contributed to schism. As Yves Congar has shown, secular factors such as the division between the Eastern and Western Empires and the interruption of normal communication by reason of Islamic control of the Eastern Mediterranean helped to set the stage for misunderstanding and eventual rupture between Eastern Orthodoxy and Western Catholicism.[19] Something similar happened in the Western church in the sixteenth century. The rise of national consciousness, the wealth of the monasteries, the political involvements of popes and bishops, together with a multitude of cultural, linguistic, and philosophical differences, added fuel to the doctrinal disputes and prevented them from being

[18] Pope Paul VI, 'Remarks at the Canonization of the Forty Martyrs', ibid., pp. 42–3.
[19] Yves Congar, *After Nine Hundred Years: The Background of the Schism between the Eastern and Western Churches* (New York: Fordham Univ. Press, 1959), chap. 2, pp. 7–28.

settled through dispassionate theological consultation.

A frequent source of schism and a major impediment to its healing has been what Congar calls 'powerful and voracious nationalism'.[20] It is no secret that Orthodox Christianity, since the collapse of the Byzantine Empire, has been plagued by the tendency to interpret autocephaly as demanding total autonomy for each of the new national churches, organized on predominantly secular principles.[21] In the West the Catholic Church has had to struggle against Gallican separatist tendencies in France and against analogous nationalistic movements in other countries. In Germany powerful political figures such as Bismarck have at times tried to manipulate the Protestant churches for political ends. The Church of England has at times been dominated by kings and parliaments, and one of the great merits of the Oxford Movement was its reassertion of the spiritual independence of the Church. In the volume, *Lux Mundi*, the Anglican theologian W. J. H. Campion showed the connection between the catholicity of the Church and its independence from national politics. He concluded:

. . . the Church is essentially Catholic, and only incidentally national. It is their Catholic character so far as it remains, at least their Catholic ideal, which gives the different fragments of the Church their strength and power. The 'Church of England' is a peculiarly misleading term. The Church of Christ in England is, as Coleridge pointed out, the safer and truer phrase.[22]

Karl Barth in his *Church Dogmatics* makes much the same point. If the Church is to remain the true Church, he says, it cannot allow itself to be determined by any state or secular authority. 'There is a Church in England,' he adds, 'but in the strict sense there is no Church of England.'[23] Catholicity in his view demands that any local or regional church be linked to the *una sancta*.

The emergence of the World Confessional Families

[20] Congar, *Divided Christendom*, pp. 112–13.

[21] This statement applies particularly to the Balkans. See John Meyendorff, *Orthodoxy and Catholicity* (New York: Sheed & Ward, 1966), pp. 42–4.

[22] W. J. H. Campion, 'Christianity and Politics', in Charles Gore (ed.), *Lux Mundi* (10th edn.; London: John Murray, 1890), pp. 435–64; quotation from p. 464.

[23] Karl Barth, *Church Dogmatics*, vol. iv.1 (Edinburgh: T. & T. Clark, 1956), p. 703. In a similar vein, Henry de Lubac warns against speaking, for example, of a 'French church' (*The Motherhood of the Church* (San Francisco: Ignatius Press, 1982), p. 231).

represents, to my mind, a partial but significant recovery of catholicity. I therefore look with some misgivings on certain efforts to set up 'union churches' along purely geographical lines. In this category I would place the proposal that there should be in England three autonomous churches, English, Scottish, and Welsh, each absorbing the functions of the previous denominational churches in its own area.[24] Given the doctrinal divergences, this proposal seems unrealistic. From an ecumenical point of view, John Macquarrie's comment is appropriate: 'The last thing the world needs is a series of national churches reduplicating the political divisions that already exist, and in some cases breaking up the international Christian communions (Roman, Anglican, Lutheran, etc.) which transcend national and racial borders.'[25]

Because of its historical experiences with Protestantism, Anglicanism, and Gallicanism, the Catholic Church since the Reformation has been wary of regional variations, whether in doctrine, in ritual, or in canon law. The efforts of Jesuit missionaries in Asia to adapt Catholic Christianity to the traditions and sensitivities of the Chinese and the Indians were condemned by Rome. The Counter-Reformation trend towards uniformity continued well into the twentieth century, but was checked by Vatican Council II, which aimed to restore the proper balance. The council's stress on 'legitimate variety' in doctrine, liturgy, and canon law (*UR* 17) has encouraged Anglicans, Lutherans, and others to entertain the possibility of union with Rome on the basis of 'reconciled diversity' without capitulation or absorption.

Catholic ecumenism, as here understood, avoids the over-simplification of extreme positions. It neither canonizes differences by accepting indiscriminate pluralism nor does it seek to obliterate all differences by imposing uniformity. It seeks rather to discern what differences are compatible with the gospel and Catholic unity, and to accept, with necessary corrections, as much as it can. Catholicism, in this field as in others, works in the tension-filled no-man's-land in which patient dialogue is required. The practice of such ecumenism is

[24] This proposal is mentioned by John Macquarrie in his *Christian Diversity and Christian Unity* (Philadelphia: Westminster, 1975), p. 12.

[25] Ibid., p. 26.

a Catholic imperative because, as Vatican II pointed out, the existing divisions among Christians make it difficult for the Church 'to express in actual life her full catholicity in all its aspects' (*UR* 4).

(5)

In Chapter 3 we have seen that Catholic differs from sectarian Christianity in so far as the latter, convinced that the world is doomed to perdition, withdraws into an isolated, self-centred community, intent upon the salvation of its own members. Catholicism, while open to the whole world as the sphere of God's redemptive action, recognizes a distinction between the Church as the body of Christ and a 'world' that has not explicitly accepted the gospel. Brotherhood for the New Testament writers, as Joseph Ratzinger shows, is a narrower concept than it was for Stoic philosophers such as Epicetus and Marcus Aurelius, and for the philosophers of the Enlightenment who prepared the slogans of the French Revolution. For rationalistic humanism all men and women are brothers and sisters by virtue of their common nature. For the New Testament a brother or sister is a member of the community of Jesus' disciples. And yet this view is not sectarian, because it recognizes that all human beings share a common vocation to eternal life and a consequent orientation to Christ and the Church. Loving every human being in Christ, the Church labours for all, prays for all, suffers for all. Only thus can it remain Catholic. In the words of Ratzinger:

In external numbers it [the Church] will never be fully 'catholic' (that is, all-embracing), but will always remain a small flock—smaller even than statistics suggest. . . . In its suffering and love, however, it will always stand for the 'many', for all. In its love and suffering it surmounts all frontiers and is truly 'catholic'.[26]

Whereas the sectarian may look upon the Church as a vanguard of heroic individuals who can be true to the gospel without needing the support of a Christian environment, the Catholic vision is that of a Church made up of saints and sinners together, so intermingled that only at the last day will

[26] Joseph Ratzinger, *The Open Circle: The Meaning of Christian Brotherhood* (New York: Sheed & Ward, 1966), p. 120.

they be sorted out by the Judge of the world and his angels (cf. Matt. 13: 24–30, 36–43). The Church is for the weak as well as for the strong, or those who think they are so strong as not to need it. It is a community in which each may find support from all.[27]

Immediately after the 'holy catholic Church', the Apostles' Creed mentions the communion of saints. The exact meaning of this term has been much disputed, but according to J. N. D. Kelly, whose authority in the matter is considerable, the phrase was originally understood as signifying that in the Church one can have fellowship with God's holy ones, including the saints of the Old Testament and probably the angels.[28] As the cult of the martyrs and their relics became established, about the fifth century, Faustus of Riez felt it proper to insist on the merits which the saints have received from God. 'They deserve to be venerated worthily,' he wrote, 'forasmuch as they infuse into us, through their contempt of death, the worship of God and the yearning for the life to come.'[29]

At the root of this Catholic doctrine is the principle that there is a communication of spiritual gifts among all the redeemed, including those who have passed into the life to come. As God unsparingly bestowed upon us the gift of his Son, so the Christian, filled with a like charity, becomes fruitful for others. The members of Christ's body mutually serve one another in building up the whole in unity. Since power goes out from the saints, their merits and virtues may be said to constitute, metaphorically speaking, a treasure. Thanks to this conception of spiritual communication, we become more conscious both of our obligation to contribute to the common good and of the extent to which we are indebted to others for our spiritual blessings. Those who contribute the most through their example, prayer, and sacrifice may be poor, sick, or imprisoned, perhaps unaware of their ability to do anything for others. The cult of the martyrs, though it may have grown to excess, was based on the sound principle that the Cross is fruitful. Only

[27] See Jean Daniélou, 'The Church of the Poor', chap. 1 of his *Prayer as a Political Problem* (London: Burns & Oates, 1967), pp. 9–22. See above, p. 66.
[28] J. N. D. Kelly, *Early Christian Creeds* (3rd edn.; New York: D. McKay, 1972), pp. 390–7.
[29] Faustus of Riez, *Hom.* II in C. P. Caspari, *Ungedruckte Quellen*, vol. ii, p. 197; quoted by Kelly, ibid., p. 391.

after the saints have died, in most cases, does it become apparent to what degree they were, and continue to be, living channels of God's grace. Their God, like that of Abraham and Isaac, 'is not the God of the dead, but of the living' (Mark 12: 27).

The horizontal aspect of an exchange of gifts among God's people was still vivid in the piety of Luther, before that aspect was overlaid by the verticalism that later became characteristic of Protestant theology. Dietrich Bonhoeffer, in his early dissertation, *The Communion of Saints*, consciously strove to retrieve this lost dimension. Echoing the very language of Luther, he maintained that Christians exist not only *with* but also *for* one another:

Just as no man can live without the church, and each owes his life to it and now belongs to it, so his merits too are no longer his own, but belong to the church too. It is solely because the church lives as it were one life in Christ that the Christian can say that other men's chastity helps him in the temptations of his desires, that other men's fasting benefits him, and that his neighbour's prayers are offered for him.[30]

Hardly any practice is so distinctively Catholic as the cult of the saints. The Catholic esteems the saints as living embodiments of the gospel and archetypal instances of its transforming power. By their example and intercession, they not only constitute the communion of saints but effect and maintain that communion. Having received in abundance from God's self-communication in Christ, they share in his altruistic love. Christ's 'being for others' takes root in them.[31]

The merits of the saints, though they serve to build up the Church, are not directed only to the Church as a closed community. The Church would not be Catholic if it were simply a mutual aid society based on enlightened self-interest. Its catholicity requires it to be open without restriction. The saints are those in whom Christ's totally selfless love is present and operative.

[30] Dietrich Bonhoeffer, *The Communion of Saints* (New York: Harper & Row, 1964), pp. 129-30.

[31] On the Catholic understanding of the communion of saints see Hans Urs von Balthasar, *Katholisch: Aspekte des Mysteriums*, pp. 45-64; id., *Elucidations* (London: SPCK, 1975), pp. 57-63, cf. 213-15; Robert P. Imbelli, 'Toward a Catholic Vision: The Theology of the Communion of Saints', *Review for Religious*, xlii (1983), pp. 289-96.

It might be conjectured that a universally open society could be constituted from below through a mere intensification of the gregarious instinct or through the indefinite expansion of a social contract based on mutual advantage. Henri Bergson weighed this hypothesis and came to the conclusion that the particular, 'closed' society and the universal, 'open' society are essentially different, so that the transition from the one to the other cannot be accomplished simply by increasing the size of the group.[32] According to Bergson a radical change of motivation is required to pass from self-interest, whether individual or collective, to an all-embracing charity. An authentically universal society, he argued, must be rooted in a transcendent love, one that comes from God and transforms its bearers into the likeness of what the Christ of the Gospels was most perfectly.[33]

In the context of our own theme, Bergson's thesis may be translated into the statement that the horizontal catholicity of the Church discussed in this chapter depends upon its vertical catholicity analysed in the preceding two chapters. Only the fullness of God, communicated through Christ and the Holy Spirit, can give the Church the dynamism and inclusiveness implied in the concept of extensive catholicity.

[32] Henri Bergson, *The Two Sources of Morality and Religion* (Garden City, NY: Doubleday Anchor, n.d.), pp. 38, 234, 267.
[33] Ibid., p. 240.

5

Catholicity in Length: Tradition and Development

In Chapter 4 we considered catholicity as extensive, inclusive, or expansive; that is to say, the breadth of the Church, her horizontal catholicity. But there is another dimension to horizontal catholicity, which might be called length, namely, catholicity in time.

(1)

The concept of catholicity in time strikes us as unusual because we generally place the historical continuity of the Church under the caption of apostolicity rather than catholicity. But since the theme of apostolicity would raise more specialized questions, such as the succession in the ordained ministry, I prefer to speak first of the abiding identity of the Church as a whole through the centuries. The medieval authors commonly looked on this as an aspect of catholicity. Thomas Aquinas, for example, in his commentary on the Apostles' Creed, held that the church is called catholic or universal for three reasons: (*a*) geographically it extends everywhere, not only on earth but even beyond it, to purgatory and heaven; (*b*) with respect to persons, it is open to all, regardless of natural and social differences such as sex or class; (*c*) in the dimension of time, it stretches back to Abel, the just one, and forward to the end of the ages and even into eternity.[1]

This Thomistic conception of catholicity in time, which had some patristic foundation in Vincent of Lerins and Augustine, continued to figure in the ecclesiology of the later Middle Ages and early modern times, as may be verified from the works of James of Viterbo (fourteenth century), Juan de Torquemada

---

[1] Thomas Aquinas, *In symbolum Apostolorum, Opusculum VII* (Parma edn.), vol. xvi, pp. 135–51, art. IX, p. 148. See Appendix.

(fifteenth century), Francisco Suárez (sixteenth century), and Jacques-Bénigne Bossuet (seventeenth century).[2]

Besides this grounding in the tradition there is another reason why the concept of catholicity in time appeals to me. As I hope to show in this chapter, the principles governing the historical continuity of the Church through the centuries are analogous to the principles governing its spatial extension throughout the world. Continuity in the temporal dimension corresponds to communion in the spatial. The Church spans the centuries somewhat as it spans the nations and continents. In each of these dimensions the Church is a symbolic centre *from* which the divine fullness of life, as given in Jesus Christ, radiates outwards to all creation, and *towards* which that life, diffused through all creation, gravitates for its conscious and socially palpable expression. With regard to both place and time, moreover, we have a mystery of identity within difference. A catholic ecclesiology, therefore, implies a distinctive attitude towards temporal succession as well as towards geographical extension. My principal purpose in these pages will be to identify this catholic attitude towards time, in so far as it affects one's understanding of the Church.

Modern Christians might find it surprising that Saint Thomas speaks of the Church as having existed since the time of Abel. Since the Reformation even those who call themselves Catholic have lost something of the universalism of the Catholic tradition. The second-century *Shepherd* of Hermas portrays the Church as a very old woman, created before all things; and Greek Fathers of the next few centuries, such as Origen, Athanasius, Eusebius, Gregory Nazianzen, and John Chrysostom, regularly allude to the pre-existence of the Church as being, next to Christ, the first-born of all creation.[3] Ambrose speaks of Abel as a type of the Church, and Augustine, particularly in his controversial works against the

[2] References to the pertinent texts may be found in Wolfgang Beinert, *Um das dritte Kirchenattribut* (Essen: Ludgerus-Verlag, 1964), vol. i, pp. 86–91, 128–38; Gustave Thils, *Les notes de l'Église dans l'Apologétique catholique depuis la Réforme* (Gembloux: Duculot, 1937), pp. 215–44.

[3] For specific references see Yves Congar, 'Ecclesia ab Abel', in M. Reding (ed.), *Abhandlungen über Theologie und Kirche* (Festschrift für Karl Adam; Düsseldorf: Patmos, 1952), pp. 79–108; also Henri de Lubac, *The Splendour of the Church* (London: Sheed & Ward, 1956), pp. 38–9.

Manichaeans, develops the theme of the Church having existed from the time of Abel. This idea was almost universally accepted in Western theology throughout the Middle Ages and early modern times. The Roman Catechism (sixteenth century) teaches that the Church includes all true believers since Adam. Seeing Christ as the source of all redemptive grace, these authors hold that all who live by that grace belong in some sense to Christ's Body, the Church. One of the leading commentators on Saint Thomas, Juan de Torquemada, holds that it would be an indefensible error to deny the existence of the Church before the advent of Christ. After the Reformation some Roman Catholic apologists such as Peter Canisius and Robert Bellarmine began to define the Church primarily in institutional terms, putting the accent on the divinely established hierarchy, and in this new approach it was no longer meaningful to speak of a Church in pre-Christian times.

Recovering something of the older tradition, Vatican Council II's Constitution on the Church states explicitly that the Church 'transcends all limits of time' (*LG* 9). The council distinguishes four stages of the Church's existence: prefigured from the beginning of the world, she was prepared in the history of ancient Israel, constituted in the final age of history (that is to say, our own), and gloriously consummated in eternity (*LG* 2). The Constitution quotes Saint Gregory the Great on the Church existing since Abel (ibid.), and later recalls that Israel in the desert was already called the 'Church of God' in the Old Testament (*LG* 9).

The idea of the Church 'since Abel' could be distorted so as to suggest that in addition to the visible Church there is a second, invisible one, which might even be considered the more spiritual of the two. The Catholic tradition, as we shall see in the coming chapters, insists on visibility. There is only one Church, and it comes to visibility first under the figures and sacraments of the Old Law, and more fully in the apostolic body that stems from Jesus Christ. Those who lived under the Old Law, according to the Letter to the Hebrews, did not receive what they hoped for, and were not to be made perfect without the fulfilment given in Christ (11: 39–40). Similarly, one may argue, the Church of the Old Testament was oriented towards, and needed to be perfected by, the Church of the New.

(2)

At the other end of the spectrum, when the Church enters into its final glory, the institutional element will be absent, for there will no longer be any need of sacraments and other means of grace. The economy of symbols will pass away and yield to an immediate vision of the reality signified. The Church itself will not pass away but, on the contrary, will be realized more perfectly than ever. In the New Testament the glorious Church is frequently described through metaphors such as the marriage of the Lamb, the heavenly banquet, the sabbath rest, and the new Jerusalem, the completed Temple. The mystical marriage of Nazareth and Calvary will be completed and, as it were, consummated when Christ returns in glory. Only then will the Church be entirely pure, without spot or wrinkle or any such thing (cf. Eph. 5: 27). Thus Henri de Lubac is justified in writing: 'At the Day of the Lord when the *catholica societas* will be realized in its perfection, everything will be at once unified, interiorized and made eternal in God, because "God [will be] all in all".'[4]

The panoramic vision implied in this eschatological view of the Church has been narrowed in modern ecclesiology, both Protestant and Catholic. Protestants have tended to define the Church in terms of faith, as the *congregatio fidelium*, and Catholics in terms of the hierarchy, as the body subject to the legitimate pastors. Both these views apply not to the heavenly but only to the pilgrim Church. Many contemporary theologians apparently hold that when the Kingdom of God arrives, the Church will wither away.[5] Yet in terms of the biblical and Catholic tradition, nothing could be further from the truth. Here again Vatican II recovered an important Catholic theme, for it devoted an entire chapter of its Constitution on the Church to 'The Eschatological Nature of the Pilgrim Church and Her Union with the Heavenly Church'. This chapter

---

[4] De Lubac, *Splendour of the Church*, p. 50.

[5] E.g., Hans Küng, *The Church* (New York: Sheed & Ward, 1968), pp. 92–3. Wolfhart Pannenberg, in his *Theology and the Kingdom of God* (Philadelphia: Westminster, 1969), pp. 76–7, speaks of the final Kingdom of God as being 'without any Church at all', but in *The Church* (Philadelphia: Westminster, 1983) he holds that 'only in the glory of the eschatological consummation will the Church be fully and completely catholic' (p. 62, cf. p. 68). See below, Conclusion, note 18.

teaches that the Church 'will attain her full perfection only in the glory of heaven' (*LG* 48).

The eschatological aspect of the Church, since it is so heavily stressed in the New Testament, has naturally been affirmed not only in Roman Catholicism but also in other communions. In World Council circles this theme has been the subject of some controversy. During the 1950s a few Lutheran theologians, including Edmund Schlink, emphasized the sinfulness and deficiency of the pilgrim Church, suggesting that it could be called one, holy, and catholic only because it believes in Christ, who has these qualities.[6] The Second Assembly of the World Council of Churches, meeting at Evanston in 1954, seemed to identify the pilgrim Church with the multitude of humanly constituted, denominational churches and to imply that these churches could not enter into the one glorious Church except by obedience unto death. The Orthodox delegates at Evanston found the Assembly report on 'Our Oneness in Christ and Our Diversity as Churches' too one-sided. They submitted a dissenting Declaration in which they affirmed that the perfect unity of Christians should not be interpreted exclusively as something to be realized at Christ's Second Coming. The unity of the Church, they insisted, is a present reality that will receive its consummation at the Last Day. The Orthodox added that although repentance was appropriate for members of the Church, the Church itself was not sinful and did not have to repent.[7]

In this disagreement the Lutherans and the Orthodox may be said to have been insisting on different aspects of a complex truth that can only be held together in a wider Catholic synthesis. According to a fully Catholic view the Church of God, with all its essential attributes, does exist in the present age, but it remains to be perfected in the age to come. It would be wrong to hold that the Church is perfectly one, holy, or catholic on earth or, alternatively, that it has these qualities only in hope and promise.

[6] See Edmund Schlink, *The Coming Christ and the Coming Church* (Edinburgh: Oliver and Boyd, 1967), esp. pp. 96–118, 245–55, and 256–68.

[7] 'Declaration of the Orthodox Delegates', *The Evanston Report. Second Assembly of the World Council of Churches, 1954* (London: SCM, 1955), pp. 92–5.

(3)

From these debates within the World Council of Churches it becomes evident that the disagreements have less to do with the glorious heavenly Church, to which all look forward, than with the pilgrim Church within historical time. We must therefore consider more carefully the condition of the Church in the centuries between Pentecost and the Parousia. I shall maintain that in the Catholic view, the Church at this stage already participates in a real, definitive, though imperfect manner, in the fullness of God's gift in Christ; secondly, that this participation brings about a real continuity or communion between different generations of Christians; and thirdly, that the different periods of the Church, notwithstanding this continuity, have their own distinctive character, so that the later is able to complement and complete what has been initiated by the earlier.

First, then, let me propose as a thesis that the Church in historical time really participates in the redeeming grace of Christ. The catholic fullness or *plērōma* of Christ's living presence really inheres in the Church. Christ has suffered and has by the shedding of his blood gained for himself his beloved Bride (Eph. 5: 25). From that time forth, he has showered benefits upon her. Having risen from the dead, he makes intercession 'for those who draw near to God through him' (Heb. 7: 25). Bestowing upon his community the eschatological gift of the Holy Spirit (Acts 2: 33), he makes the Church a sharer in his own divine life (John 20: 22). Although the Bride is not as yet perfectly sanctified, she ought not to be called simply sinful or faithless. Even now she is sustained by the grace of the Lord.

In contrast to this view, some Protestant ecclesiologists seek to exalt Christ alone in contrast to the Church. Edmund Schlink applying to the Church the Lutheran theology of justification, implies that the Church is devoid of beauty in herself but that God imputes to her, as it were by a kind of fiction, the merits that are really Christ's.[8] Karl Barth, in his *Church Dogmatics*, says that the Church should be like John the Baptist in Grünewald's painting of the Crucifixion, with outstretched finger pointing away from himself to the Lord.[9]

[8] See note 6, above.

[9] Karl Barth, *Church Dogmatics*, vol. i.1 (New trans.; Edinburgh: T. & T. Clark, 1975), pp. 112, 262–3.

Rudolf Bultmann, emulating the actualism of Barth's dialectical period, denies that the Church as a continuing institution is one or holy. 'Just as the Word of God', he writes, 'becomes his Word only in event, so the Church is really the Church only when it too becomes an event. For the Church identity with a sociological institution and a phenomenon of the world's history can be asserted only in terms of paradox.'[10]

During the debate on the report of the Amsterdam Assembly of the World Council concerning the unity of the Church, the Anglican, Canon Leonard Hodgson, made an intervention to the following effect:

. . . there were two distinct points of view which it was impossible to reconcile. The one was that the Church was meant to be a body in space and time, continuing down history as an earthly body, the continuity being that of an actual historical body. The opposite view was one which maintained that the only continuity necessary was not in this sphere of space and time at all but was in the invisible sphere of our risen Lord Jesus Christ, the same yesterday, to-day, and for ever, Who embodies Himself as and when He will, in this or that group of human beings, whom He calls and who make the response of faith.[11]

Yves Congar, commenting on this intervention, agrees that it accurately describes the deepest cleavage between the typically Protestant and Catholic approaches. The 'vertical' ecclesiology, he says, implies 'acts of God wholly gratuitous and therefore free, unpredictable, and discontinuous'.[12] For Barth and his disciples, then, the Church is comparable to the people of Israel at the time of the Judges, when their vocation was to subsist without regularized ordinances, living by occasional divine interventions which, like the manna in the desert, were new each day. But already under the Davidic monarchy, which foreshadows the reign of Christ, Israel enjoyed, according to Congar, a permanent covenant guaranteeing the presence of the Spirit 'from that day forth and forever' (1 Sam. 16: 13). Unlike the ancient Israel and John the Baptist, the Church

[10] Rudolf Bultmann, *Jesus Christ and Mythology* (London: SCM, 1958), pp. 82–3.

[11] Summary of Leonard Hodgson's intervention in Willem A. Visser 't Hooft (ed.), *The First Assembly of the World Council of Churches* (London: SCM, 1949), p. 60. For the text under debate, see ibid., pp. 51–2; cf. above, Chapter 1, note 15.

[12] Yves Congar, *Christ, Our Lady and the Church* (London: Longmans, Green, 1957), p. 10.

cannot be content to point forward to something not yet given; it must guard and dispense what has been irrevocably given in the definitive sending of the Son and of the Holy Spirit. In the perspectives of an incarnational theology the Barthian image of grace as a tangent touching a circle is misleading. The gift of God has truly entered the world and is at work transforming it.

Karl Rahner writes in much the same terms as Congar. He holds that the Church, even in her pilgrim condition, is already the final, eschatological community, bearing within herself the reality of the divine self-communication. Since the time of Christ, he declares,

The grace of God no longer comes (when it does come) steeply from on high, from a God absolutely transcending the world, in a manner that is without history, purely episodic; it is permanently in the world in tangible historical form, established in the flesh of Christ as part of the world, of humanity and of its very history.[13]

Recognizing this, one may conclude with Vatican Council II that the unity of the Church is given to her 'as something she can never lose', but still capable of being increased in the course of time (*UR* 4). The same may be said of the Church's holiness and catholicity. These gifts are inseparable from the very being of the Church and are therefore, like the Church itself, indefectible.

No Catholic author, of course, would deny that the Church is subject to Christ or that every member of the Church can, as an individual, fall away. The Church continually depends on the graciousness of the Holy Spirit, who remains free to act beyond and outside the normal channels of grace. Catholicity, since it looks upwards to God as the source of all blessings, is not sheer horizontalism. But it relies on the instituted means of grace to keep people receptive to God's gifts.

(4)

Once this is granted, further questions arise about the relationships between the various eras of Church history. Should the history of the Church be seen as a decline from the original purity, as unbroken progress towards a future fullness, or as a

---

[13] Karl Rahner, *The Church and the Sacraments*, reprinted in his *Inquiries* (New York: Herder and Herder, 1964), pp. 191–299; quotation from p. 197.

simple perpetuation of the original endowment? All three of these positions have been proposed and defended, but how are they to be assessed by the standard of catholicity?

The Church historian, Ferdinand Christian Baur, writing towards the middle of the nineteenth century, complained that up to his own day Protestants had tended to regard the history of the Church as a progressive falling away from the gospel.[14] The sixteenth-century Reformers, he explained, aimed to weed out the accumulated errors and restore the original purity. For them the privileged moment of Church history was the first, the time of foundation. Although some Protestants, like Baur himself, reject this schematization, Baur undoubtedly hit upon a characteristic and recurrent trend. Down to our own time, many Protestants hold that true Christianity can be found only in the apostolic Church and the apostolic writings of the New Testament. These alone, for them, are the criterion by which all else is to be judged.

The sixteenth-century Reformers were not themselves critical of the dogmas of the early centuries, because they were convinced that the councils had defined only what was already the teaching of Scripture. But as Protestantism went on, there was an increasing disposition to invoke the Bible alone and to use it critically against the Fathers and the early councils. A distinguished biblical theologian, Oscar Cullmann, comes close to this position. He regards apostolic tradition as divinely authoritative, but looks on ecclesiastical tradition, beginning with the second century, as highly untrustworthy. Generally speaking, Cullmann accepts the New Testament as a pure deposit of the original apostolic tradition.[15]

The logic of this primitivist approach can be applied against the New Testament itself. Some nineteenth-century liberal theologians, including Adolf Harnack, took the teaching of Jesus as the supreme norm for judging even the theology of John and Paul. Early in the twentieth century it became common to characterize the Christianity of the subapostolic period (roughly from AD 95 to 150) as being—in a pejorative

[14] Peter C. Hodgson (ed.), *Ferdinand Christian Baur on the Writing of Church History* (New York: Oxford Univ. Press, 1968), pp. 14–16, 79–81, 115.
[15] Oscar Cullmann, 'The Tradition', in his *The Early Church* (Philadelphia: Westminster, 1956), pp. 59–99.

sense—'early Catholic'. Contemporary exegetes such as Ernst Käsemann and Willi Marxsen have taken a further step. Finding traces of early Catholicism in the New Testament itself, they compare the relatively late writings of Luke and the Pastoral Letters unfavourably with what they regard as the original gospel, as found, for example, in the authentic epistles of Paul. Behind this analysis we can detect the tendency to equate development with decline. What was first given is taken as normative. What comes later, it is assumed, will inevitably be a deviation, infected by human sinfulness.

This schematization is, of course, contested by scholars of a Catholic orientation—and not only by members of the Roman Catholic Church. A few contemporary Lutherans such as John Elliott and Robert Wilken have questioned the premises of their colleagues' reasoning. Wilken, for instance, protests:

We cannot discover what Christianity 'is' by an exegesis of biblical texts or by uncovering the earliest strata of the Christian tradition. The Christian movement can be understood only in light of its historical development, i.e., what it *became* within the course of its history. The New Testament has a *future* as well as a past. What *becomes* of a historical phenomenon is as much a statement of what it is as what it was at the beginning.[16]

In Wilken's opinion Harnack and Käsemann, like many earlier Christians, have been beguiled by what he calls 'the myth of Christian beginnings'—that is to say, the illusion that there was a primitive golden age and that any departure from it must be a corruption.

From a Roman Catholic perspective, Johann Sebastian Drey, early in the nineteenth century, pointed out a serious weakness in the Protestant appeal to Scripture alone. Christianity, he objected, cannot be reduced to an occurrence in the remote past as attested by contemporary witnesses. Protestants themselves have recognized the impossibility of deciding the questions of a later age without supplementing the Bible. Deprived of any authoritative tradition, they have been constrained to rely on subjective human efforts to breathe life into the dead records. Their arbitrary constructions cannot

---

[16] Robert L. Wilken, *The Myth of Christian Beginnings* (Garden City, NY: Doubleday, 1971), pp. 155–6.

claim the authority of God's word. The actual and lived Christianity of Protestants is thus a product of human subjectivity.[17]

Anglicans and Orthodox, as well as Roman Catholics, have generally rejected the Protestant position, in so far as this is purely biblicist, and have insisted that the Bible cannot be the rule of faith except when conjoined with a continuous Church tradition. In this perspective, which is fundamentally Catholic, the very sections of the New Testament which the liberals tend to discount as too far removed from the events can be seen as providing privileged interpretations, for, as Newman pointed out, events of great importance require a considerable span of time in order to be rightly comprehended.[18] On the same principle, the traditionalists argue that the assimilative process was not complete even with the last books of the New Testament. Only when Christianity became a historical religion through some distance from the apostles, and a universal religion through some dispersion from its Palestinian matrix, could certain important questions arise and be addressed. The New Testament, therefore, gives only the early stages of a continuing process whereby the revelation of Christ perpetuates itself in the Church.

The Orthodox differ on one important point from Roman Catholics, and on this the Orthodox were, at least in the nineteenth century, joined by many Anglicans. They hold that Christianity must meet the test of antiquity, and that doctrines not attested by the consensus of the Fathers must be set aside as unfounded. John Henry Newman for a time accepted this position, and attempted to defend it in his *The Via Media of the Anglican Church*. But he soon became dissatisfied with his own arguments, which he then answered in his *Essay on the Development of Christian Doctrine*. The consensus of the Fathers, he concluded, gave only feeble support to certain basic beliefs of the Church of England, such as the Trinity, original sin, and the real presence. On the other hand, the Fathers were relatively concurrent in professing the universal authority of the successors of Peter, which the Anglicans rejected. Thus to

[17] Johann Sebastian Drey, 'Vom Geist und Wesen des Katholizismus', *Tübinger Theologische Quartalschrift*, i (1819), 8–23, esp. pp. 20–3.

[18] Cf. John Henry Newman, *An Essay on the Development of Christian Doctrine* (Garden City, NY: Doubleday Image, 1960), Part I, Introduction, sec. 21, p. 53.

Newman it began to appear that the principle of development, if it applied to the early centuries, must apply to subsequent centuries as well. The truth or falsehood of a doctrine could not be established by the date when it came to be believed, but by other criteria which Newman attempted to spell out in his famous *Essay* and in several other works.

In contrast to those theories which exalt the past at the expense of the present, there are others, equally opposed to authentic catholicity, which canonize the present or the future, and depreciate the past. As an example of this distortion one may cite the work of Alfred Loisy. Influenced in part by Newman's developmental theories, he wrote a mordant book-length response to Harnack's *What Is Christianity?*[19] Ridiculing Harnack's effort to find a stable essence of Christianity in the message of the historical Jesus, he maintained on the contrary that the Church, as a living organism, was destined to develop far beyond all that Jesus had foreseen and all that the apostles had believed. In Loisy's theology, Christianity was portrayed as a movement that took its departure, and even its inspiration, from Jesus and the apostles, but was not governed by them as its norm. Loisy was a brilliant writer. He argued his case with an extraordinary command of the biblical and historical materials, and inserted a number of cautionary remarks to forestall exaggerations. But the Roman authorities understood him as advocating an extreme historical relativism that would make the demands of the passing situation in effect the norm of faith. They accordingly condemned Loisy's doctrine and labelled it Modernism. The label has stuck.

Whatever judgement is to be passed on Loisy and his associates, we must, I think, grant that Catholic Christianity is committed to a fundamental continuity. It holds that the Holy Spirit, having inspired the apostolic Scriptures, continues to be with the Church at every stage of her development preventing her from betraying the apostolic heritage. Hence it must be possible to trace a direct line from past to present. Tradition is not infinitely fluid.

Catholicism accordingly opposes both the archaism of Harnack and the Modernism of Loisy. For much the same

[19] Alfred Loisy, *The Gospel and the Church* (Eng. trans. 1903; reprinted Philadelphia: Fortress, 1976).

reasons, Catholic Christianity has always resisted futurist movements that sought to play off both the past and the present against a coming golden age that was thought to be at hand. At various times sects have arisen proclaiming that the period of institutional Christianity was coming to an end and was about to be superseded by an age of the Spirit in which every individual would be guided by the inner leading of grace without need of external authority. These movements, from Montanism, through Joachim of Fiore, to some more recent apocalyptic sects, have regularly led to bizarre exaggerations and have quite properly been repudiated as diverging from Catholic Christianity.

The position I have been advocating is not limited to Roman Catholics. It is defended, for example, in the report, *Catholicity*, submitted to the Archbishop of Canterbury in 1947 by a committee under the chairmanship of the future archbishop, Arthur Michael Ramsey. This report declares: 'Protestantism has not really come to terms with the reality of history as the scene of the continuous presence of Divine life that flows from the Incarnation.'[20] This sentence, however, raises the question how such continuity can be asserted notwithstanding the vicissitudes the Church has undergone in its two-thousand-year history.

(5)

It must be admitted, I think, that Catholic theology has not always found it easy to come to terms with the realities of history. F. C. Baur, who objected to the Protestant tendency to look on history as a continual defection, held that Catholicism, committed to the thesis of continuity, could not do justice to the phenomenon of change. In effect, he argued, Catholics remove the Church from the realm of history.[21] These charges were not wholly unfounded. Just as in early modern times Catholics tended to confuse universality with uniformity, so they tended to equate continuity with immutability. The great Counter-Reformation historian, Caesar Baronius, composed his twelve-

---

[20] *Catholicity: A Study in the Conflict of Christian Traditions in the West* (Westminster: Dacre Press, 1947).

[21] Hodgson, *Baur on Church History*, pp. 13–14, 33, 115, and *passim*.

volume *Annales ecclesiastici* to demonstrate that in the Catholic
fold the divinely given constitution of the Church 'was
preserved inviolate, was guarded scrupulously, and was never
broken or interrupted but perpetually maintained'.[22] Shortly
afterwards, Bossuet was to write an apologetic work in which
he argued that, while the doctrines and systems of the Protestants continually change, the Catholic Church, unalterably
attached to the institution of Christ, is so stable 'that not the
least variation since the origin of Christianity can be discovered
in her'.[23]

With the expanded historical consciousness of later centuries, this extreme conservatism became untenable. At the
very time when Baur was complaining about Catholic
immobilism, theologians such as Möhler and Newman,
without questioning the continuity, were excogitating theories
of development. They appealed not only to the analogy of
organic growth, whereby plants and animals develop from a
tiny seed, but also to the analogy of consciousness. Just as a new
idea, after taking root in the mind, gradually achieves its own
proper formulation, so likewise, they argued, the Christian
idea, though fully given at the beginning, takes time to find its
appropriate expression in doctrines and institutions. Unlike
some other Catholic theologians, Möhler and Newman did not
require that the development of doctrine be homogeneous, in
the sense that the later formulations could only explicate what
was logically implicit in earlier formulations.

At Vatican Council II the views of Möhler and Newman,
mediated by Blondel, Geiselmann, Congar, and others, seem to
have prevailed. The Constitution on Divine Revelation opts for
a dynamic, progressive theory of tradition. Inhering in the
collective consciousness of the Church, tradition is said to
develop constantly through the active assistance of the Holy
Spirit, so that as a result 'the Church constantly moves forward
toward the fullness of divine truth until the words of God reach
complete fulfilment in her' (*DV* 8).

It must be admitted, I think, that Catholic authors until the
middle of the present century have tended to speak as though

---

[22] Quoted by Baur, ibid., p. 108, from Preface to Baronius's *Annales ecclesiastici*.
[23] Jacques-Bénigne Bossuet, *The History of the Variations of the Protestant Churches*, 2
vols. (Dublin: R. Coyne, 1829), vol. ii, p. 388.

the Church moved ahead without reference to its changing environment, but with Vatican Council II we begin to get a certain recognition that this is not the case. As a principal motive for calling the council, Pope John XXIII spoke of the need to bring the Church abreast of the times where required.[24] The Declaration on Religious Freedom was self-confessedly written as a response to the newly developing consciousness of the dignity of the human person (*DH* 1). The Pastoral Constitution on the Church in the Modern World, after commenting on the Church's obligation to read and respond to the signs of the times, observed: 'In this way, revealed truth can always be more deeply penetrated, better understood, and set forth to greater advantage' (*GS* 44). The council makes it clear that the structures of the Church, although fundamentally given by Christ, must continually be adjusted to the times (ibid.).

These recent teachings add a further nuance to the Catholic insistence on continuity. Continuity is not best served by an endless repetition of the same rites and formulas, but periodically requires new doctrinal assertions, liturgical symbols, and pastoral structures to transmit the 'fullness' of Christ effectively to new generations. The faith, constantly present in a global way in the consciousness of the total Church, has to be articulated in forms appropriate to the place and time. Changes in the cultural climate thus introduce a certain discontinuity in the self-understanding and self-expression of the Church. A number of contemporary authors—Anglican, Lutheran, and Roman Catholic—speak in this connection of alterations in perspective. 'Historical perspective', writes Gabriel Daly, 'is rapidly becoming a normal characteristic of contemporary Roman Catholic theology.'[25]

It could easily seem that the Church's catholicity in time is impaired by the inevitability of change. Does not the Church, in accepting historical consciousness, renounce the continuity in which she has traditionally gloried? To answer this question, we need only recall the constant refrain of this study, that catholicity is not homogeneous but heterogeneous unity; it is

[24] John XXIII, Opening Speech to the Council (11 Oct. 1962), in Walter M. Abbott (ed.), *Documents of Vatican II* (New York: American Press, 1966), pp. 710–19, esp. p. 712.
[25] Gabriel Daly, *Transcendence and Immanence* (Oxford: Clarendon Press, 1980), p. 227.

unity in difference. Catholicity in time, therefore, includes an element of discontinuity. Just as the Church's geographical catholicity requires a variety of cultural forms, so her temporal catholicity calls for responsiveness to the times and seasons. 'The present form of the apostolic mission', writes Wolfhart Pannenberg, 'has the task of bringing to new expression in each age the catholic fullness of the church.'[26]

Carrying this thought a stage further, we may perhaps surmise that each major era of Church history has a special task or vocation. By living out the integral Christian reality in its own way, it makes a distinct contribution to the ongoing tradition. The task of the apostolic age was to formulate the basic Christian message and to lay the foundations of the Church once and for all. The Church of succeeding generations can build on no other foundation than that which has been laid (cf. 1 Cor. 3: 11; Eph. 2: 20). One would, however, look in vain to the apostolic period and its Scriptures for detailed prescriptions by which to answer the problems of a later age. Fundamentalist Protestantism, with its rallying cry of 'Scripture alone', fails to make this important distinction.

The task of the patristic period was to establish the classic patterns of doctrine, church organization, and liturgical worship. In its own characteristic style—a style not ours—that age gave definitive answers to a number of central and recurring questions, such as the unity of the godhead, the Trinity of divine persons, and the full divinity and humanity of the incarnate Word. No subsequent age will be required to do again what the Fathers accomplished. But in building on the work of the Fathers we are not obliged to repeat mechanically what they did and said. Their venerated formulations have to be reinterpreted through modern patterns of thought, probed with the help of contemporary investigative techniques, and restated in terms intelligible to present-day believers.

The work of subsequent centuries lacks the same foundational importance for the Church. We are not related in the same way to the medieval churchman and theologians, for example, as we are to the apostles and the Fathers. Standing further from the sources, these later figures could not so significantly shape the future of the Church, but they could

[26] Pannenberg, *The Church*, p. 68.

explicate certain logical implications of what had already been defined. By their creative efforts, moreover, the medieval monks, academicians, and prelates illustrated the possibilities of adapting the Christian faith, as previously set forth, to the needs and possibilities of a very different culture. What the churchmen and theologians of the Middle Ages and early modern times did for their own day, we must do for ours, profiting as much as possible from their accomplishments.

(6)

One final caution may be in order. I have spoken of the unfailing assistance given to the Church by the Holy Spirit, and consequently of the docility with which we should approach the past. This attitude could be carried too far if it were not tempered by the realization that the Church, within history, always falls short of the perfection to which it is called. In spite of the assistance of the Holy Spirit, the Church, as a human community, is not, in the strict sense, a continued Incarnation of the Word, nor is it, properly speaking, an Incarnation of the Holy Spirit. It is a group of graced but humanly limited, often sinful, men and women like ourselves. There is some truth, therefore, in the Lutheran axiom that the Church is simultaneously righteous and in need of forgiveness. Vatican Council II was on guard against triumphalism and warned against glorifying the Church to the point of idolatry. Far from her heavenly home, the pilgrim Church, it taught, 'is at the same time holy and always in need of being purified' (*LG* 8). Only the divine assistance can enable her, amid afflictions and hardships, 'to show forth in the world the mystery of the Lord in a faithful though shadowed way, until at last it will be revealed in total splendor' (ibid.).

All of this can be admitted without prejudice to catholicity. As has been said in Chapter 4, the Church is a great crowd of saints and sinners so inextricably intermingled that only the angels at the last day will be able to sort out the good from the evil (cf. Matt. 13: 28–30, 40–3). Once this is recognized, one's conception of tradition and development must be adjusted. Tradition is not simply a matter of handing on what has been thought and said, but also a matter of sifting out the truth of the

Christian witness from the distortions of human blindness and ignorance. It has a corrective as well as an interpretative function. As stated in the Decree of Ecumenism, 'Christ summons the Church as she goes her pilgrim way to that continual reformation of which she always has need insofar as she is an institution of men here on earth' (*UR* 6). Even the official formulations of doctrine, said the council, since they are not identical with the deposit of faith itself, may be in need of rectification (ibid.).

Those who aspire to correct and update official Church teaching run an evident risk of introducing new errors and even compounding them with those of the past. While striving to improve upon their predecessors, they must be aware of their own limitations and of their need for enlightenment from above. To serve the Church's catholicity in time, they must cultivate the qualitative or vertical catholicity that derives from vital communion with Christ the Head. They will also need the support of the whole body of the faithful in order to discern the signs of the times (*GS* 4), to distinguish the 'many voices of our age, and to judge them in the light of the divine Word' (*GS* 44).

Because reform can easily lead to schism, and has frequently done so in the past, one must take the necessary measures to keep it truly Catholic. On this subject the pioneering work of Yves Congar, *Vraie et fausse Réforme dans l'Église*, first published in 1950, has not been surpassed. Already at that time Congar recognized the insufficiency of a reform that restricted itself to the correction of abuses. He saw that the culture-conditioned forms and structures of Christianity, once they ceased to be suitable and credible, could conceal the gospel rather than radiate it. But he also saw the danger that in the name of reform zealous innovators might do violence to the essential structures of the Church, including its heritage of faith, sacraments, and ministry. To avoid such deviations Congar proposed four principles.[27]

First, he insisted on respect for the given reality of the Church and on willingness to work within that given. This precept Congar put under the heading of charity and pastoral sensitivity.

---

[27] Yves Congar, *Vraie et fausse Réforme dans l'Église* (2nd edn., revised, Paris: Cerf, 1968), pp. 211–317.

Secondly, he required concern for communion with the whole—a concern brilliantly articulated by Augustine in his controversies with the Donatists. The full truth of Christian revelation, having been committed to the Church as a whole (the *Catholica* of Augustine), lies beyond the grasp of any isolated individual or group.

Thirdly, according to Congar, the Catholic reformer must be patient with delays. As Newman was fond of saying, paper logic can lead to instant conclusions but does not yield real and lasting benefits. 'Great acts take time.'[28]

Fourthly, an authentic Christian and Catholic reform must be based on the authentic principles given in the gospel and the tradition. It must be renewal rather than innovation.

These four principles exhibit different aspects of what in these pages I have been calling the Catholic principle. They provide for that continuity in time without which there can be no true catholicity. At the same time they raise the question as to what structures are to be reckoned as irrevocably given and essential to the Church. These questions will be addressed, within the limited scope of the present study, in the next two chapters.

[28] John Henry Newman, *Apologia pro vita sua* (Garden City: Doubleday Image, 1956), p. 264.

The Structures of Catholicity: Sacramental and Hierarchical

IN the last four chapters we have surveyed four salient characteristics of catholicity, schematized under the rubric of dimensions:

– Being filled with the fullness of God, made present in Christ and the Holy Spirit. This aspect of catholicity, commonly called vertical, I have considered under the analogy of height.

– Rootedness in the natural and the human, which are healed and elevated by grace. This I have called catholicity in depth.

– Unlimited spatial, ethnic, and linguistic transcendence, corresponding to the dimension of breadth.

– Unlimited transcendence of the barriers of time, constituting the Church's catholicity in length.

In the present chapter I shall deal with an additional feature commonly recognized in Catholic Christianity, namely, its reliance on institutional or sacramental structures to mediate the truth and grace of Christ. Such structures, in the Catholic view, are necessary to sustain all four of the 'dimensions' of catholicity: the height, because the divine presence must be continuously mediated in order that God's gift in Christ be made accessible; the depth, because the fruits of Christ's redemptive action must be applied to the human and the cosmic; the breadth, because without such structures the world-wide Church would break apart; and the length, because these structures are needed to preserve continuity amid change. Without visible mediations even the spiritual aspects of redemption would be compromised by being isolated from the material. The institutional, according to the Catholic view, is not just tolerated as a necessary evil; it is positively cultivated as having intrinsic religious value.

Although this chapter follows logically from those that have preceded, it introduces a new aspect of catholicity. We begin at this point to consider the means whereby the catholicity of the

Church is maintained. If it is helpful to make a distinction between catholicity and Catholicism, one may say that at this point we are entering upon a consideration of Catholicism—a consideration that will be continued and narrowed down in our next chapter.

(1)

The subject of mediation may fittingly be broached with a reference to Friedrich Schleiermacher, who in a justly famous passage of his *Christian Faith* summed up the differences between Protestantism and Catholicism under this heading. For Protestants, he said, the individual's relationship to the Church depends upon a relationship to Jesus Christ, whereas in Catholicism the reverse is true.[1] Schleiermacher himself recognized that neither position could be defended in pure form, for adherence to Christ and to the communion are not separable. He was therefore convinced that the Protestant–Catholic antithesis was not insuperable and that it would one day be overcome. But so long as it persisted, the churches would be divided on the question of ecclesiastical mediation. His views on this subject in some ways anticipate the contrast between the vertical and the horizontal forms of Christianity expressed by the World Council at Amsterdam.

Although this type of schematization can be misleading, it can also be useful for illuminating much of the theological literature on both sides of the divide. In Chapter 1, passing reference was made to the views of certain liberal Protestants, especially in the late nineteenth and early twentieth centuries, who blamed Catholicism for setting the institutional Church between the believer and God. A little more must now be said about this tendency.

Adolf Harnack in his *What Is Christianity?* gave the classic expression of the liberal position. The Church, according to him, sacrificed its original freedom in the system that emerged from the struggle with Gnosticism in the second century. 'It was now forced to say: You are no Christian, you cannot come into any relation with God at all, unless you have first of all

---

[1] Friedrich Schleiermacher, *The Christian Faith* (New York: Harper Torchbooks, 1963), sec. 24, p. 103.

acknowledged these doctrines, yielding obedience to these ordinances, and followed out definite forms of mediation.'[2] Traditionalism, orthodoxy, ritualism, and monasticism: these are the four traits Harnack singled out as common to Greek and Roman Catholicism. The distinguishing feature of Roman Catholicism was, over and above these four, the legalism that it allegedly inherited from pagan Rome.

A contemporary of Harnack, the Lutheran historian of canon law, Rudolph Sohm, carried Harnack's critique one stage further, notably in his book on *The Essence and Origin of Catholicism*.[3] He identified the rise of Catholicism with the introduction of ecclesiastical law under the influence of Rome. He believed that not only legalism, but law itself, was incompatible with the nature of the Church as a spiritual community.

Ernst Troeltsch, a sociologist of religion from the same period, in his *The Social Teaching of the Christian Churches* (1911), connected Catholicism with the emergence of the church type of religion.[4] While he saw this type as having clear advantages over the other two types in his typology (the sectarian and the mystical), he considered that Catholicism, especially in the form it had assumed in the medieval West, carried objectification and institutionalization to excess, so that the originally free movement of the spirit became imprisoned in a hierarchical, episcopally ordered organization of sacrament and tradition. Although he found limitations in all forms of Christianity, he apparently thought that the Protestant form of the church type gave greater scope to the gospel than did medieval or modern Catholicism.

In summary, Catholicism as viewed by liberal Protestants is pre-eminently the religion of dogma and law, tradition and hierarchy, sacrament and monasticism. These institutional elements, it is alleged, are foreign to the religion of Jesus. They come either from Greco-Roman paganism or from a reversion

[2] Adolf Harnack, *What Is Christianity?* (New York: Harper Torchbooks, 1957), Lecture XI, p. 208.

[3] Rudolph Sohm, *Wesen und Ursprung des Katholizismus* (Leipzig: Teubner, 2nd edn., 1912). Harnack replies to Sohm in his *The Constitution and Law of the Church in the First Two Centuries* (New York: Putnam's Sons, 1910), Appendix I, 'Primitive Christianity and Catholicism', pp. 176–258.

[4] Ernst Troeltsch, *The Social Teaching of the Christian Churches*, 2 vols. (New York: Macmillan, 1931).

to Judaism. Catholicism not only accepts these foreign elements but treats them as divinely authoritative. It thus puts obstacles between the individual Christian and God, destroying the direct relationship required by the gospel in its original and authentic form.

(2)

More recent scholarship has pointed out that liberal Protestantism diverges at vital points from the teaching of Luther and Calvin. These Reformers may have been critical of certain late medieval institutions, but they insisted that the grace of God is mediated to the believer not only by Jesus Christ but also by the Church with its ministry of word and sacrament. Luther and Calvin both repudiated the 'heavenly prophets'—i.e. the radical reformers who sought to bypass the visible mediation of the Church and to achieve union with God in pure spirituality and inwardness.

What can fairly be said of Luther and Calvin is that they stressed the priority of the Word in the process of mediation. Harnack may have exaggerated but he was not far from the truth when he wrote that for Luther religion was 'reduced to its essential factors, to the Word of God and to faith', and that for him 'the Christian religion was given only in the Word of God and in the inward experience which accords with this Word'.[5] Luther did in fact write: 'The Word, I say, and only the Word, is the vehicle of God's grace.'[6] The Smalcald Articles, drafted by Luther, state unequivocally: 'We must hold firmly to the conviction that God gives no one his Spirit or grace except through or with the external Word which comes before'[7]—a principle by which Lutheranism differentiated itself from the Radical Reformation on the one hand and from the papal church on the other.

Calvin likewise looked upon the Word as the primary vehicle of grace. In his theology sacraments are described as supplements to the preached and written word, necessary conces-

---

[5] Harnack, *What Is Christianity?*, pp. 269–70.

[6] Martin Luther, Commentary on Galatians (1519), on Gal. 3: 2–3; in *Luther's Works* (J. Pelikan and H. Lehmann, gen. eds.), vol. xxvii (St Louis: Concordia, 1964), p. 249.

[7] Smalcald Articles, Part III, art. 8, no. 2; in Theodore G. Tappert (ed.), *The Book of Concord* (Philadelphia: Fortress, 1961), p. 312.

sions to human weakness, 'shut up as we are in the prison house of our flesh'.[8] Accommodating himself to our limited capacity, God furnished outward helps to beget and increase our faith.[9] The 'one function' of the sacraments for Calvin is, in his own words, 'to set his [God's] promises before our eyes to be looked upon'.[10] They are therefore supplements to doctrine, visible words. In view of statements such as these, Karl Barth seems justified in holding that the Reformation 'restored' (or should Barth have said 'refashioned'?) 'the Church as the Church of the Word'.[11]

Catholicism is at one with the Reformation in accepting the mediation of the Church and the Word. Catholics are accustomed to declare that faith comes from hearing the Christian proclamation, that the Church which proclaims is in a real sense prior to its members, and that it begets them. Luther and Calvin could say much the same. 'The Christian Church is your mother,' wrote Luther, 'who gives birth to you and bears you through the Word.'[12] The first chapter of the section on the Church in Calvin's *Institutes* bears the title: 'The True Church with Which as Mother of All the Godly, We Must Keep Unity.' He writes: 'There is no other way to enter into life, unless this mother conceive us in her womb, give us birth, nourish us at her breast.'[13] Although Calvin here says explicitly that he is referring to the visible Church, he asserts only a few pages later that the true Church is invisible except to the eyes of God, and that it consists only of the elect.[14] Thus he seems to be ambivalent about the motherhood of the visible Church.

In Roman Catholic ecclesiology the idea of the Church as mother, well founded in the New Testament and in the patristic tradition, has remained vital to the present day. Vatican Council II in its Constitution on the Church teaches that the

---

[8] John Calvin, *Institutes of the Christian Religion* (Library of Christian Classics, vol. xxi; Philadelphia: Westminster, 1961), Part IV, chap. 1, sec. 1, p. 1012.

[9] Ibid.

[10] Ibid., Part IV, chap. 14, sec. 12.

[11] Karl Barth, 'Roman Catholicism: A Question to the Protestant Church' (1928), reprinted in his *Theology and Church: Early Theological Writings* (London: SCM, 1962), p. 324.

[12] Martin Luther, 'Ten Sermons on the Catechism' (1528); in *Luther's Works*, vol. li (Philadelphia: Fortress, 1959), p. 166.

[13] Calvin, *Institutes*, Part IV, chap. 1, sec. 4, p. 1016.

[14] Ibid., Part IV, chap. 1, sec. 7, p. 1022.

Church, like Mary, becomes a mother by accepting God's word in faith (*LG* 64). Among living theologians, Henri de Lubac has developed this theme most extensively and profoundly. One of the values of this analogy, for him, is its accentuation of the vital, organic relationship of the individual to the Church. Reborn in the Church, we continue to be nourished by the Word and the sacraments in her womb. Christian adulthood, according to de Lubac, is achieved not by becoming separated, but by continually deeper immersion. Unlike our natural mother, he points out, the Church bears us not by expelling us from her womb but by receiving us into it.[15]

The maternal function implies that the Church is prior to her members and that they depend upon her for the origin and continuation of their new life in Christ. Every movement towards God in grace is at the same time a movement towards the Church, a deeper affinity with, or incorporation into, her. Grace therefore emanates from the Church, like a magnetic field, and at the same time draws people towards the Church as the place where all sanctity finds its connatural home. In this sense one may continue to say with Cyprian and Augustine: No one has God for a Father who does not have the Church for a mother.

As visible bearer of the invisible grace of God, the Church is often described as a sacrament. This concept, although acceptable to theologians of many traditions, has found particular favour among Roman Catholic theologians of the twentieth century.[16] In a key text, the first article of its Constitution on the Church, Vatican Council II described the Church as a kind of sacrament, that is to say, a sign and instrument of union with God in Christ (*LG* 1). The concept of sacrament in Catholic theology involves not only signification but also the dynamic presence of the reality signified. The Church and grace are essentially connected. Grace itself has an incarnational struc-

[15] Henri de Lubac, *The Motherhood of the Church* (San Francisco: Ignatius Press, 1982), p. 69. For some playful but insightful reflections on the Church as 'domineering mother', see Rosemary Haughton, *The Catholic Thing* (Springfield, Ill.: Templegate, 1979), Introduction and Chapter 7. Haughton's work will be further discussed at the end of Chapter 8 below.

[16] Among prominent representatives of this group of theologians one may mention George Tyrrell, Henri de Lubac, Otto Semmelroth, Karl Rahner and Edward Schillebeeckx. For a study of the concept see Leonardo Boff, *Die Kirche als Sakrament im Horizont der Welterfahrung* (Paderborn: Bonifacius, 1972).

ture, for it seeks to express itself in a palpable and social form, and does not fully achieve itself until it succeeds in doing so. The Church, as a visible entity, comes into being at the point where believers in community recognize themselves as recipients of God's gift in Christ.

(3)

In modern theology it has become common to contrast Protestant churches as churches of the Word with Catholic churches as churches of the sacrament. Many Catholic ecumenists, with Gregory Baum, have acknowledged the debt that Catholics owe to Protestants for having kept alive a powerful theology of the Word at a time when this theme was neglected by Catholics.[17] Conversely, many Protestants would agree with Paul Tillich when he writes: 'The permanent significance of the Catholic Church for Protestants is its powerful representation of the priestly and sacramental element, the weakness of which is the specific danger of Protestantism.'[18]

Neither form of Christianity, of course, denies either Word or sacrament, and neither totally separates the one from the other. Broadly speaking, a sacrament can itself be called a word, in the sense that it is a sign expressing the mind and intention of God who is at work in it. The Word of God, conversely, has a sacramental quality, since it is charged with divine power. Yet word and sacrament in the strict sense are not identical. The word does not derive its identity from any particular shape or sound: the same letter *A* can be written several different ways, and the same sound 'bear/bare' can stand for several words. The word is constituted as such by the meaning it bears. The sacraments, by contrast, are not reducible to their intelligible import. Though they are signs, they are closely bound up with material elements and gestures, which convey not simply a meaning, but a spiritual effect that comes from the power of Christ. In the sacramental action, however, the verbal component may, and usually does, play a crucial role. This is notably the case when the priest stands at the altar and says,

---

[17] Gregory Baum, *Progress and Perspectives: The Catholic Quest for Christian Unity* (New York: Sheed & Ward, 1962), pp. 143–4, 168.

[18] Paul Tillich, 'The Permanent Significance of the Catholic Church for Protestantism', *Protestant Digest*, iii (1941), pp. 23–31; quotation from pp. 23–4.

'This is my body', or when, in the confessional, he says, 'I absolve you'. These words themselves are quasi-sacramental, inasmuch as they are charged with the power of Christ.

If Catholic Christianity tends to put special emphasis on the sacraments, this is, I think, because of the characteristics already noted. Catholicism is a thoroughly incarnational faith. Just as in the Incarnation, the Word is made flesh, so in the sacraments the prescribed word becomes embodied in the elements, the gestures, the persons. In opposition to certain schools of Protestantism, Catholicism is unwilling to describe the efficacy of the sacraments simply in terms of the enhancement of the faith of the recipients. The sacraments are seen as working not only on the mind and will but on the whole person, and as bringing about a real transformation in Christ. This view is bound up with the optimism and realism of the Catholic doctrine of grace, already noted in Chapter 3.

The social or ecclesial dimension of the sacraments calls for some additional comment here. According to the Catholic understanding, the grace that inhered in Jesus in concentrated form was, as it were, universalized through the Ascension and the sending of the Holy Spirit, who thereby became the unifying principle of the expanding community. The sacraments are the visible means whereby the Church organically structures itself as the body of Christ. In early modern times, the sacramental doctrine and piety were thwarted by the reigning individualism. Catholics as well as Protestants, looking on the sacraments principally as means for achieving their own personal salvation, neglected the sacraments as means of celebrating and building up the Church in its multiform unity.

In 1938 Henri de Lubac published his influential work, *Catholicism: A Study of Dogma in Relation to the Corporate Destiny of Mankind*.[19] Drawing on an astonishing familiarity with the Fathers and medieval doctors, he pointed out that the sacraments are sources of grace precisely because and in so far as they draw their recipients into a new or closer union with the Church. All sacraments are, in the first instance, sacraments of the Church. Whenever they are administered, the whole Church is involved. The celebrant, especially if he is a bishop or

---

[19] Henri de Lubac, *Catholicism* (London: Burns, Oates, and Washbourne, 1950).

priest, publicly represents Christ and the Church, but each member participates in an active capacity.

The theses of de Lubac's early work, confirmed in scholarly studies by many other theologians, gradually won common acceptance in the theological community and received official confirmation in the Constitution on the Church and the Constitution on the Liturgy of Vatican Council II.

Each of the sacraments is a particular actualization of the Church's essence and gives an ecclesial grace specific to itself. Baptism actualizes the Church's maternal role in begetting new members of Christ's body. From the standpoint of the baptized, it is the sacrament of visible incorporation into the one Church. It is not only this or that individual who is incorporated, but all the members who are, so to speak, 'concorporated' and made 'members of one another' (Rom. 12: 5) in the body of Christ. As Paul says in First Corinthians, 'By one Spirit we were all baptized into one body . . . and all were made to drink of one Spirit' (1 Cor. 12: 13). In the ancient ceremonies of baptism on the vigils of Easter and Pentecost—ceremonies that are just beginning to be restored—the community welcomed its new members, thus making it clear that, in the words of Emile Mersch, baptism 'is the act of the Church because it is the act of the whole of Catholicism, a liturgy, a public cult'.[20]

The social aspect of sin and repentance is only very gradually reasserting itself. In the later Middle Ages the sacrament of penance was excessively individualized. The early Church by its public penitential liturgies expressed better the realization that every sin is an offence against the Church, as well as against God, and to some extent separates from the Church. Reconciliation, likewise, should have an ecclesial dimension. The Church must act through her public leadership to grant pardon to the sinner. Thus in this sacrament the Church carries out her mission to represent Christ in his role as merciful judge. In the words of Karl Rahner, the Church 'effectually fulfills her own nature as the abiding sacrament of God's mercy in the world'.[21] Christ acts in and through the Church. From the standpoint of the penitent, this sacrament readmits its recipient

[20] Emile Mersch, *The Theology of the Mystical Body* (St. Louis: B. Herder, 1951), p. 562.

[21] Karl Rahner, *The Church and the Sacraments*, reprinted in his *Inquiries* (New York: Herder and Herder, 1964), pp. 189–299; quotation from p. 277.

to the bosom of the Church as one of her penitent members. Vatican Council II clearly taught that this sacrament effects reconciliation both with God and with the Church, but left open the question how the two aspects are connected.[22]

In a report developed for the 1983 world Synod of Bishops, the International Theological Commission carried forward the teaching of Vatican II on the ecclesial dimension of the sacrament of penance. It stated: 'Thus in sacramental penance the readmission to full sacramental communion with the church is the sacramental sign (*res et sacramentum*) of the renewed communion with God (*res sacramenti*).'[23] The Commission accepted the teaching of many contemporary theologians that the sinner is reconciled to God precisely by achieving peace with the Church (*pax cum Ecclesia*).

More than any other sacrament, the Eucharist expresses the unitive role of the Church. Thomas Aquinas and many other scholastic theologians call it the 'sacrament of church unity' (*sacramentum ecclesiasticae unitatis*).[24] In this they are only taking up the teaching of Paul, 'Because there is one bread, we who are many are one body, for we all partake of the one bread' (1 Cor. 10: 17)). As this text suggests, the symbolism of the elements invites a unitive interpretation. Various Fathers of the Church, including Cyprian and Augustine, wrote eloquently of the way in which many grains of wheat are made into one loaf and many grapes pressed into a single chalice of wine. From this they concluded that all the faithful are to be formed into one flock, one body, one mystical person.

'O sacrament of devotion! O sign of unity! O bond of charity!'[25] This triple exclamation of Augustine, quoted by Vatican Council II (*SC* 47), magnificently summarizes the ecclesial dimension of the Eucharist. The Constitution on the Church quotes the medieval liturgical prayers, 'that by the flesh and blood of the Lord's body the whole brotherhood may be joined together' (*LG* 26). Recent revisions of the liturgy,

[22] Vatican II, *Lumen gentium*, no. 11. See Aloys Grillmeier, Commentary on *Lumen gentium*, chap. 2, in Herbert Vorgrimler (ed.), *Commentary on the Documents of Vatican II* (New York: Herder and Herder, 1967), vol. i, p. 162, note 15.

[23] International Theological Commission, 'Report on Penance and Reconciliation', *Origins*, vol. xiii, no. 31 (12 Jan. 1984), pp. 513–24; quotation from p. 519.

[24] Thomas Aquinas, *Summa theologiae*, Part III, qu. 73, art. 2, *sed contra*.

[25] Augustine, *In Iohannis Evang.*, Tract XXVI, chap. 6, no. 13; *PL* 13: 1613; cf. Vatican II, *SC*, no. 47.

designed to emphasize the meal aspect and the solidarity of all who partake in it, remind us of this unitive universalism. According to Vatican II's Decree on Ecumenism, Holy Communion is both a celebration of existing unity and a means of deepening that unity (*UR* 8).

Churches of the Catholic type, including the Roman Catholic Church, tend to be somewhat restrictive in admitting non-members to Holy Communion. This strictness is not motivated by a pharisaical intention of reserving the sacrament to the righteous. Rather, the concern is to protect the integrity of the sign. It would not be correct to argue: 'I believe that the Lord is really present, therefore I have a right to receive.' By receiving in a given church one gives a sign of solidarity with that community and its pastors. If one does not share the faith of the community and does not wish to join it as a member, one should not ordinarily be receiving its Eucharist. This normative principle, of course, admits of exceptions, but to discuss them would take us beyond our present subject.

The philosopher Hegel made some interesting observations on the doctrine of the Eucharist, which he regarded as the most fundamental and indeed the only significant point of difference between Catholicism and Protestantism.[26] He granted that the divine had to appear on earth in bodily form, as it did at the Incarnation, in order to bring about divine–human unity. But since the Ascension, Hegel held, the divine is removed from the senses and must be grasped in an interior, spiritual way. Catholicism, with its doctrine of the objective real presence in the consecrated elements, appeared to him to be a vain attempt to prolong the sensory stage of the absolute religion. The Reformed churches made the opposite error, reducing the Eucharist to a mere commemorative rite. The Lutherans, according to Hegel, achieved the correct synthesis by holding that the presence of Christ is real but spiritual, and achieves itself not objectively but dynamically in the very act of partaking, which is an act of faith. This analysis neatly schematizes the views of the three church traditions, but at the price, I think, of distorting the true positions of each. Catholics, for

---

[26] Georg W. F. Hegel, *The Christian Religion. Lectures on the Philosophy of Religion*, Part III, *The Revelatory, Consummate, Absolute Religion* (ed. Peter C. Hodgson; Missoula, Mont.: Scholars Press, 1979), pp. 271, 274–6, 334–43.

their part, do not hold a material or physical presence but a sacramental one which, while real in its own order, is effected by the faith of the Church and perceptible only in faith. The Eucharistic presence, moreover, is directed primarily to the religious actions of eating and drinking. The Catholic doctrine may therefore be seen as mediating between the extremes of external physicism and mere commemoration. As recent dialogues have shown, many Lutherans and Calvinists, as well as Anglicans, are in substantial accord with the Roman Catholic Church on the question of real presence.

Seen in this sacramental perspective, the Eucharist is pre-eminently a Catholic sacrament. It is offered on behalf of the entire human family, both living and dead. Celebrated from East to West and among all nations, according to the prophecy of Malachi taken up into the liturgy (Mal. 1: 11), it binds together the sacrifice of Abel and Melchizedek with that of Christ the high priest. A participation in the heavenly liturgy of the risen Christ, it also looks forward to this return in glory. Since it is the glorious Christ who makes himself present, this sacrament has not only a human but a cosmic significance. In the words of Teilhard de Chardin: 'When Christ says through his priest, "This is my body", these words overflow the piece of bread upon which they are pronounced; they bring to birth the entire mystical Body. Beyond the transubstantiated host, the priestly action extends to the cosmos itself. . . . All matter submits, slowly and irresistibly, to the great consecration.'[27] Teilhard did not mean that the universe would be literally turned into Christ's eucharistic body, as some have imagined, but that the glorified Christ who makes himself really present in the Eucharist is the source from which the final glorification of the universe radiates like light from a burning torch. He gave poetic expression to this thought in his inspiring meditation, 'The Mass Over the World'.[28]

When we speak of the Eucharist as sacrament of unity, therefore, it is possible to distinguish three levels. It effects community within the Church; it establishes communion between humanity and God; and finally, it is a communication

[27] Quoted by Norbertus M. Wildiers in his 'Introduction' to Pierre Teilhard de Chardin, *Hymne de l'Univers* (Paris: Seuil, 1961), p. 14.
[28] Teilhard de Chardin, 'La Messe sur le Monde', ibid., pp. 17–37.

of life to the material world. Jesus, according to the Fourth
Gospel, said: 'The bread which I shall give for the life of the
world is my flesh' (John 6: 51). In the consecration bread and
wine, which are elements of the world, are transformed into the
final reality, making the new, eschatological creation prolepti-
cally present.[29]

(4)

The public character of the sacraments is assured, to a great
extent, by the representative role of the hierarchy who direct
the Church. In our discussion of mediation, therefore, we must
include some consideration of the priestly office. In Catholic
churches the priestly ministry is exercised not only on the local
level but also on the level of supervision, which is called, in
Greek, *episkopē*. The Bible, although it occasionally uses the
term *episkopos* (meaning bishop), does not mention episcopacy
as an order distinct from the presbyterate except, according to
some interpreters, in the Pastoral Letters. On the whole, the
New Testament portrays the Church of the first generation
after Christ, when the apostles themselves were in general
charge. In the Pauline lists of offices and ministries in the
Church (1 Cor. 12: 28; Eph. 4: 11), that of the apostles regularly
holds the first place.

Only in post-apostolic times did it become apparent that the
unity and continuity of the Church as a whole required a body
of leaders who would carry on the supervisory role originally
performed by the apostles. Hence arose the doctrine of apostolic succession, which has become for many the very hallmark
of Catholic Christianity. For Catholics there is no entry into the
highest governing body of the Church except by the consent
and action of those who already belong to that body. The
normal practice of having three consecrating prelates is a sign
that the bishops are collegially co-opting a new member into
their ranks.

The responsibility for the direction of the Church includes
not only the power to enact and enforce practical regulations
but also to make final decisions about doctrinal matters. From

[29] See Wolfgang Beinert, 'Eucharistie als Sakrament der Einheit', *Catholica*, xxxvi
(1982), pp. 234–56, esp. 244–5.

a Catholic perspective these powers cannot properly be committed except to a body of pastors selected for their reliability and installed into office by a sacred rite. The ordination of bishops (and correspondingly of prebyters, as priests of the second order) is viewed as a sacrament, since it is one of those crucial acts whereby the Church actualizes her own essence as an organically structured body. Although the Church has great flexibility in adapting the forms of her ministry to changing situations, she can never be without a supreme directive body succeeding to the apostles. In that sense episcopacy belongs to the essence of the Church, not simply to her well-being (*bene esse*).

Thanks to its body of bishops the Church can preserve continuity and unity notwithstanding her vast extension in space and time. They are responsible for seeing that the full heritage of faith is not corrupted and that the regional churches do not become alienated from one another. On the other hand, they bring to the universal Church the particular insights and riches of their own local churches. Thus they represent the universal Church to the particular, and the particular church to the universal.

The liberal theologians whom I mentioned at the beginning of this chapter were correct in discerning a gradual development in the emergence of the ecclesiastical hierarchy. The Church did borrow certain elements from the Hellenistic world and from the political organization of the Roman Empire. Since the Church is a historical reality, this should be expected. To imagine that the Church should never develop beyond her primitive and rudimentary forms and should draw nothing from the surrounding secular culture, would be to ignore all that we have said in these pages about the historicity of the Church and her Catholic openness to the world.

What is essential to episcopacy, however, is not the particular features borrowed from secular organizations but the existence of a body of pastors having apostolic authority. The true source of this authority is neither the episcopal office nor the apostolic but, more fundamentally, Christ the Lord. It is he who speaks and acts in and through his authorized witnesses, according to the gospel saying, 'Whoever hears you, hears me' (Luke 10: 16). Without anyone in the Church who can say with finality, 'Thus says the Lord', the Church would lack one of her essential qualifications for perpetuating Christ's presence in the world. The reliability of such witnesses makes it possible for Christians of each generation to hear God's word coming to them in the particular circumstances of their own lives.

Karl Barth, though often critical of Rome, holds that on this point Roman Catholicism safeguards the substance of the Church, which was eroded, in his opinion, in the liberal Protestantism of Schleiermacher, Ritschl, and Troeltsch. Barth quotes Karl Adam as saying that Christ is the real 'ego' of the Church, the one who primarily acts in the Church's ministry.[30] Granting that this is a dangerous doctrine, easily perverted, Barth nevertheless addresses to his fellow Protestants the question: 'Should Protestantism be understood as a dilution of the Catholic idea of God's presence? Is Protestantism to mean an exchange of roles—God the object and Christians the subject of the Church?'[31] Barth then goes on to ask whether the idea of the Church as a merely human organization concerned with God as an object can be squared with the views of Luther and Calvin and with the teaching of Scripture itself.

The apostolic succession, consequently, is intended to safeguard the faithful transmission of the word so that it can be heralded with confidence and lead to the firm assent of faith. Understood in this way, the apostolic succession is the institutional counterpart of the apostolic tradition. The Word of God, as understood by Catholics, is not simply the written word of Scripture, but especially the spoken word, which makes it possible for belief to come from hearing (Rom. 10: 14). For the preaching to be authoritative it must be done by persons who are duly sent. Since the Church is a visible continuation of Christ's presence, ordination in the apostolic succession is the appropriate means of entering her official ministry. The office gives authority to the spoken word so that hearers can allow it to judge them, rather than make themselves its judges.[32] The doctrine of the apostolic succession therefore upholds the

---

[30] Barth, 'Roman Catholicism' (cited above, n. 11), pp. 313–14; cf. Karl Adam, *The Spirit of Catholicism* (Garden City, NY: Doubleday Image, 1954), p. 14.

[31] Barth, ibid., p. 316.

[32] Cf. Joseph Ratzinger, 'Primacy, Episcopate, and Apostolic Succession', in Karl Rahner and Joseph Ratzinger, *The Episcopate and the Primacy* (New York: Herder and Herder, 1962), pp. 37–63, esp. pp. 53–4.

function of the Church not only as sacrament but also as herald of the word.

(5)

Catholic Christianity, with its doctrine of the apostolic succession, attributes to the hierarchy, and those commissioned or approved by them, a genuine teaching authority, technically called 'magisterium'. The faithful may and must presume that when the bishops define the faith, as they can do by their corporate action, they are trustworthy witnesses. But there are limits to hierarchical authority, and these must be discussed in the final portion of this chapter.

Some Catholics, enthusiastically affirming what they regard as the Catholic principle of authority, put their trust in the hierarchical magisterium as if it were the sole norm of truth. They would like to see every religious and theological question promptly and definitively settled by a peremptory pronouncement. Is this tendency truly Catholic, or does it err by excess? Like those rigoristic views that would deny the existence of grace and salvation outside the Church, for fear of compromising the necessity of the Church, this magisterial monism seems to be 'Catholicist' rather than authentically Catholic; for catholicity, as we have repeatedly observed, consists in a dynamic interplay of mutually opposed but complementary principles. To obtain support for the pluralistic position on this question I should like to draw on three notable prefaces by modern English-speaking authors: Newman, von Hügel, and George Bernard Shaw.

Cardinal Newman in his introduction to the third edition of the *Via Media* (1877) maintained that the Church inherits from Christ three distinct offices, the priestly, the prophetic, and the royal. While all three functions could conceivably be combined in a single individual, they are more commonly distributed, he believed, among different persons. It is rare for a single individual to possess the devotion of the saint, the learning of the scholar, and the practical skills of the ruler. The over-all performance of the Church results from a continual interaction of the three offices, whose bearers, having different abilities and concerns, co-operate and occasionally check one another's

excesses. Church history is therefore not a rectilinear movement but is marked by frequent detours, compromises, and
adjustments, as Newman illustrated with abundant examples.
Hierarchical authority, while it plays an indispensable role, is
not totally self-sufficient or in every instance blameless.

> Nothing but the gift of impeccability granted to her [the Church's]
> authorities would secure them from all liability to mistake in their
> conduct, policy, words and decisions, in her legislative and her
> executive, in ecclesiastical and disciplinary details; and such a gift
> they have not received.[33]

The royal power of the pastors, Newman concluded, must
function in tension with the unofficial authority of saints and
scholars, who in turn stand in some tension with one another.

With explicit references to Newman's work just cited,
Friedrich von Hügel further developed the same line of
thought, especially in the introduction to his great work on the
life of Saint Catherine of Genoa (1908). He spoke of the
mystical, the rational, and the institutional components of
religion, connecting them with the Johannine, the Pauline, and
the Petrine tendencies in the New Testament. On the ground
that 'every truly living unity is constituted in multiplicty', von
Hügel rejected the Draconian solution of establishing order by
letting one of the three elements suppress the other two. In the
body of his work von Hügel went on to argue from his concept of
catholicity. 'The Church's life and spirit,' he wrote, 'which is
but the extension of the spirit of Christ Himself, is, like all that
truly lives at all, not a sheer singleness, but has a mysterious
unity in and by means of endless variety.'[34] St. Catherine of
Genoa, in his estimation, had a truly Catholic spirit because
she did not allow the mystical and individual aspects of her
religion to extinguish or be extinguished by the social and the
institutional.

My third preface is that of George Bernard Shaw to his play,
Saint Joan (1924). Under the sub-title 'Catholicism not Yet
Catholic Enough', Shaw states that the apostolic succession
does not prevent all blunders, and that the bishops blundered

---

[33] John Henry Newman, *The Via Media of the Anglican Church*, vol. i (third edn., 1877;
new impression; London: Longmans, Green, 1911), p. xliii.
[34] Friedrich von Hügel, *The Mystical Element in Religion as Studied in Saint Catherine of
Genoa and Her Friends*, vol. i (2nd edn.; London: J. M. Dent, 1923), p. 123.

badly when they condemned St. Joan to the stake. But he adds that in canonizing St. Joan the Church made a magnificently Catholic gesture. Where did Shaw, no theologian himself, get his concept of catholicity? He speaks of having received a letter from a Catholic priest, containing the following words:

In your play I see the dramatic presentation of the conflict of the Regal, Sacerdotal, and Prophetical powers, in which Joan was crushed. To me it is not the victory of any one of them over the others that will bring peace and the Reign of the Saints in the Kingdom of God, but their fruitful interaction in a costly but noble state of tension.[35]

Some think that the letter was actually written by von Hügel, who was a layman,[36] but, however that may be, Shaw made its sentiments his own. He commented: 'The Pope himself could not put it better; nor can I. We must accept the tension, and maintain it nobly without letting ourselves be tempted to relieve it by burning the thread. This is Joan's lesson to the Church.'[37]

Vatican Council II, although in certain texts it strongly emphasized hierarchical authority, made many statements that would have gratified Newman and von Hügel. The Constitution on the Church, in its second chapter, taught that charismatic gifts are widely diffused among the faithful and are highly useful for the Church as a whole (*LG* 12). The Pastoral Constitution on the Church in the Modern World emphasized the inherent claims of truth upon the assent of the mind, and the freedom of every individual to seek the truth and to decide responsibly in conformity with the dictates of personal conscience. It likewise encouraged all the faithful, according to their respective gifts and competences, to speak with courage in the Church (*GS* 62). The traditional virtues of obedience and docility, important though they be, are no substitute for personal integrity and open dialogue. The Pastoral Constitution recognizes this when it states that the Church, by reason of its unifying mission, 'stands forth as a sign of that brotherliness which allows honest dialogue and invigorates it'. With mutual

---

[35] George Bernard Shaw, *The Complete Prefaces of Bernard Shaw* (London: P. Hamlyn, 1965), p. 623.

[36] See Haughton, *The Catholic Thing* (cited above, note 15), p. 19.

[37] Shaw, *Complete Prefaces*, p. 623.

esteem and full recognition of legitimate diversity, pastors and faithful can engage in fruitful interchange (*GS* 92).

(6)

One of the most distinctive features of Catholic Christianity is the emphasis it gives to the hierarchical ministry, but this emphasis can lead to distortions. The dominant temptations of Catholicism are, on the one hand, clericalism, and on the other, by way of reaction, anti-clericalism. Both these deformations derive from a failure to appreciate the mutual complementarity of the many states of life within the Church, which serve on occasion as checks and balances.

Among these various states monasticism, as a form of the vowed life according to the evangelical counsels, deserves special mention as a characteristically Catholic institution. This form of life, more than others, bears witness to the over-riding importance of the Kingdom of God and to the all-sufficiency of Christ and his gospel. Over the centuries, monks and members of active religious communities have done much to sustain idealism in the Church and to keep her from becoming a prisoner to the demands of corporate self-interest. The religious orders have often been prime agents of reform and renewal.

Not a few Protestant theologians have recognized this value. Harnack, for one, wrote feelingly of Greek monasticism as providing a 'leaven and a counterpoise' to ritualism and traditionalism. 'Here', he declared, 'there was freedom, independence, and vivid experience.'[38] Monasticism, in his judgement, generated 'figures of such strength and delicacy of religious feeling, so filled with the divine, so inwardly active in forming themselves after certain features of Christ's image, that we may, indeed, say: here there is living religion, not unworthy of Christ's name.'[39] Monasticism in the West, he believed, prevented ecclesiasticism from suppressing the power of the gospel.[40] In assessing the 'dark side' of the Reformation, Harnack lamented the disappearance of monasticism. The Church, he wrote:

[38] Harnack, *What Is Christianity?*, p. 240.
[39] Ibid.
[40] Ibid., p. 266.

. . . needs volunteers who will abandon every other pursuit, renounce 'the world,' and devote themselves entirely to the service of their neighbor; not because such a vocation is 'a higher one,' but because it is a necessary one, and because no Church can live without also giving rise to this desire. But in the evangelical Churches the desire has been checked by the decided attitude which they have been compelled to adopt towards Catholicism. It is a high price that we have paid. . . .[41]

The clerical and religious states, of course, are only two of many vocations in the following of Christ. According to the Catholic view, the Church has many aspects and functions, not all of which can be performed by any one class. As an anticipation of the heavenly Kingdom, she contemplates and gives thanks. As the body of Christ, she seeks to become a community of love and mutual concern. As a leaven in the world, she promotes justice and peace among all individuals and nations. The full realization of the Church demands members specially dedicated to each of the various functions. There must be contemplatives and activists, persons withdrawn from worldly preoccupations and persons who introduce Christian values into the heart of secular life.

In traditional terms it is customary to speak of clergy and laity. This dichotomy can be defended, but it tends to classify everyone too narrowly with reference to ordination. More authentically Catholic, in my opinion, is the idea that every Christian has some special gift or grace, which must be cultivated and faithfully lived out.

Combining these observations with the findings of earlier chapters, we may conclude with a typically Catholic 'both/ and'. The Church is greatly blessed by her sacramental structures, which mediate to her members the fullness of God's gift in Christ. But these structures must be rightly used. They are intended to help the faithful develop their personal powers and gifts, whether of prayer, of understanding, or of action. If all initiative is left to the highest office-holders—the bishops—not even they can function well. Their proper role is not to initiate all action, but rather to recognize, encourage, co-ordinate, and judge the gifts and initiatives of others. Where the community is inert, the hierarchy becomes paralysed. Having no material

---

[41] Ibid., p. 288.

on which to work, it is forced to be idle or to assume functions not properly its own.

The idea of a complementarity of roles, without confusion of functions, is more Catholic and more faithful to the Scriptures than the idea of unilateral subordination, with an active hierarchy dictating to a passive laity. The Church needs teachers and prophets as well as apostles. It also needs members who 'seek the kingdom of God by engaging in temporal affairs and by ordering them according to the plan of God' (*LG* 31). In this polycentric community, neither the eye nor the ear can say to the other, 'I have no need of you' (cf. 1 Cor. 12: 21).

The mission of the Church is too vast to be accomplished by any single group of members. It requires the kind of unity in variety of which Möhler spoke in his analogy of the choir.[42] In this choir Christians of every social condition and calling can find their place provided that they allow the leaven of the gospel to permeate their activity, and do not cut themselves off from the total Catholic communion.

[42] See above, Chapter 4, note 13.

7

The Centre of Catholicity: Roman Primacy

CHAPTER 6 introduced the theme of Catholicism, a term here taken to mean the set of structures that serves the Church's catholicity in all its dimensions. Continuing this theme, we must now consider whether Roman primacy is one of these structures. Our views on this question will greatly affect the way in which we conceive of the relationship between Catholicism as such and Roman Catholicism.

(1)

In the present chapter we have to deal with issues that are divisive among Catholic Christians. Many who profess catholicity and even Catholicism, as hitherto described, do not acknowledge papal primacy. Thus there are different answers to questions such as the following: can one be both Catholic and Roman? Must one be Roman in order to be truly Catholic? Three main positions must be distinguished.

(1) The relationship is contingent, or accidental. The Catholic Church can be, but does not have to be, Roman. Similarly, according to this first position, an individual may be either a Roman Catholic or some other kind of Catholic. One can cease to be Roman without ceasing to be Catholic.

From a historical point of view this position is ably expounded by the Lutheran Jaroslav Pelikan, who considers himself a catholic Christian (and prefers to spell 'catholic' with a small initial 'c'). He recognizes a double development in the early centuries. First there was a process by which Christianity became catholic. This process for him involved five elements, seminally present from the beginning, which became manifest in the second and third centuries: missionary expansion, an ordered episcopal ministry, a sacramental system, standards of orthodoxy (such as creeds and canonical scriptures), and

finally a *modus vivendi* with the secular state. In a second phase of
evolution catholic Christianity became Roman. This happened
through a combination of historical circumstances, partly
religious and partly secular. Pelikan particularly emphasizes
the fact that in the fourth century the mantle of the emperor fell
upon the shoulders of the pope, who then assumed the old
sacerdotal title of supreme pontiff, *pontifex maximus*.[1] With Leo I
this process became substantially complete, though papal
centralization was to be carried further under the medieval
popes from Gregory VII to Boniface VIII.

Even after the schism with the East, according to Pelikan, the
Roman communion remained practically coextensive with
Western Christianity and could therefore present itself as the
catholic Church for the Christians of the West. After the
sixteenth century, however, the Church of Rome lost this
characteristic. In the divided church that resulted from the
Reformation neither Roman nor Protestant Christianity could
claim to be truly catholic, though some elements of catholicity
survived in both. 'Everyone has lost something by the division
of the Church. It has made a travesty of the word "catholic"
in the title "Roman Catholic".'[2] Pelikan's conclusion is
reminiscent of William Temple's quip, 'I believe in the holy
Catholic Church and sincerely regret that it does not at present
exist.'[3]

There is a second form of the first position which affirms that
the Catholic Church does still exist in those churches which,

[1] Jaroslav Pelikan, *The Riddle of Roman Catholicism* (Nashville: Abingdon, 1959), p.
38. Pelikan here gives the impression that Leo I took over the title, *Pontifex maximus*.
Relying on the more recent research of R. Schieffer, Yves Congar writes:

> *Pontifex maximus*, the pagan title abandoned by the emperors Gratian and
> Theodosius in 382, was never a title taken by the popes. A number of manuals
> mistakenly attribute it to St. Leo. Only in the fifteenth century, in the humanistic
> context of a rediscovery of the ancient monuments, was this appellation given to
> popes in their funeral inscriptions, on coins, even in their biographies, and, at the
> beginning of the sixteenth century (for example at Lateran V) in discourses
> addressed to them.

(Y. Congar, 'Titres donnés au pape', *Concilium* (French edn.), no. 108 (1975), pp. 55–
65; quotation from pp. 62–3; reprinted in Y. Congar, *Droit ancien et structures ecclésiales*
(London: Variorum Reprints, 1982).)
[2] Ibid., p. 52.
[3] Quoted in Frederic A. Iremonger, *William Temple* (London: Oxford Univ. Press,
1948), p. 387.

since the Reformation, have rejected Protestantism.[4] According to Edward Pusey and many leaders of the Oxford movement, there are three varieties of Catholic Christianity—Roman, Orthodox, and Anglican. These Catholic churches, unfortunately separated from one another by schism, are obliged to labour for reunion. In 1857 there was founded in England an 'Association for the Promotion of the Reunion of Christendom', with vigorous participation of some Roman Catholics and the approval, initially, of the English Catholic hierarchy.

In 1886 the American Episcopal Church in Chicago drew up a list of four essential features 'exemplified by the undivided Catholic Church during the first ages of its existence'—namely the Holy Scriptures, the Nicene creed, the two sacraments of baptism and the Lord's Supper, and the historic episcopate. With slight modifications this 'Quadrilateral' was reaffirmed by the Lambeth Conferences of 1888 and 1920.[5]

In 1933, on the hundredth anniversary of the launching of the Oxford movement, Norman P. Williams proposed a modified version of the Branch Theory in which the third branch was 'Northern Catholicism' rather than simply Anglicanism.[6] This new terminology made room within Catholicism for certain continental Lutheran churches as well as for groups such as the Jansenists of Utrecht and the Old Catholics. For Williams the Catholic Church was the inner circle or nucleus of Christendom, itself divided, which possessed the full apostolic heritage, while around it was an outer circle of communities which in various degrees lacked the marks of catholicity. Like the original Branch Theory and the Lambeth Quadrilateral, this theory implied that the papacy was neither a part of the full apostolic heritage nor totally incompatible with it.

(2) The second position is that the attributes Roman and

---

[4] A very complete statement of this type of ecclesiology may be found in William Palmer, *A Treatise on the Church of Christ* (2nd edn.; 2 vols.; New York: Appleton, 1841).

[5] On the Chicago–Lambeth Quadrilateral see Ruth Rouse and Stephen C. Neill (eds.), *A History of the Ecumenical Movement 1517–1948* (London: SPCK, 1954), pp. 264–5, 447–8. The text of the Lambeth Appeal of 1920 is printed in George K. A. Bell (ed.), *Documents on Christian Unity* (Oxford: Oxford Univ. Press, 1924), pp. 1–12.

[6] Norman P. Williams, 'The Theology of the Catholic Revival', in Norman P. Williams and Charles Harris (eds.), *Northern Catholicism* (London: SPCK, 1933), pp. 130–234, esp. p. 220. Williams's views of the papacy are more fully set forth in his earlier book, *Our Case As against Rome* (London: Longmans, Green, 1918).

Catholic are mutually exclusive, at least if Roman is understood as it is in the modern papal church. As an example one may mention the chapter on the 'Essence of Catholism' in Friedrich Heiler's massive work, *Catholicism: Its Idea and Its Manifestation* (1923). He assailed the Roman practice of identifying Roman with Catholic, and argued that Rome commits the anti-Catholic heresy of making the particular into the universal.[7] By its narrow self-definition Rome has forced other Catholics into a situation of division.[8] Rome, according to Heiler, is not Catholic, for it wants to rule in the spirit of the Caesars rather than serve in the spirit of the gospel.[9]

In an article published in 1957 another high-church Lutheran, Bishop Wilhelm Stählin, took a similar position, opting, as did Heiler, for 'evangelical catholicity'. The 'ism' in both Catholicism and Protestantism, he maintained, implied a polemical orientation against the other. Catholicism, a product of the Counter Reformation, was exclusive and intolerant, and therefore uncatholic. Protestantism, on the other hand, was involved in negative protest and anti-Catholicism. Both Catholicism and Protestantism, therefore, were defections from catholicity. Speaking for himself and his colleagues Stählin proclaimed: we cannot become Roman because we are Catholic.[10]

(3) The third position, at the opposite extreme from the second, asserts that there is a necessary conjuction between Roman and Catholic. This view has occasionally been held even by Protestants. For example, a small group of high church Lutherans in Germany, known as *Die Sammlung* (The Gathering), held in the late 1950s that there can be no true Catholicism without union with Rome as the visible centre of the universal Church. The papacy, according to these theologians, could properly be criticized, but not discarded. The intention of the Reformers, as they interpreted it, was not to form a new Church but to reform the existing Church. That intention could not be fulfilled until evangelical Christianity

[7] Friedrich Heiler, *Der Katholizismus: seine Idee und seine Erscheinung* (reprint of 1923 edn.; Munich and Basel: E. Reinhardt, 1970), p. 633.

[8] Ibid., pp. 634–5.

[9] Ibid., p. 657.

[10] Wilhelm Stählin, 'Katholizität, Protestantismus, und Katholizismus', in Hans Asmussen and Wilhelm Stählin (eds.), *Die Katholizität der Kirche* (Stuttgart: Evangelisches Verlagswerk, 1957), pp. 179–204, especially p. 202.

became integrated into the Roman Catholic Church.[11]

Within what is today called Roman Catholicism this third position has had an interesting development. In the Middle Ages partisans of the Gregorian Reform took the position that the Roman Church, without being itself identical with the Catholic Church, was 'the mother of all the faithful'.[12] The *Dictatus papae* of Gregory VII (AD 1075) contains the proposition, 'Whoever does not agree with the Roman Church is not to be considered Catholic.'[13]

In the ensuing centuries the Roman Church was called holy and apostolic and was virtually identified with the one, holy, catholic, and apostolic Church of the creeds. According to Robert Bellarmine the term 'catholic' in the creed had been a mere synonym for 'Roman' even before the twelfth century.[14] In 1864, in a condemnation of the Branch Theory, the Holy Office wrote a letter to the English bishops affirming that the Roman Church is not just a part of the Catholic Church. 'There is no other Catholic Church except that which, having been built on the one man, Peter, is "joined and knit together" (Eph. 4: 16) and grows up in the unity of faith and love . . .' (DS 2888).

Several years later, at Vatican Council I, the expression 'holy Roman Catholic Church', which appeared in the schema on the Catholic Faith, was found objectionable, especially by the papalist party, who feared that it might be taken as implying that such a thing as non-Roman Catholicism could exist. The text was accordingly modified to read, 'The holy, catholic, apostolic, and Roman Church' (DS 3001). This title raised in some minds the question whether *romanitas* might not be a fifth mark of the true Church in addition to the four traditional ones (oneness, holiness, apostolicity, and catholicity).

Some apologists of the Roman school in the nineteenth and

---

[11] See Hans Asmussen and others, *The Unfinished Reformation* (Notre Dame: Fides, 1961), notably the contribution of Max Lackmann, pp. 66–112.

[12] Fifth Council of Rome (1078), Mansi, 20: 512. Cf. Tridentine Profession of Faith (1564), DS 1869.

[13] 'Quod catholicus non habeatur qui non concordat Romanae ecclesiae', *Dictatus papae*, no. 26; text in Mansi, 20: 169.

[14] Robertus Bellarmine, *De controversiis christianae fidei*, Fourth General Controversy, *De Conciliis*, Bk. IV, chap. 4 (Paris: Vives, 1870), vol. ii, p. 367.

early twentieth centuries did actually use submission to the authority of Rome as a criterion of the true Church. Gustave Thils, in surveying the apologetics of this period, observes that many of the authors reduced the other three notes to that of unity, and then reduced the argument from unity to one from Roman primacy. To be one in faith, worship, and discipline, it was contended, the Church must have a single visible head on earth, namely the successor of Peter.[15]

Vatican Council II, as has been mentioned in Chapter 1, taught that the Church of Christ, with its catholicity, subsists in the Catholic Church, which preserves communion with the successor of Peter, the bishop of Rome (*LG* 8; *UR* 4). It stated that to be outside this communion is to lack some of the means of grace bequeathed by Christ to his Church (*UR* 3), but it also said that the separated churches possess elements of the true Church of Christ, and that some of these churches, such as the Orthodox (*UR* 17) and the Anglicans (*UR* 13), retain authentic Catholic traditions and institutions. Vatican II, however, did not call these other communions Catholic churches.

Like Vatican I, this council avoided the term 'Roman Catholic'. On the other hand, it also avoided the rather inflated title 'holy, catholic, apostolic, and Roman Church'. Instead it chose to use the simple term 'the Catholic Church'. In a crucial text in which one would expect the adjective 'Roman', the Constitution on the Church uses the circumlocution, 'the Catholic Church, which is governed by the successor of Peter and by the bishops in union with that successor' (*LG* 8). Only in a footnote does this text refer to documents which use the term 'Roman'—namely the Tridentine Profession of Faith and the Vatican I decrees.

Why this reluctance on the part of the Vatican II? Out of a number of possible reasons, I should like to single out two. First of all, the Council wished to respect the sensitivities of Eastern

---

[15] Gustave Thils, *Les Notes de l'Église dans l'Apologétique catholique depuis la Réforme* (Gembloux: Duculot, 1937), especially p. 248, with reference to J. Perrone, C. Mazzella, and others. Joseph de Guibert held that if the notes of unity, catholicity, and apostolicity are to be fully understood, they must be seen as involving the primacy of jurisdiction of the Roman pontiff (*De Christi Ecclesia* (2nd edn.; Rome: Gregorian University, 1928), no. 145, pp. 110–11). Yves de la Brière, however, warned that *romanitas* cannot be used as a note in apologetic arguments with dissidents, since it is the very point at issue. See his 'Église (Question des notes)', *Dictionnaire apologétique de la foi catholique*, vol. i (Paris: Beauchesne, 1911), cols. 1268–1301, esp. col. 1279.

Catholics who, though in full union with Rome, do not like to be called Roman. The Roman church, for many of them, is something Western.

Secondly, the Roman church, properly speaking, would seem to be the local church of Rome, the diocese which has the pope as its local ordinary. Vatican II was concerned to rehabilitate the doctrine of the local church, which had been obscured in post-Tridentine theology. This shift in ecclesiology is crucially important for understanding the status of the papacy in contemporary theology.

Prior to Vatican II it had become quite common to look on the Church as a gigantic corporation in which all true authority is located at the top, and flows downwards through the bishops to the laity at the bottom. This monolithic ecclesiology did not do justice to the idea of catholicity as identity in diversity—the idea that has been the leitmotiv of the present study. Because it did respect this idea, Vatican II was forced to take a different view of the local church. Thanks to preparatory studies of a number of theologians, it was able to introduce elements of what we may call an 'ecclesiology from below'.

According to the Constitution on the Liturgy, the Church most clearly reveals itself when the eucharistic liturgy is celebrated by the bishop accompanied by his priests and assistants, with the active participation of the laity (*SC* 41). The same doctrine is repeated in substance in the Constitution on the Church (*LG* 26) and in the Decree on the Pastoral Office of the Bishops (*CD* 11). This last text is of special interest for our purposes because it describes the diocese as a particular church in which 'the one, holy, catholic, and apostolic Church of Christ is truly present and operative'. Catholicity, therefore, is to be predicated not only of the universal Church but also of the local churches, though always in reference to the universal. Thus in another text we read: 'The variety of local churches with one common aspiration is particularly splendid evidence of the catholicity of the undivided Church' (*LG* 23; cf. *LG* 13).

Long forgotten in the West, the catholicity of the particular church has recently become a major theme in theological literature. 'The local Churches', writes Joseph Ratzinger, 'are not administrative units of a large apparatus but living cells, each of which contains the whole living mystery of the one body of the Church.'[16] The particular church has a certain inviolability, for it is the place where the Lord makes himself specially present through the ministry of word and sacrament, building up a living community of faith. Yet the particular church is never isolated. For the sake of its catholicity, it must cultivate communion with its sister churches. The universal Church, for its health, depends on the vitality of the member churches, each of which is expected to make a contribution to the life of the whole. Thus there is a kind of mutual indwelling, or circumincession, between the universal and the particular Church.

(2)

The case for Roman primacy has been differently stated in different eras of Church history. In the patristic period the argument was made chiefly on the grounds of apostolicity. When doctrinal disputes came up, they were normally settled by seeking out the traditions of the apostolic sees. Because both Peter and Paul had taught at Rome and had sanctified its soil by the shedding of their blood, Rome was considered to have a richer and more glorious apostolic inheritance than any other apostolic see. For St. Irenaeus the apostolic tradition was most surely present in what he called 'the greatest, most ancient, and generally known church, founded and established by the two most glorious apostles, Peter and Paul'.[17] The Roman tradition, therefore, was the very touchstone of gospel truth. When Irenaeus wrote it was still possible to believe that the oral doctrine of the apostles survived in the churches over which they had presided.

In the later patristic period, when ecclesiastical authority was seen as requiring doctrinal and administrative decisions,

---

[16] Joseph Ratzinger, 'The Pastoral Implications of Episcopal Collegiality', in *Concilium*, vol. i, *The Church and Mankind* (Glen Rock, NJ: Paulist, 1965), pp. 39–67; quotation from p. 44. On the catholicity of the local church see Emmanuel Lanne, 'The Local Church: Its Catholicity and Apostolicity', *One in Christ*, vi (1970), pp. 288–313; Henri de Lubac, 'Particular Churches and the Universal Church', in his *The Motherhood of the Church* (San Francisco: Ignatius Press, 1982), pp. 171–355. For a Lutheran perspective, see Timothy F. Lull, 'The Catholicity of the Local Congregation', in Carl E. Braaten (ed.), *The New Church Debate* (Philadelphia: Fortress, 1983), pp. 138–54.

[17] Irenaeus, *Adversus haereses*, Bk. III, chap. 3, nos. 1–2; *PG* 7:848.

the authority which Irenaeus had ascribed to the local church of Rome was increasingly shifted to the bishop of Rome, who was looked upon as the successor of Peter, the apostle upon whom the Lord had chosen to build his Church. By the fifth century Leo I was appealing to a kind of mystical presence of Peter in his own person.[18] This identification was recognized at the Council of Chalcedon, when Leo's tome was greeted with the acclamation, 'Peter has spoken through Leo!' This argument from mystical identity was quite different from the earlier argument from a historically continuous tradition, but the two both pointed to the same conclusion: that the approved doctrine of the Roman church was the most reliable witness to the faith of the apostles.

In the late Middle Ages and in early modern times, still another shift took place. Under the influence of political theory, theologians began to argue that for the maintenance of unity the most suitable form of government is a monarchy.[19] The Church as a vast society would fall apart unless it had a single head in whom all authority is vested. According to Boniface VIII, in the fourteenth century, the fullness of power (*plenitudo potestatis*), both spiritual and temporal, was conferred upon Peter by Christ under the figure of the two swords (Luke 22: 36). Papalist theologians of the period taught that the pope could at any time suppress the episcopal powers of any bishop, that bishops derived their episcopal powers from the pope, and that the same was true of the powers of the emperor and other earthly rulers, who were mere delegates of the pope.[20]

Beginning with the seventeenth century, when a clearer distinction was made between the ecclesiastical and the secular spheres, less extravagant claims were made for the temporal authority of the pope, but still the papacy was studied principally in terms of the category of power. With the development of the doctrine of sovereignty in political theory, primacy

[18] On Leo I see Jean M. R. Tillard, *The Bishop of Rome* (Wilmington, Del.: Michael Glazier, 1983), p. 118, with reference to the previous studies of Walter Ullmann and Philip A. McShane.

[19] E.g., Thomas Aquinas, *Summa Contra Gentiles*, Bk. IV, chap. 76.

[20] See the views of Agostino Trionfo (Augustinus Triumphus) summarized by Tillard, *The Bishop of Rome*, pp. 57–8; also those of Herveus Natalis summarized in Joseph Ratzinger, 'Primacy, Episcopate, and Apostolic Succession', in Karl Rahner and Joseph Ratzinger, *The Episcopate and the Primacy* (New York: Herder and Herder, 1962), p. 43, note 15.

came to be seen as the supreme jurisdiction enjoyed by the ruler of a 'perfect society'.

Unlike Boniface VIII, the Fathers at Vatican I were conscious that papal power in the Church was limited, but they were unable, in terms of their own categories, to specify any limiting principle.[21] Excessively influenced by the Ultramontane majority, the council spoke as though the pope were the sole vicar of Christ. It was not difficult for a hostile critic like Otto von Bismarck to misread the documents as if they deprived the other bishops of their pastoral authority and made them mere agents of the pope. In the Roman Catholic responses to these criticisms of Vatican I we find the beginnings of a reassertion of episcopal authority.[22]

(3)

We have seen, then, that papal primacy in the first millennium was envisaged principally as witness, and was closely linked to what has been called the apostolicity of the Church. In the second millennium, until Vatican Council II, papal authority was understood as a matter of power, and was linked to the Church's attribute of unity. A more recent kind of theology, reflected in the documents of Vatican II, links papal primacy rather with service, and interprets it in relation to the catholicity of the Church. According to this third view the Petrine see and the particular church may each be said to enjoy a certain primacy, and the two primacies, far from conflicting, require one another.

The particular churches, as we have noted, are not mere fragments of a large whole, but are realizations of the essence of the Church itself, with all its essential attributes, in a particular place and time. The bishop, who officially represents the universal Church in the particular church, has a catholic function. As a sign and instrument of unity, the bishop governs his individual church by building up consensus among its

[21] This observation is made by Garrett Sweeney, 'The Primacy: The Small Print of Vatican I', in Adrian Hastings (ed.), *Bishops and Writers* (Wheathamstead: A. Clarke, 1977), pp. 179–206, esp. p. 203. See also Basil Christopher Butler, *The Church and Unity* (London: G. Chapman, 1979), p. 233.

[22] See particularly the collective declaration of the German bishops (1875), DS 3112–6.

members and by giving official expression to that consensus in his public words and actions. He is also an agent of unity among the sister churches that belong to the Catholic communion. The communion of churches is maintained by the interrelations of the bishops, who mutually question, criticize, advise, and support one another.

The college of bishops corresponds on the universal level to the college of presbyters on the diocesan level. The presbyters constitute a college by being gathered under a single head, the chief presbyter who is the bishop. Hence it is to be expected that on the universal scale there will be a chief bishop serving as centre of unity for the college.

Unlike Vatican I, Vatican II approached the question of papal primacy in the light of several other ecclesiological doctrines, such as the relative autonomy of the particular church, the *communio* concept of the universal Church, and the collegiality of the bishops as agents of communion. In this perspective the role of the pope becomes far clearer. He is, in the words of Jean Tillard, 'a bishop among bishops who is commissioned, on the basis of the shared grace of episcopacy, to gather his brother bishops into a college of which he is the *centrum unitatis*'.[23]

Putting the same idea in other words, we might say that the pope is responsible for the catholic unity of the whole Church, and that by assuring this unity he performs a service for all the particular churches. The other bishops need to have standards to which they can look for guidance in maintaining the catholicity of their respective churches. Thanks to the apostolic succession they have the means of keeping their churches diachronically in communion with the Church of apostolic times. They also need a standard for the maintenance of simultaneous or synchronic communion with the other particular churches that are faithful to the apostolic heritage. The primatial see gives the needed reference point.[24]

The universal responsibility of the pope, explained in these terms, does not reduplicate that of the local bishop, although

[23] Tillard, *The Bishop of Rome*, p. 157.
[24] Tillard explains how communion with Rome assists individual bishops in their task of allowing 'the catholicity of the Church to reveal itself in a particular place' (ibid., p. 153).

there will often be problems about where to draw the line. In general terms it may be said that the local bishop, rather than the pope, has the duty to build up the particular church and keep it in faith and communion.[25] According to the principle of subsidiarity, the higher authority must not intervene in local affairs except where the local church cannot bring a remedy.[26]

(4)

From the standpoint of credibility, the collegial understanding of the papacy, which emerges from Vatican II, has distinct advantages over the older theories. It is not necessary to prove that the local church of Rome has a purer faith or richer traditions than all other local churches, for the pope, even though he be bishop of Rome, is not seen as specifically representing the characteristics of that particular church. The fact that the pope can come from Cracow underlines this point.

Whether the papacy could be transferred away from Rome is debatable. Theologians such as Domingo Bañez held that the Petrine see would not necessarily have to remain forever identical with the Roman, and Vatican Council I carefully refrained from repudiating Bañez's opinion. From the New Testament it is evident that Peter exercised a ministry at Jerusalem and Antioch before coming to Rome, and it is problematic what kind of ministry he did perform at Rome. Before its destruction Jerusalem, rather than Rome, held the primacy. If Rome were to be destroyed, as Jerusalem was, it would still be possible to call the pope titular bishop of Rome, but there would be little point in maintaining that fiction. The primacy, I suspect, could be transferred to another see, which would by that very fact become 'Petrine'.[27]

Whatever one may think about this hypothetical case, it is clear that the primacy has been held by Rome ever since there

---

[25] Ibid., p. 154.

[26] Tillard rightly sees in the principle of subsidiarity an important corrective for the excesses of centralization in the modern period (ibid., pp. 183–4). On the principle of subsidiarity as applied to the papacy see Patrick Granfield, *The Papacy in Transition* (Garden City: Doubleday, 1980), pp. 76–8; also de Lubac, *Motherhood of the Church*, pp. 297–304.

[27] For further discussion of the connection between the Petrine office and Rome see Granfield, *The Papacy in Transition*, pp. 146–7; also Avery Dulles, *The Resilient Church* (Garden City: Doubleday, 1977), pp. 119–20.

was a papacy at all. The United States Lutheran–Catholic Dialogue, in its statement on Papal Primacy, acknowledged the importance of this fact. 'Structures invested with powerful symbolic meaning cannot be created at will'[28] The Anglican–Roman Catholic International Commission (ARCIC) in its Venice statement stated even more pointedly: 'The only see which makes any claim to universal primacy and which has exercised and still exercises such *episcopē* is the see of Rome, the city where Peter and Paul died. It seems appropriate that in any future union a universal primacy such as has been described should be held by that see.'[29]

To reinforce the significance of Rome it could be helpful to show that Peter did in fact perform a ministry of leadership there, and was martyred there, but it is probably not essential to prove these points. Still less is it essential to prove that Rome or its bishop consciously exercised a universal primacy from the first century onwards. From history it seems evident that the Church only gradually came to see the necessity of having within its episcopate someone who could speak and act for the whole Church. This insight, though gradually achieved, has lasting validity.

It might be objected that if all the bishops, as members of the college, have universal supervisory functions, the papacy is superfluous. Could not the college govern by consensus or by majority vote? Possibly the Lord could have provided for a headless college but it would seem less suited to the nature of the Church. Just as in the eucharistic assembly there must be a presiding priest, specially representing Christ as head, and just as in the diocese there must be a single bishop to govern as 'vicar of Christ' (*LG* 27), so in the universal Church it is important to have one bishop who can personally address all the pastors and faithful in the name of Christ.

Vladimir Soloviev, the nineteenth-century theologian sometimes called the 'Russian Newman', made a strong case for a monarchical primacy. If vested solely in the collective administration of a council, he held, corporate decisions would

[28] Paul Empie and T. Austin Murphy (eds.), *Papal Primacy and the Universal Church. Lutherans and Catholics in Dialogue*, vol. v (Minneapolis: Augsburg, 1974), Part II, no. 36, p. 31.
[29] Anglican/Roman Catholic International Commission, *The Final Report*, Windsor, 1981 (London: CTS and SPCK, 1982), no. 23, p. 64.

fall prey to unstable majorities and political compromises. Different interest groups, he suggested, would sometimes combine to defeat what was required to maintain the Church in the truth of Christ. He summed up his argument as follows:

> The perfect circle of the Universal Church requires a unique center, not so much for its perfection as for its very existence. The Church upon earth, called to gather in the multitude of the nations, must, if she is to remain an active society, possess a definite universal authority to set against national divisions; if she is to enter the current of history and to undergo continual change and adaptation in her external circumstances and relationships and yet preserve her identity, she requires an authority essentially conservative but nevertheless active, fundamentally unchangeable though outwardly adaptable; and finally if she is set amid the frailty of man, to assert herself in reaction against all the powers of evil, she must be equipped with an absolutely firm and impregnable foundation, stronger than the gates of hell.[30]

Such a universal authority, Soloviev was convinced, was provided for in Christ's words to Cephas, 'You are Peter and on this rock I will build my church' (Matt. 16: 18).

As shown by the collaborative study, *Peter in the New Testament*, commissioned by the United States Lutheran–Catholic Dialogue, contemporary biblical scholars generally agree that Peter is portrayed in the New Testament as having the first rank among the apostles and as being charged with special responsibility for the unity and mission of the entire Church.[31] The development of the images of Peter throughout the New Testament, according to this joint study, was oriented in the direction of the later institution of papacy, which can therefore claim a good measure of biblical support, even though it cannot be proved from Scripture alone. In Vatican II the argument is that if the college of bishops succeeds to the college of the apostles there must be in the episcopal college someone who succeeds to the headship of Peter.

On the basis of this line of reasoning, the Lutheran members of the American dialogue in 1974 accepted the concept of a 'Petrine' ministry to the universal Church. They put to their

[30] Vladimir Soloviev, *Russia and the Universal Church* (1889; London: G. Bles, 1948), pp. 107–8.

[31] Raymond E. Brown and others, *Peter in the New Testament* (Minneapolis: Augsburg, and New York: Paulist, 1973).

own churches the question whether 'they are prepared to affirm with us that papal primacy, renewed in the light of the gospel, need not be a barrier to reconciliation'. They acknowledged the desirability of a 'papal Ministry, renewed under the gospel and committed to Christian freedom, in a larger communion that would include the Lutheran churches'.[32]

ARCIC was even more positive, especially at its Windsor meeting of 1981. Notwithstanding certain remaining difficulties about the 'divine right' status of the papacy, its infallibility, and its universal primacy of jurisdiction, the Anglicans were able to join the Roman Catholics in declaring:

We can now together affirm that the Church needs both a multiple, dispersed authority, with which all God's people are actively involved, and also a universal primate as servant and focus of visible unity in truth and love. This does not mean that all differences have been eliminated; but if any Petrine function and office are exercised in the living Church of which a universal primacy is called to serve as a visible focus, then it inheres in his office that he should have both a defined teaching responsibility and appropriate gifts of the Spirit to enable him to discharge it.[33]

It would be possible to quote a great number of individual theologians, both Lutheran and Anglican, who agree with the dialogue findings and would perhaps wish to go still further. To mention only one, John Macquarrie argues strongly that papacy, far from being an additional structure over and above the four named in the Lambeth Quadrilateral, is 'included within the structure of the episcopate'. He concludes:

At the very least we have to affirm that any vision of a reunited Church, one, holy, catholic and apostolic, must envisage it in communion with the most illustrious of the apostolic sees. Anything short of this can be regarded as only an interim step; and anything that might make this ultimate consummation more difficult should be scrupulously avoided.[34]

In another work Macquarrie speaks specifically of the relationship between Rome and catholicity:

[T]he Roman Catholic Church is, in a unique way, the guardian of

---

[32] *Papal Primacy*, Part I, no. 32, pp. 22–3.
[33] *The Final Report*, no. 33, pp. 97–8.
[34] John Macquarrie, *Principles of Christian Theology* (rev. edn., 1977; London: SCM, 1979), p. 416.

catholicity. Rome claims to have the fullness of the catholic faith, and even if this claim is controversial, one cannot deny the further claim that, of all Christian communions, the Roman communion is the most truly international and worldwide. . . . I think . . . that Anglicans and others would be ready to acknowledge that their catholicity would be deepened and enhanced through a closer relation to Rome, considered as the centre.[35]

Quotations such as these, which could be multiplied many times over, prove beyond question that we are today at a unique moment of ecumenical history. Never since the Reformation has there been such readiness on the part of Protestants, Anglicans, and Orthodox to acknowledge the value of the papacy as a bond of unity. This recognition is in great part a response to the new image given to the papacy by Vatican Council II and by recent popes since John XXIII. It may also be a response to the new situation of the pluralistic world Church. Now that Christianity is becoming for the first time truly planetary and culturally pluralistic, it is more important than ever to have a central authority that will keep the regional groupings in communion. The centrifugal forces of social and cultural diversity must be counterbalanced by the centripetal attraction of a symbolic focus of unity.

Within Roman Catholicism steady efforts are being made to implement the principles of subsidiarity, diversification, and collegiality. Many dioceses have equipped themselves with pastoral councils and senates of priests; national and regional conferences of bishops have been established all over the world; the college of cardinals has assumed new roles; the papal curia has been restructured and internationalized; and there have been periodic meetings of the world-wide Synod of Bishops. Not content with these measures, Popes Paul VI and John Paul II have made long and exhausting pastoral visits to all parts of the world. Extending their vision beyond the Roman Catholic community, they have striven to make ecumenical contacts with the leaders of other churches. They have likewise concerned themselves with issues of peace and social justice, which can never be alien to the gospel. Doubtless the record of these popes has not been in every respect perfect. Like all their

[35] John Macquarrie, *Christian Unity and Christian Diversity* (London: SCM, 1975), pp. 51–3.

predecessors, including Peter, they have had their human limitations; but they have surely given unprecedented prominence to the catholic dimensions of the papacy.

The concept of collegiality, as approved by Vatican II, has often been misrepresented through excessive reliance on political models. In liberal societies there has been a tendency to imagine that the Church, having previously been an absolute monarchy, has now become a limited monarchy or even a parliamentary democracy. Like Bismarck's reading of Vatican I, this interpretation runs counter to the texts. The collegial mode of papacy, promoted by Vatican II, requires the pope to be in a vital relationship with the whole body of bishops and to be responsive to their pastoral concerns. But collegiality, as explained by the councils, takes account of the unique position of the pope as head, and accords to him powers that the other bishops do not have. For example, it pertains to the pope to decide when and how to call the episcopate as a whole to collegiate action. For the good of the Church it is important that the pope should have such discretion. If Pope John XXIII had not been free to act on his own initiative, in response to what he regarded as an inspiration from on high, there would probably have been no Vatican Council II.

Whether inside or outside a council, the pope cannot be outvoted by a majority of the bishops. The ecumenicity of a council depends essentially on the participation of Rome, the supreme apostolic see, and unless approved by the pope, as the catholic bishop *par excellence*, the conciliar decrees would lack decisive force. But precisely because of the pope's universal status he cannot, by appealing to his office, stand against the consensus of the universal Church. Primacy and collegiality, though they stand in tension with each other, cannot exist except in unison. The episcopacy is structured as a duality in unity, and this dialectical structure makes it truly catholic.

To delve into the vexed problem of papal infallibility would take us far afield. The problem has been discussed at length by many contemporary authors; I have written on it myself.[36] In

---

[36] Avery Dulles, *A Church to Believe In* (New York: Crossroad, 1982), chap. 9, with references to much recent literature. For an additional contribution see Alexis van Bunnen, 'Infaillibilité et logique', *Revue des Sciences philosophiques et théologiques*, lxvii (1983), pp. 45–86.

the perspectives of catholicity, it is important to recognize that the pope, as universal teacher, is not an isolated voice. As Joseph Ratzinger has put it, 'Precisely because of the inner nature of his [the pope's] infallibility, he needs the testimony of the "ecumene" '[37]—that is, of bishops who are not just papal delegates or shadows of the pope, but true pastors of other particular churches.

Infallible doctrine, moreover, must necessarily resonate with the faith of the whole people of God. Such doctrine is not an external decree imposed on the faithful from without, but an articulation of what was already, in a less articulate way, their own faith. Vatican II, by bringing out the links between the infallibility of the pope, that of the college of bishops, and that of the whole believing Church, made it clear that the primary seat of infallibility is the total Church, even though on occasion the pope may become its primary spokesman. Any dogmatic definition will, by the nature of the case, emerge from long and wide consultation and will predictably win the acceptance of the Church as a whole. As understood in contemporary theology, the particular churches and their faithful are not merely passive subjects upon whom truth is impressed from outside. As active bearers of the faith, they will often nuance and enrich the very doctrines that they accept on the word of authoritative teachers.

(5)

On the basis of these reflections we may now return to the questions posed at the beginning of this chapter. What is the relationship between Roman and Catholic? Are the two concepts mutually exclusive, merely compatible, or necessarily conjoined?

It should be clear in the first place that the term 'Roman' in this context is not used in the usual civic or geographical sense. In an authentically Catholic theology 'Roman' does not mean Western, Latin, Mediterranean, Southern, or Italian. It simply designates the centre of communion, which happens to be linked, for historical reasons, with the city of Rome. The primacy as such is no more Italian than it is Polish, British, Argentinian, or Indian.

---

[37] Ratzinger, 'Primacy, Episcopate, and Apostolic Succession', p. 62.

In answer to those who hold for a contradiction, we may concede that papal primacy, if exercised in a way that hampers the leadership of other bishops and pastoral authorities, can stand in the way of true catholicity. The extreme papalism of certain fourteenth-century popes and theologians, for example, was an uncatholic distortion. Such papalism is as unacceptable as the the anti-papalism to which it was opposed. A Catholic understanding of papacy has to transcend the opposition between these attitudes. Authors such as Heiler and Stählin, although dissatisfied with what they saw as Roman Catholicism, were denouncing papalism rather than papacy as such.

Can Catholicism exist without a papacy, as many Lutherans, Anglicans, and Orthodox have held? This question can be answered in more than one way, depending on how much content one puts in the term 'Catholic'. Although the evidence is complex, Pelikan is not wholly incorrect in saying that even after the Church had become manifestly 'catholic' there was for some time no papacy in the modern sense of that word. Only gradually did it become apparent that the Church needed within her own episcopate a permanent organ of universal unity. But once that need had become apparent it was no longer possible for Catholicism to be integral and complete without communion with the primatial see and its bishop.

It is true that numerous Catholic elements, such as the word of God, the sacraments, and the hierarchical ministry, exist with varying degrees of efficacy outside the Roman communion, but they do not in that situation have their full potency. The sacraments, when administered in separation, no longer express or promote—at least to the same degree—the unity of the Church, and the hierarchy, without its centre of unity, cannot achieve its full collegial value. In a reunited Church the Catholic elements of all the uniting churches would be included, not destroyed. The splendours of the liturgy, theology, and spirituality of Lutherans, Anglicans, and Orthodox Christians would be preserved. If Roman forms were to be substituted for this rich heritage, the catholicity of the entire Church would be diminished. For catholicity consists in a rich, diversified unity.

If Roman and Catholic imply each other, as the third position maintains, should they be treated as synonyms? Our investigation points to the conclusion that they are polar opposites. Rome is the centre, the principle of unity; Catholic is the periphery, the principle of diversity. There can be no centre without a circumference, no circumference without a centre. If, *per impossibile*, the see of Rome were to cut itself off from the other sees, so that the bishop of Rome ceased to be in communion with the other Catholic bishops, Rome would no longer hold the primacy.[38] The church of Rome would have, in effect, become a mere sect. And if, on the other hand, other sees are content to live in isolation from the centre, and if they cease to measure themselves in relation to it, the catholicity that they possess is jeopardized. Conversely, as they come into closer communion with the Petrine see, giving what they have to give, and receiving what they have to receive, their catholicity takes on new life. Roman primacy and Catholic communion, therefore, are dialectical opposites which exist and flourish in mutual relatedness.

[38] Cf. ibid., p. 61.

8

Catholic and Protestant: Contrary or Complementary?

WE have been dealing with Catholic Christianity, mentioning Protestantism only to bring out more clearly what is distinctive to the Catholic tradition. Before ending this study it will be appropriate to say something of Protestantism as the principal type of Christianity that does not consider itself, and is not generally considered, Catholic. In some ways this chapter will complete what was begun in Chapter 7, where we considered the relationship between Roman Catholicism and Catholicism in a wider sense. Further enlarging the circle, we shall here deal with the relationship between Catholicism, especially Roman Catholicism, and Protestantism.

(1)

As Johann Adam Möhler noted 150 years ago, there has been a varied history of Protestant–Catholic relations, moving from hostile polemics through irenic controversy to comparative symbolics.[1] Since Möhler's time this history has gone several stages further. We cannot here trace the full course of the development, but we must say something about how these changing relationships have affected the way in which both Protestantism and Catholicism have been understood.

In the sixteenth and seventeenth centuries Protestant and Catholic Christianity were still in many ways quite similar. Both sides recognized that there was only one Church, the true Church of Jesus Christ, and that this Church was catholic, as well as holy and apostolic. Each side claimed that the true Church was present in itself, whereas in the other there were only vestiges of true Christianity. The two sides had a common method of argument, proceeding by deductive proofs from authoritative texts. The primary authority for both was the

[1] Johann Adam Möhler, *Symbolik*, vol. i (Cologne: J. Hegner, 1960), pp. 44–54.

Bible, but both also made use of proofs from the consensus of the Fathers and from the creeds of the early, undivided Church. Both sides claimed to have remained faithful to the original patrimony and accused the other of having introduced novelites. Even when I myself studied theology in the 1950s, the Protestant Reformers were still called *Novatores* (innovators).

While claiming catholicity for themselves, the two sides differed somewhat in their interpretation of the term.[2] On the Protestant side, Luther and Calvin saw the Church as catholic in the sense of universal. There could be only one true faith, and hence only one Church in which that faith was believed, confessed, and practised. The true Church was present wherever the gospel was purely preached and the sacraments were rightly administered, and nowhere else. Early Lutherans such as Philipp Melanchthon and Johann Gerhard, taking up this line of argument, held that the Church was catholic in so far as it was faithful to the gospel as attested by the Scriptures and the early Christian authorities. The Roman Church, with its medieval doctrines and practices, had allegedly departed from the original patrimony, and was thus no longer catholic.

Christians still loyal to Rome took their concept of catholicity chiefly from Augustine, who had used against the Donatists the argument of universal extension. Dismissing the Protestant churches as mere sects, they argued that the Roman obedience, spread everywhere in the world, was alone catholic. In answer to Protestant objections they contended that the sacramental and institutional features of Roman Catholicism were supported by the Bible and by patristic tradition.

The controversies of this period, initially acrimonious and later more polite, as in the correspondence between Bossuet and Leibniz, proved rather unfruitful. Yves Congar notes five common defects:[3]

(1) Concerned with achieving immediate results, this controversial literature adopted a tactical rather than a strategic plan of operation. It failed to produce works of lasting value.

---

[2] For early Lutheran views on catholicity see Wolfgang Beinert, *Um das dritte Kirchenattribut*, vol. i (Essen: Ludgerus-Verlag, 1964), pp. 93–127. On Calvin see his *Institutes of the Christian Religion*, Book IV, chap. 1, no. 2.

[3] Yves Congar, 'The Encounter between the Christian Confessions: Yesterday and Today', in his *Dialogue Between Christians* (London: Chapman, 1966), pp. 135–59, esp. pp. 136–9.

(2) It attempted to prove its points by deductive argument from biblical and patristic texts, without attention to the real situation out of which those texts had emerged and to the changing intellectual environment. Subsequent developments have shown the importance of resources other than authoritative proof-texts and syllogistic reasoning.

(3) Issues were atomized, and no real effort was made to understand the mentality that made the positions of the other side seem coherent and even obvious to their adherents.

(4) Neither party to the debate showed any capacity or willingness to recognize that its own positions might be subject to revision. Self-criticism was not seen as a virtue.

(5) As a result of all the foregoing faults, the controversies had the net effect of hardening the oppositions and locking each side into its own limited perspective. Congar quotes in this connection the saying, 'It is a great misfortune to have learned one's catechism against someone else.'[4]

(2)

This kind of controversial apologetics, though perpetuated in apologetic manuals until our own day, became outdated about the beginning of the nineteenth century with the foundation in Germany of the new science of comparative symbolics. Among the founders were two important Protestants, Philipp Marheineke and Friedrich Schleiermacher. Influenced by Romantic organological thinking, they were convinced that each confessional group was a living whole, to be understood through its fundamental idea (*Grundidee*). Under the impact of the new idealistic philosophy, they further sought to apply to the Christian divisions the distinction between essence and manifestation (*Wesen* and *Erscheinung*). They tended to believe that the oppositions were chiefly on the phenomenal level, and could be transcended by a higher synthesis that would see both as different manifestations of the same fundamental reality.[5]

The philosopher Hegel,[6] whose work was in part paralleled

---

[4] Ibid., p. 138.

[5] See J. R. Geiselmann, Introduction to Möhler, *Symbolik*, vol. i, pp. [1] to [148].

[6] Georg W. F. Hegel, *The Christian Religion. Lectures on the Philosophy of Religion*, Part III (ed. Peter C. Hodgson; Missoula, Mont.: Scholars Press, 1979), pp. 253, 271–5, 334–44.

by other Lutheran thinkers such as Friedrich Schelling and Ferdinand Christian Baur,[7] envisaged the dialectical opposition in historical terms. Catholicism, according to authors of this tendency, represented an earlier historical moment in which the Christian revelation was seen as an objective datum, externally imposed on the believer. The Catholic emphasis on sacramental objectivity and dogmatic authority was regarded as a relic of this outdated mentality, wherein the divine was still confused with its invisible and historical manifestations. Protestantism, in the view of these thinkers, was a basically healthy reaction towards historical consciousness and personal freedom, but was always in danger of succumbing to relativism, subjectivism, and individualism. The future could be counted upon to bring a synthesis of the relative and the absolute, so that the objective content of the Catholic religion could be combined with the subjective appropriation stressed in Protestantism.

This type of historical dialectic was imported into the English-speaking world by the German Reformed theologian, Philip Schaff. In 1844, shortly after coming to the United States, he delivered at Reading, Pennsylvania, his inaugural address, significantly entitled *The Principle of Protestantism, as Related to the Present State of the Church*. He asserted that both Catholicism and Protestantism were essential to the life of the Church as it progresses through a series of dialectical contrapositions (*Gegensätze*). Protestantism he viewed as a principle of critical protest, which had manifested itself most influentially in the Reformation. In Schaff's own day, however, protest and freedom were being carried to an excess and were provoking anti-Protestant reactions in the Church of Rome and in what he called Puseyism.

There is an opposition to the errors of Rome and Oxford, sometimes displayed in our own country, which may be said to wrong the cause it affects to defend almost as seriously as this is done by these errors themselves. In its blind zeal and shallow knowledge, it sinks the

---

[7] On Schelling see Walter Kasper, *Das Absolute in der Geschichte: Philosophie und Theologie der Geschichte in der Spätphilosophie Schellings* (Mainz: Matthias-Grünewald, 1965), pp. 412–21. The views of Baur are well presented in Peter C. Hodgson (ed.), *Ferdinand Christian Baur on the Writing of Church History* (New York: Oxford Univ. Press, 1968), esp. in the 'General Introduction'.

Church to the level of a temperance society, strips the ministry of its divine commission and so of its divine authority, reduces the sacraments to mere signs, turns all that is mystical into the most trivial worldly sense, as in fact to throw open the door to the most rampant sectarian license, in the name of the gospel, that any may choose to demand. Opposition to Oxford and Rome in this form can never prevail.[8]

Advocating what he called 'Protestant Catholicism', Schaff pleaded for a recovery of the heritage of Christian antiquity on the part of the Reformation churches. In this way he felt that divisions of the sixteenth century could perhaps be overcome. Acknowledging his indebtedness to Schelling and Neander, Schaff saw three major eras in church history. The first, or Petrine, period, that of Catholicism, was characterized by authority and law; it culminated in the medieval papacy. The second period was typified by Paul, the advocate of free justifying faith, and came to a head at the Reformation. The signs of the times in Schaff's own day called for both Catholics and Protestants to repent of their exaggerations and errors, so that a Johannine era of reconciliation might come to pass.[9] He hoped that era might be inaugurated in the land of his adoption, the United States.[10] (Ironically Schaff's address led to his trial in 1845 before the Reformed Synod on charges of Puseyism, but he was acquitted and continued a fruitful ecumenical apostolate till his death in 1893.)

Although Roman Catholics were less creative than their Protestant colleagues in the field of comparative symbolics, they did issue significant responses, at least in Germany, and especially at Tübingen. Johann Sebastian Drey, the founder of the Catholic Tübingen school, took part in the early stages of this discussion.[11] He acknowledged that a certain kind of Protestantism had existed since the beginnings, even within the Catholic Church. In ancient and medieval times many had protested against abuses of authority without departing from

[8] Philip Schaf (*sic*), *The Principle of Protestantism as Related to the Present State of the Church* (Chambersburg, Pa.: German Reformed Church, 1845), p. 214.

[9] Ibid., pp. 175–6.

[10] Ibid., p. 101.

[11] Johann Sebastian Drey, excerpts from *Tagebuch* in Joseph R. Geiselmann (ed.), *Geist des Christentums und des Katholizismus* (Mainz: Matthias-Grünewald, 1940), pp. 125–6, 131–5.

the Catholic communion. The Reformation originally appeared as a protest against abuses, but it soon became uncatholic and anti-catholic, attacking the Church itself. Granting that Catholicism needed a countervailing principle to keep it from becoming excessively authoritarian and rigid, Drey argued that this second principle should be mysticism, which allows the Church to stand but prevents it from degenerating into a lifeless mechanism. The Protestant principle of private judgement, according to Drey, could have no rightful place in Church, for it was destructive of the Church's reality.

Johann Adam Möhler, Drey's foremost disciple, distinguished between a dialectic internal to the Church and another between the Church and the heretical sects.[12] The Church could accept the internal oppositions (*Gegensätze*) as mutually complementary, but she had to reject heretical oppositions (*Widersprüche*) as incompatible with her faith and unassimilable. God, he conceded, uses heresies to make the Church reflect on her faith and thus develop her self-awareness. But, unlike Schleiermacher, Möhler was convinced that there could never be a synthesis between Protestantism and Catholicism. Dialogue with Protestantism, in his opinion, should demonstrate that Catholicism is itself the higher unity of all authentic Christian oppositions. In his great work on comparative symbolics Möhler tried to state the oppositions as sharply as he could so that, by increasing the tensions, he could intensify the motivation to overcome them.[13] Without denying the validity of certain Protestant insights, both Drey and Möhler took the position that Protestantism, as it had developed since the Reformation, was irreconcilable with Catholic Christianity, and could not be reincorporated without radically changing its nature.

(3)

The epoch of comparative symbolics, which initially seemed to point towards reconciliation, led to a heightening of confessional consciousness and thus to renewed controversy. In the

[12] Johann Adam Möhler, *Die Einheit in der Kirche oder das Prinzip des Katholizismus* (Cologne: J. Hegner, 1957), sec. 46, pp. 152–7.
[13] Möhler, *Symbolik*, Author's Introduction, p. 8.

period from 1840 to 1920 authors on both sides specialized in unflattering polemics against the other. On the continent Catholic apologists such as Jaime Balmes, Juan Donoso Cortés, and Giovanni Perrone argued that the Protestant appeal to private judgement had paved the way for a decline into rationalism and infidelity. Meanwhile the Anglo-Catholics sought to purge all Protestant elements from the Church of England and to re-establish continuity with the patristic and medieval tradition.

Conversely, liberal Protestants such as Albrecht Ritschl, followed by Adolf Harnack and Auguste Sabatier, looked upon Catholicism as the foremost adversary. They praised the Reformation for having recovered the gospel in its original purity and for having swept away many Catholic accretions—priestly, legal, sacramental, liturgical, and monastic. Modern scientific historiography, they believed, made it possible to reconstruct the original teaching of Jesus and thus to do away with the authoritarian use of Scripture. Seeking a pure religion of the spirit, they aspired to complete the work of the Reformers by eliminating the Catholic elements that survived in their own churches.

The Catholic Modernists responded sharply to the liberals. Alfred Loisy, in his book-length answer to Harnack's *What is Christianity?*, ridiculed Harnack's identification of the essence of Christianity with the teaching of Jesus.[14] George Tyrrell, like Loisy, attacked the individualism and intellectualism of the Protestants. Catholicism, he held, as the religion of the whole person, made use of symbols that spoke to the deepest levels of the human psyche. Tyrrell was also convinced that the Jesus of history bore no resemblance to the liberal reconstruction. 'The Christ the Harnack sees, looked back through nineteen centuries of Catholic darkness, is only the reflection of a Liberal Protestant face, seen at the bottom of a deep well.'[15]

(4)

A greater mutual openness began to reappear in Catholic–

[14] Alfred F. Loisy, *The Gospel and the Church* (London: Pitman & Sons, 1908), from French original of 1902.

[15] George Tyrrell, *Christianity at the Cross-Roads* (London: Longmans, Green, & Co., 1909), p. 44.

Protestant relations after World War I. On the Catholic side, von Hügel made a fair and balanced estimate of Protestanism, based on a wide familiarity with the literature. While convinced that Protestanism lacked the rich inclusivess of Catholicism in its complete and classical form, he found it possible to speak chiefly of the points held in common between Catholics and Protestants, such as the essential givenness of religion in God's historical deed in Jesus Christ. He found a 'renaissance of Catholic principles' and a 'recovery of Catholic values' in the Protestantism of his own day.[16] He was also prepared to admit the characteristic weaknesses of Catholicism. Catholics, he believed, were more tempted than Protestants to neglect the achievements of pioneers in the historical and natural sciences and to exact conformity by issuing imperialistic decrees.[17]

Meanwhile some Protestants, without any inclination to renounce their own special heritage, sought to profit from the distinctive strengths of Catholicism. The two strongest theoreticians of this new attitude were probably Karl Barth and Paul Tillich.

Barth, writing in 1928, insisted on the need of Protestantism to let itself be questioned by Roman Catholicism.[18] He respected Catholicism for holding that the Church must be able to speak and act in the name of God. In this the Catholics were closer to the Protestant Reformers, he believed, than were neo-Protestants such as Schleiermacher, Ritschl, and Troeltsch, who threw away both the substance of the Church and the restoration effected by the Reformers. If forced to choose between liberal Protestantism and Roman Catholicism, Barth confessed that he would choose the latter. But at the same time he asserted that Catholicism failed to subject the Church to the Word of God. Identifying the divine with the official actions of the ecclesiastical hierarchy, the Catholic Church ceased to be attentive to God's word in Scripture. In the last analysis

---

[16] Friedrich von Hügel, 'The Convictions Common to Catholicism and Protestantism' (1917), reprinted in his *Essays and Addresses on the Philosophy of Religion* (London: J. M. Dent and Sons, 1921), pp. 243–53.

[17] Friedrich von Hügel, 'The Catholic Contribution to Religion' (1921), reprinted in his *Essays and Addresses ... Second Series* (London: J. M. Dent and Sons, 1926), pp. 245–51.

[18] Karl Barth, 'Roman Catholicism: A Question to the Protestant Church' (1928), in his *Theology and Church* (London: SCM, 1962), pp. 307–33.

Catholicism, like Protestant Modernism, ended by making the Church dependent only on itself.[19] Barth issued a powerful call for a return to Reformation Christianity, which he understood in terms of the sovereignty of the Word of God.

Paul Tillich, in numerous books and essays, took up the ideas of Schelling and Hegel on the dialectical opposition between Protestant and Catholic Christianity. Christianity, he held, is essentially constituted by a Catholic substance and a Protestant principle, each needing the other as its own counterpart. Roman Catholicism, thanks to its sacerdotal and hierarchical structures, has better preserved the Catholic substance, which tends to be dissipated in Protestantism, with its lack of symbolic mediation.[20] The chief strength of Protestantism is its commitment to the Protestant principle, which rejects the tendency to make absolute claims for any relative or finite reality. Tillich makes rather absolute claims for this principle: 'The judge of every religious and cultural reality, including the religion and culture which calls itself "Protestant", is the Protestant principle.'[21] The specific weakness of Roman Catholicism, according to Tillich, is its tendency towards idolatry or, in his own words, 'a sacramental objectification and demonization of Christianity'.[22] The doctrine of transubstantiation, according to Tillich, transforms the symbol into a thing to be handled, and thus borders on the magical.[23]

Tillich's assertions concerning the 'Protestant principle' and the 'Catholic substance' have had enormous influence on authors of many traditions, but especially on several prominent American Lutherans. Jaroslav Pelikan, as a historian of the Reformation, holds that Luther kept the Catholic substance and the Protestant principle in proper balance, and that both must be combined in any future unity of the Church. The Protestant principle, he observes, must always be applied with critical reverence.[24]

---

[19] Karl Barth, *Church Dogmatics*, vol. i.1 (Edinburgh: T. & T. Clark, 1975), pp. 40–4.

[20] Paul Tillich, 'The Permanent Significance of the Catholic Church for Protestantism', *Protestant Digest*, iii (1941), pp. 23–31.

[21] Paul Tillich, *The Protestant Era* (Chicago: Univ. of Chicago Press, 1948), p. 163.

[22] Ibid., p. 94.

[23] Paul Tillich, *Systematic Theology*, vol. iii (Chicago: Univ. of Chicago Press, 1963), p. 123.

[24] Jaroslav Pelikan, *Obedient Rebels: Catholic Substance and Protestant Principle in Luther's Reformation* (New York: Harper & Row, 1964), pp. 11–24.

George Lindbeck, another American Lutheran, points out that Tillich himself deplored the disastrous loss of spiritual substance in modern Western culture. But in attempting to speak to the secular mentality of his day, Tillich failed to bring a remedy, and perhaps even aggravated the problem. Lindbeck, for his part, advocates a reinstatement of the 'symbols, rites, and disciplines transmitted by concrete religious communities'. In the early centuries, he points out, the Christians who adhered most staunchly to the Catholic substance were best able to resist the false absolutizations of Gnosticism, millennialism, and pagan emperor worship. In recent centuries the Protestant principle has tended to operate against the Catholic substance, but in our day there is reason to hope that the two will once again converge. A re-catholicized Christianity, Lindbeck concludes, might very well be the triumph, rather than the failure, of the Reformation.[25]

Roman Catholics, in my judgement, could accept Tillich's Protestant principle with two important qualifications. First, the principle itself must be very carefully formulated—more carefully than it was by Tillich himself—if it is not to erode the Catholic substance. It is quite proper to protest, as Tillich does, against the elevation of the finite symbols of religion to divine status. But he often seems to suggest that God cannot freely communicate himself to any created reality, as occurred, for example, in the Incarnation. In repudiating Jesus-centred religion as idolatrous Tillich can easily be read as denying the divinity of the man Jesus.

In our Introduction we have noted some weaknesses in Tillich's Christology. Similar criticisms may be made of Tillich's ecclesiology, which minimizes God's presence with those who constitute Christ's body. In his doctrine of the sacraments, Tillich recognizes that the symbols are charged with the power of the divine, but he seems unable to admit that Christ may be adored as truly present in the consecrated elements of the Eucharist. Thus the Protestant principle, in Tillich's system, appears to banish God from his creation, relegating him to a sphere of inaccessible transcendence. In this Tillich deviates not only from Catholic faith but from the very heart of biblical

[25] George Lindbeck, 'An Assessment Reassessed: Paul Tillich on the Reformation', *Journal of Religion*, 63 (1983), pp. 376–93; quotation from p. 388.

religion, which celebrates God's astonishing gift of himself to his people.

My second difficulty has likewise been stated in the Introduction. In Tillich's system there is a lack of parity between the Catholic substance and the Protestant principle. The Protestant principle becomes the judge, and indeed the only judge, of a miscellaneous body of materials handed down as the Catholic substance. That substance, unprotected by any positive principle, gets worn away under the persistent chafing of the Protestant principle. I would prefer to say that if there is a Protestant principle that questions and protests, there is also a Catholic principle that affirms and defends the Christian substance. Protest will at times be appropriate, but in the Tillichian system it comes too soon. Admitting no principle except one that severs the divine from its created embodiments, Tillich greatly weakens what he calls the Catholic substance.

By calling the critical principle 'Protestant', authors such as Tillich give the impression that Protestantism is an essentially negative movement. Not all Protestants agree. Robert McAfee Brown, for instance, in the opening pages of his *The Spirit of Protestantism*, rejects as false the image of Protestantism as 'protest against'. He reminds his readers that the Latin term *pro-testari* means to bear witness in favour of. 'Protestantism is primarily affirmative,' he concludes, 'and is negative only in the sense that to affirm one thing is necessarily to deny something else.'[26]

From a Catholic point of view, Louis Bouyer has written on what he calls 'the positive principles of the Reformation'.[27] The heart of the Reformation, he contends, consisted in affirmations such as the primacy of grace (*sola gratia*), the justifying power of faith (*sola fide*), the supreme authority of Scripture (*sola scriptura*), the unique mediation of Christ (*solus Christus*), and the total sovereignty of God (*soli Deo gloria*). All these principles, according to Bouyer, are predominantly positive. To that extent, he adds, they admit of a Catholic interpretation.

[26] Robert McAfee Brown, *The Spirit of Protestantism* (New York: Oxford Univ. Press, 1961), p. 12.

[27] Louis Bouyer, *The Spirit and Forms of Protestantism* (Westminster, Md.: Newman, 1956), chaps. 1–6.

Catholicism, in fact, languishes where these principles are neglected.

(5)

Do the characteristics of Catholicism bring about imbalances, so that the Catholic Church stands in need of correctives from outside itself? The Church can certainly profit from external criticism, whether from friendly or from hostile sources. I would maintain, however, that Catholic comprehensiveness is so great that it includes the necessary principles for the self-reformation of the Church. This may be illustrated with regard to a number of Catholic themes presented in earlier chapters.

The Catholic quest for plenitude, it is often objected, promotes quantity at the expense of quality, inclusiveness at the expense of selectivity. This might be true, except that the inclusiveness of Catholicism is founded on a qualitative catholicity. It has its source in the unique fullness of Jesus Christ. By its unremitting devotion to personal holiness and evangelical perfection, Catholicism fosters a deep concern for spiritual excellence. Since the Catholic Church is confessed in the creed as holy, the principles of plenitude and of purity may be seen as co-constituents of Catholicism. To preserve without error 'the purity of the Gospel itself' has been a prime concern not only of the Council of Trent (DS 1501) but of the majority of conciliar teaching.

In comparison with some forms of Protestantism, especially among the early Lutherans, Catholicism may appear too optimistic regarding the powers of nature and the healing effects of grace. It has often been accused of verging on Pelagianism. Deviations in this direction have undoubtedly occurred, but the necessary correctives are at hand. If Catholicism celebrates our solidarity with Christ in grace, it also recognizes our solidarity with the first Adam in sin. The Augustinian doctrine of original sin can counteract any naïve complacency.

The Catholic emphasis on continuity in time may have seemed to Baur to preclude a realistic acknowledgement of the Church's involvement in the vicissitudes of history. On the other hand, Catholic incarnationalism favours attention to the concrete and the historical. Newman and Loisy argued impressively that historical consciousness could not achieve its full development except in Catholicism. The mystery of the Church, as it exhibits itself in history, is marked by discontinuity as well as continuity.

The Catholic accent on community and universality could, if unchecked, occasion a kind of ecclesiastical totalitarianism. In certain periods the Church has been seen as a quasi-incarnation of the divine. While exorbitant claims have been made for the institutional Church and its hierarchical leadership, the individual believer has been, so to speak, swallowed by in the divine organism. The machinery of ecclesiastical mediation has been exalted to the point of becoming oppressive. Catholicism has been subject to the extremes of papalism, legalism, dogmatism, ritualism, and sacramentalism.

These aberrations, however, are not endemic or inevitable. They can be corrected from within Catholicism by a broad theological vision that recognizes the sanctity and inviolability of the individual before God, the rights of personal conscience, the limitations of the hierarchical leaders, and the power of God to act outside the normal channels of grace. The Catholic mystical tradition has emphasized the immediacy of the believer to God. Zealous reformers in every century have castigated the sins and blindness of popes and bishops. Thus institutionalism has not gone unchecked.

Vatican II was in many ways a council of reform. In the first session the spirit of the council was brilliantly summarized in an eloquent speech by Bishop Emile De Smedt of Bruges, denouncing the preparatory schemata for the three cardinal errors of triumphalism, clericalism, and juridicism.[28] In opposing these distortions the council took into account various criticisms that had been voiced by Protestants. To illustrate the balancing efforts of the council it may suffice to recall a few of its main teachings.

(1) The traditional Catholic insistence on manifest unity throughout the whole expanse of the Church can, if unchecked, lead to the imposition of uniformity and to unhealthy

---

[28] See Avery Dulles, *Models of the Church* (Garden City, NY: Doubleday, 1974), pp. 35–6. The text of Bishop De Smedt's intervention is published in *Acta synodalia sacrosancti Concilii Oecumenici Vaticani II*, vol. ii, part 4 (Vatican City: Typis Polyglottis, 1971), pp. 142–4.

centralization. Vatican II, seeking to prevent such distortions, emphasized the collegial structure of the episcopate, the relative autonomy of local and regional churches, and the importance of adaptation to different cultures.

(2) The characteristically Catholic stress on the historical continuity of the Church from age to age can lead to a neglect of the need to shift, sometimes in an abrupt and discontinuous manner, so as to meet the needs, possibilities, and opportunities of a radically changed culture. Vatican II, with its call for sensitivity to the signs of the times, made it clear that the Church cannot always develop in a homogeneous, rectilinear fashion, but must sometimes adopt new styles of thought, speech, and behaviour without losing its bonds with the Christian past.

(3) Protestant scholars have sometimes objected that the Catholic Church, as it understands itself, is not amenable to reform. Thanks to the preparatory work of theologians such as Congar, Vatican II was able to dispel this erroneous impression. Frankly acknowledging the presence of sin within the Church,[29] the council taught that the Church, 'at the same time holy and always in need of being purified, . . . incessantly pursues the path of penance and renewal' (*LG* 8). The Decree on Ecumenism declared that Christ summons the Church, as she goes her pilgrim way, to continual reformation (*UR* 6). In statements such as these the council picked up certain Lutheran themes on which we have commented in Chapter 5.

(4) Catholicism has traditionally laid heavy emphasis on the mediation of God's gifts through the structures of the Church, even to the point of urging the maxim, 'Outside the Church no salvation'. Vatican II, by contrast, took pains to assert that the grace given in Christ is available to every human being, and that God is not bound to the sacramental and ecclesiastical structures.[30] Although it did not endorse the discredited idea of an 'invisible Church', the council recognized a certain distinction between the spiritual community of grace and the society equipped with hierarchical agencies (*LG* 8).

(5) In Protestant–Catholic controversy, Catholics have com-

---

[29] See on this subject Karl Rahner, 'The Sinful Church in the Decrees of Vatican II', in his *Theological Investigations*, vol. vi (Baltimore: Helicon, 1969), pp. 270–94.

[30] See the texts on this point cited in Chapter 4, above.

monly put greater emphasis on the sacraments, Protestants on the Word of God. Here again, Vatican II sought to restore a proper balance. Without neglecting the sacraments, the council wrote at greater length on the Word of God, especially in the Dogmatic Constitution on Revelation, entitled *Dei Verbum*. Strongly influenced by the theology of the word, as developed by Barth and others, this Constitution restored the Bible to its central place in Catholic theology and spirituality. It stated unequivocally that the ecclesiastical magisterium is not above the Word of God, but under it (*DV* 10). The Constitution on the Liturgy likewise gave welcome stress to the reading and proclamation of the Word of God—a theme repeated in many other council documents, such as the Decrees on the Pastoral Office of Bishops and on the Ministry of Priests.

(6) Protestants have often been critical of the Catholic theory that revelation is to be found in two sources, Scripture and tradition. They are generally uncomfortable with the idea of any tradition unconnected with the Bible. Recognizing what was legitimate in this concern, the Constitution on Revelation refused to speak of two sources, but spoke instead of the Word of God as a single source, and of Scripture and tradition as indivisibly transmitting that Word (*DV* 9).

(7) There has been a tendency in Catholic Christianity to see worship as consisting essentially of the official, publicly approved ritual of the Church, and to minimize the importance of personal participation on the part of the individual worshipper. The Constitution on the Liturgy gave unprecedented attention to the active participation of all the faithful (*SC* 14), and made this a key principle for what it called 'the reform of the liturgy'. The same Constitution taught that features which have crept into the liturgy with the passage of time ought to be discarded if they are 'less harmonious with the intimate nature of the liturgy' (*SC* 21).

(8) Catholicism has always attached great importance to the priestly hierarchy, often in such a way as to give the impression that the laity were somehow inferior or of small account. Protestant churches, by contrast, emphasized the 'priesthood of every Christian believer'. Vatican II, anxious to reactivate this dormant theme, unequivocally taught that all the faithful have a common priesthood, which is a participation in the one

priesthood of Christ, although it is different in kind from the hierarchical priesthood of the ordained (*LG* 10). Generally speaking, the council sought to clarify the rights and freedom of the laity. Far from restricting the workings of the Spirit to priests and bishops, it spoke of the graces and charismatic gifts which the Holy Spirit freely distributes among the faithful of every rank (*LG* 12).

(9) The official statements of the Catholic Church since the Middle Ages have regularly underlined the importance of law and obedience, thus arousing Protestant suspicions that the freedom of the gospel is suffocated in the Catholic system. Here again Vatican II supplied a valuable corrective, not only in its Declaration on Religious Freedom but also in the statements on conscience, and on freedom of inquiry, thought, and expression within the Church, set forth in the Pastoral Constitution (*GS* 16, 62).

(10) A final difficulty, already noted, is that the Catholic Church, in its emphasis on completeness, tends to obscure what is central. At worst, Catholicism seems to ask for an act of faith in 'whatever the Church teaches' rather than in the good news of the gospel. In one of its most important statements, Vatican II observed that 'there is an order or "hierarchy" of truths, since they vary in their relationship to the foundation of the Christian faith' (*UR* 11). In other words, not every doctrine is equally important or central. The council did not explicitly state what is the core of Christian faith, but in the following article (*UR* 12) it made reference to the Trinity and the Incarnation, thus suggesting their centrality. In the Decree on Missionary Activity the council expressed the basic Christian message in rather existential categories. For Christian conversion, said the council, it is sufficient for the convert to apprehend 'that he has been snatched away from sin and led into the mystery of the love of God, who has called him to enter into a personal relationship with him in Christ' (*AG* 13). Since Vatican II the Catholic Church has been striving to develop an effective programme of evangelization, aimed in part to bring Catholics themselves to a deeper realization of the Lordship of Jesus in their lives.

These examples, which are merely a selection, do not address the full range of traditional issues between Protestant and

Catholic Christianity, but they may suffice to indicate a pattern
by which such conflicts can be harnessed and put to good use.
In each case Vatican II reaffirmed the distinctive Catholic
principle, but tempered it so as to recognize the legitimacy of
the criticism that may be provoked by an excessive reliance on
the Catholic principle.

(6)

In the light of these reflections we may attempt direct answers
to the questions implied in the title of this chapter. Are
Protestantism and Catholicism complementary? Are they
compatible?

It seems clear that the Catholic principle, calling for
acceptance of the given, for mediation, and for conformity,
must be balanced by some other principle that gives scope to
criticism, immediacy, and spontaneity. Many of the wisest
theologians have seen the need for some such countervailing
principle. From a Protestant point of view, Heiler and Stählin
spoke of the evangelical element, Sohm and Weber of the
charismatic factor, and Tillich and Pelikan of the Protestant
principle. Among Catholics, Drey spoke of mysticism, Newman of the prophetic office, and von Hügel of the mystical
element in religion. More recently Guitton and Congar have
contended that Christianity is always under a twofold imperative to achieve both the fullness cherished by Catholicism and
the purity demanded by Protestantism,[31]

Rosemary Haughton in a recent book, *The Catholic Thing*,
describes Catholicism in terms of an allegory of two sisters.[32]
The elder sister, Mother Church, is a domineering old lady,
often making large and public errors, but courageous, devoted,
and, for all her faults, lovable. The younger sister, Sophia, is
wayward, adventurous, and difficult to live with. But the two
sisters, different though they be, are one in their symbolic
duality, except that Mother Church is mortal, whereas Sophia
will live forever. Although Mrs Haughton's 'Mother Church' is
not perfectly identical with what we have been calling the

[31] Jean Guitton, *The Church and the Gospel* (Chicago: Regnery, 1961), p. 225; Yves
Congar, 'The Encounter between the Christian Confessions', pp. 155–6.
[32] Rosemary Haughton, *The Catholic Thing*, pp. 7–17, 235–48.

Catholic principle, her 'Sophia' is at least suggestive of the dialectically related co-principle, so difficult to describe and name.

From this allegory, as well as from many of the theological works to which we have referred, it seems evident that the two principles can be dialectically united in a single Church. In theory they are both complementary and compatible. When we talk about the Catholic principle our attention is primarily on 'Mother Church', the visible institution with its structures of mediation. But when the mediation is successful, the members of the Church achieve a lived relationship with God in Christ, and are thereby enabled to be critical of the ways in which the gifts of the Spirit are being mediated. Thus there is more to Catholic Christianity than the Catholic principle. Catholics must be on guard against defining the Church solely in terms of what is distinctive to Catholicism. Catholicism, taken in a 'Catholicist' sense, could be the enemy of catholicity.

Protestant authors such as Tillich, Pelikan, and Brown would recognize similar limitations in the Protestant principle. They would say that this principle is insufficient in itself and that it cannot function properly in any church, whether Protestant or Catholic, except in union with the Catholic substance.

Yet it is a fact that the two principles exist and function pre-eminently in different churches. In that sense they are separable. According to Rosemary Haughton, Sophia, being a wayward sister, sometimes strays rather far from Mother Church, who tries to keep her at home. But even when she is away, Sophia remains a blood-sister, and must be so regarded. Many Catholic theologians from Augustine to Rahner have made the point that authentic prophecy, while it has its true home in the Catholic Church, can also arise among outsiders. Was not Balaam a non-Israelite? According to Vatican II, many of 'the most significant elements or endowments which together go to build up and give life to the Church herself can exist outside the visible boundaries of the Catholic Church' (*UR* 3). Many Protestants, from Luther and Calvin to our own day, have been willing to speak at least of *vestigia ecclesiae* (traces of the Church) in non-Protestant Christianity.

In the situation of separation the different churches can to some extent complement each other. In the ten points from

Vatican II considered earlier in this chapter, we have seen how certain 'prophetic' criticisms of Roman Catholicism, voiced by Protestant theologians such as Barth and Tillich, assisted the council in its efforts at Catholic self-appraisal and renewal.

Conversely, the Catholic Church, with her greater attention to the structures of mediation, has a role to perform not only for her own members but also on behalf of Protestant Christianity. She can call attention to the danger that, where the proper sacramental and ministerial structures are lacking, the Christian substance is likely to be dissolved or at least attenuated by subjectivism, relativism, individualism, and secularism. Drawing on the Catholic principle, Catholics have frequently reminded Protestants of the need to conserve and develop the apostolic heritage of faith, sacraments, and ministry.

Although von Hügel, at the beginning of this century, was already able to speak of a recovery of Catholic values in the Protestant churches, he would have had much more reason to do so today. It is no longer safe to say, as many Catholics did at the turn of the century, that Protestants neglect the importance of creation and nature, that they care nothing for sanctification, that they ignore the symbolic aspect of the liturgy and the sacraments, that they reject orderly succession in the ministry, or that they are content to see themselves as merely national or linguistic Christian groupings. Even monasticism, which Harnack regarded as a thoroughly Catholic institution, is being to some extent restored in Lutheran and Reformed churches.

We may say, therefore, that the complementarity of the churches is being perceived, appreciated, and fruitfully put to work, and is bringing about a certain convergence. Protestant and Catholic churches are responding to, and incorporating, each other's concerns. Can one, then, project the lines of convergence to the meeting point and say that, without either ceasing to be itself, these two major forms of Christianity may one day come to coincide, forming through their union a single community in which both the Catholic and Protestant principles would be fully operative? Many ecumenists have projected such a union as the final goal of their endeavours.

For the present, however, such a union remains a distant vision or a dream. The Protestant and Catholic churches are kept apart, not indeed by the Protestant and Catholic principles as such, but by the prevalent interpretations of those principles in their respective communions. Protestantism, in so far as it cultivates a free, immediate relationship to God, based on Christ and the gospel alone, views the Catholic structures as impediments to the Christian life, or at least as not being necessary for all Christians. Roman Catholicism, committed to the principle of visible and symbolic mediation, is convinced that any church lacking the full sacramental, hierarchical, and dogmatic structures, including the papacy as defined at the two Vatican councils, is institutionally deficient. Both positions cannot be simultaneously true. Thus the differences between these two major types of Christianity, at the present time, involve contradictions. Full unity cannot be achieved by convergence alone but only by conversion.

Such, at least, is my personal assessment of the current situation. For the present, each ecclesial body must both give and receive the greatest measure of enrichment and correction that it can through mutual witness and dialogue. Through this process each partner can grow in truth and love. Perhaps, as they do so, the Lord will enable them to perceive new possibilities that now lie hidden and to overcome barriers that now seem insuperable.

CONCLUSION

Prospects for Catholicity

To bring this study to a close it may be helpful to summarize some of our principal findings and to reflect on the difficulties and opportunities facing catholicity in the contemporary world.

(1)

The concept of catholicity, being analogous rather than uni-vocal, does not admit of any precise definition, but it can be distinguished from other similar concepts such as fullness and universality. Unlike universality, catholicity is a concrete term: it is predicated not of abstract essences but of particular, existing realities. Furthermore, it always implies intensity, richness, and plenitude. Unlike fullness, it implies a unitive relationship among things that are diverse. 'Catholic', writes Henri de Lubac, 'suggests the idea of an organic whole, of a cohesion, of a firm synthesis, of a reality which is not scattered but, on the contrary, turned towards a centre which assures its unity, whatever the expanse in area or the internal differenti-ation might be.'[1]

Catholicity, far from excluding differences, demands them. In all the instances of catholicity we have considered—Trinity, Incarnation, Church, and world—we have found a union of opposites that might, in themselves, seem incompatible.

Finally, catholicity is a dynamic term. It designates a fullness of reality and life, especially divine life, actively communicating itself. This life, flowing outwards, pulsates through many subjects, draws them together, and brings them into union with their source and goal. By reason of its supreme realization, which is divine, catholicity assures the ultimate coherence of the whole ambit of creation and redemption.

[1] Henri de Lubac, 'Particular Churches', in his *The Motherhood of the Church* (San Francisco, Ignatius Press, 1982), pp. 173–4.

In the widest sense of the term, catholicity may be predicated of the universe as a whole. The entire cosmos has in Christ its centre of unity, coherence, and fulfilment (cf. Col. 1: 17). Nature is essentially good and perfectible; it is, as Bonhoeffer said, 'directed to the coming of Christ',[2] who is at work recapitulating the cosmos under his universal headship (cf. Eph. 1: 10).

The catholicity of the Church is a more intense participation in the divine catholicity. The Church has her catholicity not from herself but from God, who makes himself present in her. Catholicity, however, is not attributed to the Church merely by extrinsic denomination, for Christ is truly present in the Church through the Holy Spirit. The Church, therefore, is a real representation of Christ. She is his new presence, not under his own proper form, but in the community of believers. Having in himself the plenitude of divine life and grace, Christ communicates this to the Church. The transformative and expansive power of the Church, as well as her continuity in time, derive from the divine source of her being. The catholicity of the Church, as we have seen, may be explicated in terms of height, depth, breadth, and length.

When in the creed we designate the Church as catholic we are going beyond the empirical data. Although something of the catholicity of the Church appears in history, we perceive only the external signs of a far deeper reality, apprehended in faith, which alone can affirm the divine dimension of the Church's life. The adjective 'catholic' in the creed does not express a mere hope or ideal, but a present, though imperfect, reality. The catholicity of the Church, coming from God as its source and tending to him as its goal, is always incomplete and in quest of its own completion.

The Church, as a real symbol, charged with the power of the divine life within her, may be called, in a true but analogous sense, a sacrament. Her catholicity achieves a certain visibility through signs that express and sustain her essential reality. The Church as sacrament is endowed with certain visible or social structures, usually considered under the heading of Catholicism. Among these structures are the sacraments, all of which

---

[2] Dietrich Bonhoeffer, *Ethics* (London: Collins, 1964), p. 144; see above, Chapter 3, note 8.

have a social or ecclesial significance, as we have seen in particular with regard to baptism, penance, and the Eucharist. The hierarchical ministry is likewise a Catholic structure, sacramental in its own way. This ministry is, in its highest exercise, episcopal. The bishop of Rome, as head and centre of the college of bishops, has a uniquely Catholic ministry, with special responsibility for the unity and mission of the universal Church.

The adjective 'catholic' may in some measure be predicated of every Christian church, for all participate in the reality of the Church which they confess as one, holy, catholic, and apostolic. All, moreover, have certain Catholic structures, such as canonical scriptures, creeds, sacraments, and ordained ministry. In a more specific sense, the term Catholic (usually with a capital C) is predicated of those churches which are conspicuous for their sacramental, liturgical, hierarchical, and dogmatic features, and those which stress continuity with the institutional and doctrinal developments of the patristic and medieval periods. In a still more specific sense, the term Catholic refers to that Church which, at Vatican II, called itself 'the Catholic Church', and which alone insists on communion with Rome as the touchstone of unity.

It has sometimes been suggested that the Church of Christ, as a complex reality, may appropriately be realized in two contrasting forms, Protestant and Catholic. This view can be misleading, at least if it is taken as implying that the Catholic features are not essential to the Church. According to the analysis given in the preceding chapters, these features belong to the Church of Christ by her very nature, for they are required to actualize, express, and safeguard her catholicity. According to Vatican II, the Catholic Church has no essential features over and above those of the Church of Christ. She claims to be the organization in which that Church subsists. The essence or idea of Catholicism is the same as that of the Church of Christ, viewed in terms of its structures of mediation and continuity.

The Catholic principle, as we have used the term, justifies and protects the mediatory structures of the Church. This principle inculcates respect for the divine presence in the cosmic and natural means whereby God communicates himself. More especially, it arouses reverence for, and confidence in, the ecclesial structures by which, in accordance with God's free promises, the grace of Christ is symbolized and transmitted. The Catholic principle defends the individual Christian and the Church from the inroads of scepticism, irreverence, and sectarian pride.

The Catholic principle, however, does not fully express the nature of the Church. It focuses on the visible and social structures of mediation rather than on the immediacy of the Holy Spirit, who animates the body and all its members. Without attention to the immediacy of grace, the Catholic structures could be alienating. There is need for a complementary principle that prevents the structures from being unduly absolutized, from becoming opaque and oppressive. Idolatry must be precluded; false and inopportune developments must be detected and pruned away. This correlative principle of immediacy and criticism corresponds to what Tillich and others have called the Protestant principle. Tillich's terminology could be misleading, since it suggests that Protestantism is essentially negative in nature, but his observations convey an important truth and one which, we have argued, is necessary for the health of Catholicism. The Protestant principle, as Tillich understands it, is not intended to dissolve the Christian substance, but to shield it against distortions. But the Protestant principle, as we have seen, can be misused to erode the Christian heritage. To protect it against its own excesses, it must be held in check by what we have called the Catholic principle.

Though the Church of Christ, according to Vatican II, 'subsists' in the Catholic Church, Catholicism does not claim perfection for itself. On the contrary, the council stated that the Church is in continual need of purification and reform. Even in her catholicity, she is deficient. Her actual, lived catholicity would be enhanced if she were holier, more faithful, more widely diffused, more deeply implanted in human cultures, and more internally unified. Catholicity, therefore, is both a gift and a task. It designates not only a present reality but also a programme for action.

(2)

In Chapter 1, allusion was made to several problem areas that make it difficult for any Church today to claim catholicity. An initial problem has to do with the inner dividedness of the Church. Christianity is split into many hostile factions that fail even to maintain communion with one another. How, then, can the Church be a sign of the coming unity of the whole human family, as the World Council of Churches claimed at Uppsala (no. 20)?

This difficulty draws attention to what we have said above, and what the Uppsala Assembly also recognized, regarding the limitations of the Church's actual catholicity. It indicates the urgency of ecumenism and the inner connection between ecumenism and catholicity. For the credibility of the Church, especially in its claim to be Catholic, it is crucial to mitigate or overcome the hostility and division among Christian groups. The ecumenical movement might also have been called the Catholic movement, so closely is it connected with the restoration of Catholic unity. The term 'ecumenical' was originally secular, referring, in Greek, to the entire inhabited earth (*oikoumenē*). In some ways this term is less suited to designate the desired unity of Christians than the term Catholic, which in its early theological usage among the Greek Fathers already refers to the universal communion among churches. Sometimes the two terms have been used as synonyms, as was done, for instance, in the Lutheran Book of Concord (1580), which begins by quoting the three ancient creeds under the title, 'The Three Catholic or Ecumenical Symbols'.[3]

The modern tendency to use 'Catholic' as a confessional designation makes it difficult to speak of a broad interconfessional movement, aiming to include Protestant communities, as 'Catholic'.[4] Since 'Catholic' has come to be connected with certain types of Church, or even a single confessional body—the 'Roman Catholic'—a distinction must be made between

---

[3] Theodore G. Tappert (ed.), *The Book of Concord* (Philadelphia: Fortress, 1959), p. 17.

[4] See Max Seckler, 'Katholisch als Konfessionsbezeichnung', *Tübinger theologische Quartalschrift*, cxlv (1965), pp. 401–31. Emphasizing the Catholic character of the current movement towards church unity, he asserts (p. 422): 'Catholic as a confessional designation is at least in the logical respect nonsense.'

Catholic and ecumenical. Many see the two terms as mutually complementary opposites. Yves Congar, for instance, holds that 'Catholicity is the taking of the many into an already existing oneness', whereas ecumenism is the introduction of unity into an existing diversity.[5] It can be persuasively argued that any successful unification will have to include a recovery of Catholic elements, for a truly universal and enduring communion cannot be maintained without the necessary structures of unity and continuity.

The connection between Catholicism and ecumenism was cogently presented by the American Episcopalian theologian, John Knox.[6] The Catholic movement of the second century, he contended, was the ecumenical movement of early Christianity. It gave rise to a firmly structured Church with sacramental worship, a biblical canon, definite creeds, and an episcopally ordered ministry. That movement produced the visible unity required for the early Church to retain her identity in the face of persecution and heresy. If the present-day ecumenical movement is to succeed, according to Knox, it must emulate the achievements of early Catholicism. The coming Great Church cannot be one and holy unless it is prepared likewise to be Catholic and apostolic.

Knox does not affirm the papacy as a Catholic structure, but if the logic of his argument were to be extended to the next few centuries it might well include this additional feature. Roman Catholics believe that the papacy is a divinely intended structure, necessary to prevent the fragmentation of Christianity and the domination of the Church by national governments.

Although ecumenism is sometimes perceived by Catholics as a threat to catholicity, Vatican II teaches on the contrary that it is to be pursued for the sake of catholicity. The council states that the separations among baptized Christians diminish the effective catholicity of the Church and make it 'more difficult for the Church to express in actual life her full catholicity in all its aspects' (*UR* 4). If the catholicity of the Church calls for expressions of the one faith in styles suited to peoples of every culture and temperament, the divisions among Christians

[5] Yves Congar, *Divided Christendom* (London: G. Bles, 1939), p. 101.
[6] John Knox, *The Early Church and the Coming Great Church* (Nashville: Abingdon, 1955).

prevent this goal from being fully achieved. The Catholic Church today lacks outward actualizations suited to peoples such as, for example, the Russians and the Scandinavians. Accordingly, as Congar remarks, the Catholic Church is 'deprived of a Slav expression, a Norse expression, of the one and many-splendoured grace of Christ'.[7] Congar also observes that by reason of the divisions, Catholics cannot corporately profit as they otherwise might from the Christian experiences and insights of religious leaders such as Luther and Wesley. These experiences and insights, in so far as they are authentically Christian, call for validation and integration within Catholic Christianity.[8]

What Knox asserts about the recovery of Catholic structures and what Congar asserts about the Catholic demand for inner diversity represent two complementary approaches addressed respectively to Protestant and Catholic readers. Both concur in stressing the Catholic import of the ecumenical movement.

(3)

Congar's observations serve well to introduce the second major difficulty: the apparent lack of universalism within each and all of the churches, not excluding Roman Catholicism. From its origins Christianity gloried in its capacity to unite in Christ people of every nation, language, and social station. The New Testament depicts Parthians, Medes, Elamites, and 'devout men from every nation under heaven' hearing Peter's Pentecost sermon in their own languages and being converted by him to one and the same faith (Acts 2: 5–13). Pentecost, therefore, is a catholic event: it represents Babel in reverse, the restoration of communication among estranged peoples.

The Pauline letters, as we have seen, depict Christ as having torn down the wall of division between Jew and Gentile, so that in him all barriers are overcome. Yet the Church of the early centuries was to develop predominantly in the Mediterranean area, in territories belonging to the Roman Empire. With the loss of the Near East and Northern Africa to Islam in the early Middle Ages, Christianity became to all intents and purposes a

---

[7] Congar, *Divided Christendom*, p. 254.
[8] Ibid., p. 256.

European religion. In later centuries Catholic Christianity was further contracted as Eastern Europe became Orthodox and Northern Europe, for the most part, Protestant or Anglican.

The great missionary thrust of modern times, combined with the emigration of many European Christians to other parts of the world, has alleviated this situation, but the majority of the world's Catholics are still of European stock. Their faith is bound up in many ways with their ethnic identity. Catholicism thus remains in many ways European—if not even Southern or South-west European. Centred in the 'eternal city', it inherits some of the mentality and aura of imperial Rome. For most purposes its official language is still Latin. A Roman legal code and a Roman liturgy are imposed on almost all Catholics, no matter what their nationality.

The complaint is therefore made that the unity of Roman Catholicism is not the kind of 'reconciled diversity' extolled in contemporary theology, but rather a uniformity based on the dominance of a single culture. This difficulty calls attention to real shortcomings in the lived catholicity of the Church. The actuality is far from the ideal. This discrepancy, however, should not be a source of discouragement. Probably no other church or religion has ever had a greater world-wide presence than Roman Catholicism in our day. Karl Rahner, as we have seen, holds that the era of Eurocentrism is coming to an end and that Catholicism is at length becoming, for the first time in history, a *de facto* planetary Church.[9] The Church of six continents, as Walbert Bühlmann calls it, is rapidly taking shape, and within this coming Catholicism the 'third Church', that of the Third World, will be demographically preponderant.[10]

In many ways Vatican II laid the groundwork for this transition. As we have noted in Chapter 4, the council affirmed that the Church is capable of entering into communion with a variety of cultures without being bound to any one of them (*GS* 58). Authorizing the use of the vernacular in the liturgy (*SC* 36, 54, 63), the council encouraged each major national group to

[9] Karl Rahner, 'Basic Theological Interpretation of the Second Vatican Council', *Theological Investigations*, vol. xx (New York: Crossroad, 1981), pp. 77–89. See above, Chapter 4, note 11.

[10] Walbert Bühlmann, *Weltkirche* (Graz: Styria, 1984). See also his earlier work, *The Coming of the Third Church* (Maryknoll, NY: Orbis, 1977).

develop its own styles of worship, its own behavioural customs, and its own modes of doctrinal expression (*GS* 44; cf. *UR* 14–18). All this it saw as part of the 'wonderful exchange' whereby the riches of the nations were given to Christ as an inheritance (*LG* 13, *AG* 22). The council introduced significant modifications of organizational structures to permit greater interplay and diversification.

Since the council, the national and regional bishops' conferences, notably in Latin America but also on other continents, have carried this process forward. Since the international Synod of Bishops in 1977 the term 'inculturation' has been extensively used to signify the adaptation of Christianity to particular ethnic groups with their own distinct cultures.

Catholics have rarely felt the suspicion and antipathy towards culture characteristic of sectarian Protestantism. In their affirmative stance towards culture, however, Catholics must be on guard against assuming that cultures are above criticism. They may profit from the warnings of Protestant authors such as Karl Barth and H. Richard Niebuhr against an excessive identification between Christ and culture.[11] Human cultures, as these theologians warn, must not be allowed to limit or distort what the gospel has to say.

By a culture we normally understand a system of meanings and values, historically transmitted, embodied in symbols, and instilled into the members of a sociological group so that they are spontaneously inclined to feel, think, judge, and behave in certain characteristic ways. If a human culture has all these functions, it is capable of being highly serviceable to Christianity, but it cannot be finally normative in matters of faith. Far from being subservient to cultures, the Church must judge them in the light of the gospel and seek to regenerate them where necessary. Paul VI for this reason called forcefully for an evangelization of cultures.[12] Recognizing the magnitude of the task, John Paul II in 1982 established a Pontifical Council for Culture.

From the standpoint of catholicity there are solid grounds for

---

[11] See especially H. Richard Niebuhr, *Christ and Culture* (New York: Harper & Row, 1951).

[12] Paul VI, *Evangelii nuntiandi* (1975), no. 20; Eng. trans. in Austin Flannery (ed.), *Vatican Council II: More Postconciliar Documents* (Northport, NY: Costello, 1982), p. 719.

favouring a measure of cultural pluralism. Because cultures are ephemeral, and because no one culture has sufficient resources for expressing the full significance of God's gift in Christ, it would be a mistake to link the Church exclusively to any one culture. Cultural monism, which in some forms tended to attribute permanent and normative value to the Greco-Roman culture of Western Europe, have proved inadequate.

Cultural pluralism, in extreme forms, is no more acceptable. It tends to divide the Church into regional and national communities having their own creeds, liturgical calendars, rituals, marriage practices, and moral codes, all determined in accord with the prevailing ethos of the region. Such unreconciled diversity would be detrimental to the catholicity of the Church, which requires that the members be able to recognize one another, across national and ethnic lines, as sharers in a single faith, servants of the same Lord, and members of one spiritual people.

Catholic unity cannot be founded on a merely transcendental experience of grace. It must be verifiable on the level of utterance and deed, and must be embodied in symbols accessible to all. To maintain itself as a universal society, the Church must have something resembling a common culture into which she can socialize her members. Up to the present the biblical symbols, modified and enriched by the cultural developments of Christian Europe, have performed this function. Although our own day calls for a greater inclusion of the experience and traditions of non-Western peoples, the inherited symbols must not be hastily abandoned on the pretext of 'cultural imperialism'. For catholicity, as we have seen, requires continuity with the Church's own past. Relying on the powerful but limited symbols and expressions of the faith in its own heritage, the Church of the future may be able to move gradually towards a greater cosmopolitanism in which different cultural expressions of the faith enrich and correct one another through reciprocal communication.[13]

The cultures of Asia, Africa, Oceania, and those of the native peoples of North and South America, are to a great extent

---

[13] I have developed the idea of a 'reciprocity of cultures' at somewhat greater length in 'The Emerging World Church: A Theological Reflection', *Proceedings of the Catholic Theological Society of America*, xxxix (1984), pp. 1–12.

bound up with traditions, practices, values, and insights from the indigenous religions. The contemporary discussion of inculturation therefore raises in sharper form the age-old question whether catholicity permits or even demands positive openness towards the other religions. The time is past when the great religions of the world, such as Islam, Hinduism, and Buddhism, can be treated as diabolical superstitions. As we have seen in Chapter 3, few Catholic theologians of our century regard these religions as untouched by grace. Some even conjecture that these religions contain elements of revelation and that their sacred books may be, at least in an analogous sense, inspired. If so, it may be possible for Catholic Christianity to incorporate features derived from the religions of those regions, just as was previously done in the Judaic and Hellenistic worlds. These questions obviously require careful study. They are mentioned here not with a view to solving them, but to indicate that they are inescapable parts of the contemporary Catholic agenda.[14]

(4)

The theme of the non-Christian religions serves to introduce our third and final problem area. In view of the statistics it appears immodest and pretentious for Christianity or Catholicism to claim universal and central significance for the ultimate destiny of the cosmos and of humanity. Other religions and ideologies appear to have comparable and perhaps even greater unitive potential.

Certain exclusivist understandings of catholicity, prevalent in past centuries, envisage the Church as holding a virtual monopoly of wisdom, culture, and excellence. They would regard it as a loss to the Church if universal human values were promoted by any other agency without dependence on the Church. A sounder theology, however, would see the Church as rejoicing in everything good and wholesome, no matter by whom achieved. According to this alternative view, the Church would use her moral influence to encourage whatever makes for truth and freedom, justice and unity. Without exceeding her

---

[14] For a preliminary orientation see Donald Nicholl, 'The Catholic Spirit and the Body of Christ', *Clergy Review*, lxvi (1981), pp. 421–8.

own proper competence in the moral and religious area, the Church would seek to integrate the partial catholicities of philosophy, science, politics, economics, art, and recreation in relation to the total destiny of the universe in Christ. Compared with all other catholicities, that of the Church is not exclusive or competitive but contributory and complementary.

This open view of catholicity has come increasingly to the fore in recent decades, and was endorsed by Vatican II. The council disavowed any desire on the part of the Church to dominate in the spheres of politics and culture. It adopted instead the posture of a servant. The Pastoral Constitution on the Church in the Modern World insisted that Christians are intimately linked with the hopes and aspirations of all human beings (*GS* 1). It sought to redefine the role of the Church in the context of a 'new humanism, in which man is defined first of all by his responsibility toward his brothers and toward history' (*GS* 55). Christians especially, according to the council, are obliged to labour not only for the Church but also for 'the fraternal unity of the one human family' (*GS* 56).

This open Catholicism was strikingly dramatized in the closing ceremonies of Vatican II in St. Peter's Square on 8 Dec. 1965. In the vast area enclosed in part by the colonnade of Bernini, which seemed to be reaching out to embrace the unenclosed world in its arms, the pope and the bishops welcomed the representatives of eighty nations and of numerous international organizations such as the United Nations, FAO and UNESCO.[15]

The messages read in French on this occasion in the name of the council Fathers were addressed respectively to rulers, intellectuals, scientists, artists, women, the poor, the sick, the suffering, workers, and youth.[16] In each of these messages the Church professed an eagerness to place her spiritual forces at the disposal of the common good of all humanity. The messages radiated the conviction that the human pursuit of truth and beauty, justice and compassion, could not fail to harmonize with the Church's heritage of faith.

[15] The Protestant theologian, Vittorio Subilia, discusses the 'Catholic' symbolism of these closing ceremonies in the final chapter of his *La nuova cattolicità del Cattolicesimo* (Turin: Claudiana, 1967), esp. pp. 259–73.

[16] These closing messages are printed in Walter M. Abbott (ed.), *The Documents of Vatican II* (New York: America Press, 1966), pp. 728–37.

The new secular catholicities are not connected in the same way with the catholicity of the Church as are the ecclesial elements of doctrine, sacraments, and ministry. Secular developments, related to Christ as the centre and crown of all creation, need not be kept under the Church's tutelage. Though the Church must esteem and encourage learning and culture, it would be a mistake to expect her to be the principal patron of such activities. Without having any special competence in the technical aspects of secular life, the Church can always encourage and direct commendable efforts in the light of the gospel and in this way show herself favourable to 'whatever is true, whatever is honest, whatever is lovely, whatever is gracious . . .' (Phil. 4: 8). Without the vision of ultimacy which the Church can provide, even worthy efforts may be one-sided and destructive.

So long as we are involved in the ambiguities of history, there will be tensions, misunderstandings, and conflicts, even among persons of good will. Nevertheless the believing Christian, assured by the promises of Christ, remains confident that the catholicity of the Church and all other catholicities are, in the long run, on a path of convergence. Christ is drawing the whole of reality towards himself so that in the end God will be not simply 'all'—which as God he can never fail to be—but 'all in all' (*panta en pasin*, 1 Cor. 15: 28). Scripture speaks of a final restoration of all things (*apokastastasis pantōn*, Acts 3: 21), and Vatican II assures us that in the glory of the coming age, 'the human race as well as the entire world, which is intimately related to man and achieves its purpose through him, will be perfectly reestablished in Christ' (*LG* 48). The eager longing for redemption that permeates all creation (Rom. 8: 18–23) will then be assuaged.

Dietrich Bonhoeffer correctly observed that the concept of the Kingdom of God, while it involves the consummation of the Church, embraces also the future of nature and civilization.[17] Wolfhart Pannenberg speaks in similar terms. The catholicity of the Church, he maintains, is in the last analysis an eschatological concept. 'Only in the eschatological glory will it attain to full reality, which will include, among other things, the

---

[17] Dietrich Bonhoeffer, *The Communion of Saints* (New York: Harper & Row, 1960), p. 199.

elimination of the contrast between church and secular society.'[18]

Until history comes to a close, catholicity will remain a challenge and a task. Sustained by great resources, it is confronted by heavy opposition. The increasing mechanization of life threatens to substitute quantity for quality, industry for nature, and planning for providence, thereby undermining what we have called catholicity in height and in depth. Catholicity in length, which creates community across the ages, is jeopardized by the acceleration of technological and social change. The new movements of emancipation that are afoot in the world today, while in many ways promising, pose a challenge to catholicity in breadth. Factionalism, resentment, and distrust seem to be the order of the day. Even the Church is in danger of being politicized by partisan groups which seek their own collective advantage, guided by their own ideology.

Under these circumstances it is not easy to cultivate the Catholic cast of mind. Great devotion and discipline are needed to maintain communion with the transcendent, fidelity to the past, and solidarity with those who belong to alien groups. The Catholic spirit, distinguished for docility, continues to cherish the wisdom handed down from earlier centuries. Self-effacing, it seeks to build on the work of others, and to contribute in modest but significant ways to a continuing tradition. This spirit, moreover, is prepared to learn from all parties, seeking out the truth in every opinion and the merit in every cause. With its long-range vision, the Catholic mentality encourages patience, subordinating superficial, momentary, and particular gains to the greater, more permanent, and more universal good. To be truly Catholic means to call into question the self-interest of any group, even that of the Church itself, and to maintain critical distance from every passing vogue. In short, catholicity seeks to foster a vision and concern as deep and comprehensive as God's creative and redemptive plan, made known to us in his Son.

---

[18] Wolfhart Pannenberg, *The Church* (Philadelphia: Westminster, 1983), pp. 62–3. Cf. H. de Lubac as quoted above, Chapter 5, note 4.

APPENDIX I

Representative Texts on the Church as Catholic

I

THE Church is called Catholic because it is spread throughout the world, from end to end of the earth; also because it teaches universally and completely all the doctrines which man should know concerning things visible and invisible, heavenly and earthly; and also because it subjects to right worship all mankind, rulers and ruled, lettered and unlettered; further because it treats and heals universally every sort of sin committed by soul and body, and it possesses in itself every conceivable virtue, whether in deeds, words or in spiritual gifts of every kind.

Cyril of Jerusalem, Catechesis XVIII[1]

2

The Church is Catholic, i.e. universal, first with respect to place, because it is everywhere in the world, against the Donatists. Romans 1: 8: 'Your faith is proclaimed in all the world'; Mark 16: 15: 'Go into all the world and preach the gospel to the whole creation.' Of old God was known only in Judea, but now throughout the whole world. This Church, moreover, has three parts. One is on earth, another is in heaven, and the third is in purgatory.

Secondly, the Church is universal with respect to the state of men, because no one is rejected, whether master or slave, male or female. Galatians 3: 28: 'There is neither male nor female.'

Thirdly, it is universal with respect to time. For some have said that the Church should last until a certain time, but this is false, because this Church began from the time of Abel and will last to the end of the world. Matthew 28: 20: 'And lo, I am with you always, to the close of the age.' And after the close of the age it will remain in heaven.

Thomas Aquinas, Opusculum VII, 'In Symbolum
Apostolorum, scil., Credo in Deum, Expositio'[2]

---

[1] From *The Works of St. Cyril of Jerusalem*, vol. ii, translated by Leo P. McCauley and Anthony A. Stephenson, The Fathers of the Church (Washington, DC: The Catholic Univ. of America Press, 1970), p. 132.

[2] From Thomas Aquinas, *Opera omnia*, Parma edition, vol. xvi (New York: Musurgia, 1950), p. 148.

3

What does Catholic mean? It means the same as universal. *Kath'holou* means 'universally', 'in general'. The king of France was called most Christian, but so that the king of Spain would not be inferior, he was given the name of Catholic.

Why is this epithet added in the article of the creed, so that the Church is called Catholic? Because it is an assembly dispersed throughout the whole earth and because its members, wherever they are, and however separated in place, embrace and externally profess one and the same utterance of true doctrine in all ages from the beginning until the very end. . . .

. . . It is one thing to be called Catholic, something else to be really Catholic. Those are truly called Catholic who embrace the doctrine of the truly Catholic Church, i.e., that which is supported by the witness of all time, of all ages, which believes what the prophets and apostles taught, and which does not tolerate factions, heresies, and heretical assemblies. We must all be Catholic, i.e., embrace this word which the rightly-thinking Church holds, separate from, and unentangled with, sects warring against that Word.

Philipp Melanchthon, 'De Appellatione Ecclesiae Catholicae'[3]

4

The word 'Catholic' also has diverse meanings. It can be used to describe the opinions and the religious attitude of those who adhere to certain positions within a divided Christendom. It can also be used to describe, not a type of thought or outlook, but certain facts whose existence and authority Christians acknowledge: the Catholic Church, the Catholic Creeds, the Catholic Faith, the Catholic Sacraments. We do not intend in this Report to use or advocate any new terminology, but we would wish to make it clear that, as Christians and theologians, our first concern is for those things which are Catholic in the latter and classical sense. In our divided Christendom we do not believe that any existing institution or group of institutions gives a full and balanced representation of the true and primitive Catholicity. It is the recovery of the principles of that Catholicity that is our quest.

Catholicity: Report Presented to the Archbishop of Canterbury, 1947[4]

[3] From *Postilla Melanthoniana*, in Corpus Reformatorum (Melanchthon), vol. xxiv, cols. 397–9.

[4] *Catholicity: A Study in the Conflict of Christian Traditions in the West, Being a Report Presented to His Grace the Archbishop of Canterbury*, by E. S. Abbott and others, with a Foreword by The Archbishop of Canterbury (Westminster, Eng.: Dacre Press, 1947), pp. 9–10.

5

All human beings are called to the new People of God. Hence this People, while remaining one and the same, is destined to spread to the whole world and to all ages. For God, who originally made human nature one, decreed that his scattered children should at length be gathered into one (cf. John 11: 52). . . .

It follows that in all the nations of the earth there is but one People of God, which takes its citizens from every nation and makes them citizens of a kingdom which is of a heavenly and not an earthly nature. . . . Since the kingdom of Christ is not of this world (cf. John 18: 36), the Church or People of God takes nothing away from the temporal welfare of any people by promoting that kingdom. On the contrary, she fosters and takes to herself, in so far as they are good, the talents, resources, and customs of each people. Taking them to herself, she purifies, strengthens, and elevates them. The Church is mindful that she must harvest with that King to whom the nations were given as an inheritance (cf. Ps. 2: 8) and into whose city they bring gifts and presents (cf. Ps. 71[72]: 10; Isa. 60: 4–7; Apoc. 21: 24). This attribute of universality which adorns the People of God is that gift of the Lord whereby the Catholic Church tends efficaciously and constantly to recapitulate the whole of humanity with all its riches under Christ the head in the unity of his Spirit. In virtue of this catholicity each individual part brings its particular gifts to the other parts and to the whole Church, so that the whole and the individual parts are enriched by the mutual sharing of gifts and the striving of all for fullness in unity. . . .

Everyone is called to be part of this catholic unity of the People of God, which both prefigures and promotes universal peace. The Catholic faithful, all who believe in Christ, and indeed the whole of mankind in various ways either belong to this unity or are positively related to it, for all are called by the grace of God to salvation.

Vatican Council II, *Constitution on the Church*, no. 13[5]

6

Yet it is within this very world that God makes catholicity available to men through the ministry of Christ in his Church. The purpose of Christ is to bring people of all times, of all races, of all places, of all

[5] From Walter M. Abbott (general editor) and Joseph Gallagher (translation editor), *The Documents of Vatican II* (New York: America Press, 1966), pp. 30–2. Translation modified.

conditions, into an organic and living unity in Christ by the Holy Spirit under the universal fatherhood of God. This unity is not solely external; it has a deeper, internal dimension, which is also expressed by the term 'catholicity'. Catholicity reaches its completion when what God has already begun in history is finally disclosed and fulfilled.

'The Holy Spirit and the Catholicity of the Church', no. 6.
From *The Uppsala Report*[6]

[6] From *The Uppsala Report 1968*, edited by Norman Goodall (Geneva: World Council of Churches, 1968), Report of Section I, p. 13.

Meanings of the Word 'Catholic'

As noted in the Introduction, the term 'catholic', with or without an initial capital, has various levels of meaning, to be distinguished in the course of the book. The following five usages may now be enumerated:

1. The adjectival form of 'catholicity', including the various aspects of catholicity described in Chapters 2 through 5. To be catholic in this sense is to share in the universal community, rooted in cosmic nature, that transcends the barriers of time and place and has its source in God's self-communication. The opposite of 'catholic' in this sense is sectarian.

2. Universal as opposed to local or particular. This seems to be the primary meaning of 'catholic' as used in a number of important texts from the early Fathers of the Church, notably Ignatius of Antioch (*Smyr.* 7:2) and the Martyrdom of Polycarp (*Insc.*; 8:1), though there is some disagreement abut the precise interpretation of these texts.

3. True or authentic as contrasted with false or heretical. This polemical use of the term is found in many church Fathers, especially after AD 150, and is much in use among Greek Orthodox theologians of our own time.

4. The type of Christianity that attaches particular importance to visible continuity in space and time and visible mediation through social and institutional structures, such as creeds, sacraments, and the historic episcopate. This sense of the word 'Catholic' (with a capital C) was prominent at the Amsterdam Assembly of the World Council of Churches (1948). The opposite was taken to be 'Protestant', although a good case could be made for regarding 'charismatic' or 'mystical' as the opposite.

5. The title of the church which, organized in the world as a society, is governed by the bishop of Rome, as successor of Peter, and by the bishops in communion with him (cf. *LG* 8). In ecumenical circles it has become common to use the term 'Roman Catholic' to designate this sociological group, partly because the term 'Catholic' has the various other meanings listed above. Some disadvantages of the term 'Roman Catholic' are mentioned in Chapter 7, section 1, above.

Indexes

A. SCRIPTURAL REFERENCES

B. REFERENCES TO VATICAN II

C. PERSONS

D. SUBJECTS